THE TRANSLANGUAGING CLASSROOM

THE TRANSLANGUAGING CLASSROOM

Leveraging Student Bilingualism for Learning

Ofelia García

Susana Ibarra Johnson

Kate Seltzer

With a Foreword by Guadalupe Valdés

Caslon • PHILADELPHIA

Para mis estudiantes y colegas en el Graduate Center, present and past, y sobre todo para el CUNY-NYSIEB team. Thanks for your wisdom and work. Y para los míos, present and future.

Ofelia

For Andrew, Aaron, Juanita and Reuben—*son mi amor, mi vida y mi esperanza.*

Susana

To all my former students who taught me to go with la corriente before I knew what to call it. To my parents and grandparents, whose multiple languages have been in my heart since before I can remember. And to Jimmy, whose love makes me better at everything.

Kate

Caslon, Inc.
825 N. 27th St.
Philadelphia, PA 19130

caslonpublishing.com

9 8 7 6 5

Library of Congress Cataloging-in-Publication Data

Names: García, Ofelia, author. | Johnson, Susana Ibarra, author. | Seltzer, Kate, author.
Title: The translanguaging classroom : Leveraging student bilingualism for learning / Ofelia García, Susana Ibarra Johnson, Kate Seltzer.
Description: Philadelphia : Caslon, [2017] | Includes bibliographical references and index.
Identifiers: LCCN 2016019210 (print) | LCCN 2016025328 (ebook) | ISBN 9781934000199 (pbk.) | ISBN 9781934000212 (ebook)
Subjects: LCSH: Education, Bilingual—United States. | Multilingualism—United States.
Classification: LCC LC3731 .G355 2016 (print) | LCC LC3731 (ebook) | DDC 370.117/50973—dc23
LC record available at https://lccn.loc.gov/2016019210

Printed in the United States of America.

Foreword

As I begin to write this Foreword, the fall quarter has just begun at Stanford and I have met the students enrolled in my course, *Issues in the Study of Bilingualism,* for the first time. The students are eager, interested, and many are dedicated to making a difference as future researchers and current and future teachers. In sharing their reasons for enrolling in the class, several students express the urgency of identifying best practices for designing dual language (bilingual) programs and two-way bilingual immersion programs, for teaching science, math, reading, and writing to English language learners, and for helping immigrant-origin students to close what appears to be an ever-widening achievement gap. There is little optimism expressed about schools' ability to make a difference in students' lives, and much concern about whether immigrant-origin children can actually be educated in U.S. schools as currently configured.

After introductions, I begin my brief lecture by talking about the shifts taking place in the field of bilingualism, about changing epistemologies, and about the excitement of moving forward by questioning the body of knowledge and the thinking that had informed us since *Languages in Contact* (Weinrich, 1979). From the questions my students ask, it is clear they have not yet heard about the *disinvention of languages* (Makoni & Pennycook, 2007), the *multilingual turn* (May, 2013), or *super-diversity* (Vertovec, 2007), and certainly not about *translanguaging* (Creese & Blackledge, 2010; Canagarajah, 2011, 2013; García, 2011a & b, 2012, 2013, 2014; García & Li Wei, 2014; Li Wei, 2010, 2013). Most have heard about code-switching and disapprove of its use, some describe their own language use as Spanglish or Chinglish, and the majority of the class fully subscribes to a narrow definition of bilingualism in which bilinguals are seen as two monolinguals in one person. It is clear that there is much work to be done if I am to move them gently from their unexamined deficit views about the flaws that they believe characterize immigrant youngsters' language(s) to embracing the richness of their present and future multicompetence. It may be even more difficult to persuade my students that an intense focus on the teaching of bits and pieces of English and the exclusion of their home language in all intellectual activities may not benefit their students in developing their very fine minds.

I will do my best. I will require the class to read both foundational works as well as the new literature (about translanguaging, pluralism, metrolingualism, and transidiomatic practices). They will read about language ideologies, language variation, societal versus individual bilingualism, and the fuzzy boundaries of "named" languages. We will engage in extensive discussions of language and identity, multilingualism, multiculturalism, and new linguistic landscapes, and we will argue about the types of instructional arrangements that might sustain and support bilingualism across generations. They will (I hope) learn a great deal and possibly begin to question many strongly rooted beliefs and perspectives.

I am painfully aware, nevertheless, that my carefully selected readings will not change students' everyday teaching. If they are to link these new perspectives on bilingualism to a transformative practice that builds on what we now know about bilingualism, they will need to go beyond the existing theoretical and research literature. They will need to read and carefully study very different works, works that begin with theory and then invite teachers to explore new ways of thinking about language and new approaches in using "named" languages in classrooms to transform their practice. Ideally such books will describe (1) how new theories can be instituted in everyday classrooms with students who are multicompetent, (2) how youngsters' needs can be identified, and (3) how particular pedagogies can respond to different students' characteristics and strengths. Such books will also provide details about designing classroom practices that meet these different needs and about the types of pedagogies that can develop youngsters' subject matter knowledge and their linguistic repertoires.

The process of translating theory to pedagogical practice is a difficult one. Teachers cannot imagine what they have not seen. Once socialized into their disciplines and professional identities and accompanying language ideologies, they cannot change their practice unless they have a solid understanding of the alternatives. Teachers may agree that established approaches have been ineffective. However, moving from that conclusion to an actionable understanding of what to do and how to do it requires detailed descriptions of what steps to take, as well as models of practice accompanied by commentaries relating particular pedagogies to their broader personal beliefs and their views on children's languages and abilities, curricular demands, policy expectations, and assessment challenges.

The Translanguaging Classroom: Leveraging Student Bilingualism for Learning provides precisely this important link between new theoretical perspectives on bilingualism and actual classroom practice. It is an important book that will significantly shift and problematize our current approaches to teaching immigrant-origin students in the years to come. I predict, moreover, that, because of this book, how researchers' and educators' view the use and role of language in the education of *all* children, especially language-minority children, will change dramatically as the ideas and practices presented here are discussed, debated, and implemented. At a time when we are engaged in a national conversation about race, inequality, poverty, opportunity, and immigration, this book brings us a groundbreaking and daring pedagogical vision. It invites us to re-examine and change the commonsense everyday classroom practices that we, as teachers and researchers, have used or recommended for (1) the teaching of content and language to immigrant-origin children in regular *and* bilingual education programs and (2) the teaching of monolingual-English-speaking children who hope to acquire a language other than English (LOTE) in two-way, dual-language bilingual programs.

I purposefully refer to the book as presenting a view that is both groundbreaking and daring. I chose *groundbreaking* because the conceptualizations of language that underlie the pedagogical practices proposed here will be both new and unprecedented for many educators. I chose *daring* because the views and perspectives on linguistic multicompetence that inform the proposed approaches to instruction directly challenge established orthodoxies about bilingualism, bilingual children, and the use of two languages in education.

The translanguaging pedagogy described in detail in the text builds directly on García & Li Wei 's (2014) book-length work on translanguaging and its role in education, which defines translanguaging as "an approach to the use of language, bilingualism, and the education of bilinguals that considers the language practices of bilinguals not as two autonomous language systems, as has been traditionally the case, but as one linguistic repertoire with features that have been societally constructed as belonging to two separate languages" (p. 2). In this book the authors describe translanguaging as "a way of *thinking about* and *acting on* the language practices of bilingual people." They then present a step-by-step guide for a pedagogy that builds on bilingualism itself—in all of its richness and complexity—and that invites teachers to see dual language competency as a repertoire of diverse and complex language practices that can be used and developed in multiple ways in everyday classrooms.

Thinking and *acting differently* about the language practices of bilingual people is fundamental to bringing about change. And change is imperative! Immigrant-origin children, in particular, are facing increasingly difficult challenges. For a number of years, those of us who work on the education of these children have continually looked for ways to call attention to the challenges facing youngsters variously classified as English language learners (ELLs) (Linquanti & Cook, 2013) as they struggle to "learn" English at the same time that they are learning challenging content. We have tried, for example, to describe ELL ghettos to those who, because they do not work in schools, imagine that "teaching" English is a straightforward, race-neutral, apolitical activity. We have also struggled to describe the disappointed faces of students who thought they would have the opportunity to learn, to excel, and to compete academically and their discouragement at being limited to meaningless drills on bits and pieces of language for hours at a time. Unfortunately, as many who spend time in classrooms with ELLs know too well, in many classes and in many schools, there is no access to age-appropriate subject matter content for students classified as ELLs, only hours of worksheets and activities that keep them both busy and quiet. They are tested endlessly, and their progress is evaluated narrowly.

This book challenges the status quo and the well-meaning pedagogies that provide few challenges for pobrecito students. It assumes that students arrive with valuable linguistic capabilities that can be leveraged to develop their fine minds and to further expand their academic and personal competencies by using their full existing language repertoires at all times. It rejects deficit perspectives and approaches to teaching bilingual students, whether emergent or established, and insists on recognizing that their multiple ways of being and speaking are an essential part of their cultural ways of knowing.

In very important ways, *The Translanguaging Classroom: Leveraging Student Bilingualism for Learning*, is by far the most compelling example proposed to date of a *culturally sustaining pedagogy* as defined by Paris (2012, p. 95):

> The term *culturally sustaining* requires that our pedagogies be more than responsive of or relevant to the cultural experiences and practices of young people—it requires that they support young people in sustaining the cultural and linguistic competence of their communities while simultaneously offering access to dominant cultural competence. Culturally sustaining pedagogy, then, has as its explicit goal supporting multilingualism and multiculturalism in practice and perspective for students and teachers. That is, culturally sustaining pedagogy seeks to perpetuate and foster—to sustain—linguistic, literate, and cultural pluralism as part of the democratic project of schooling.

As Paris (2012) argues, our search for asset or resource pedagogies, that is, for pedagogies that resist deficit perspectives and seek to honor, explore, and build on the cultures and experiences of minoritized students has been a long and challenging one. All of us, including scholars deeply committed to equity, have found it difficult to convince others to question the deeply embedded notion that students' heritage and community practices are incompatible with opportunity and academic excellence. Too often, proposed pedagogies for cultural responsiveness or relevance have not necessarily invited students to value what they bring or to proudly continue to use features of their full linguistic repertoires in both formal and informal oral and written production for a variety of purposes in and out of school.

This book is different. It explicitly takes the position that past scholarship on language has misunderstood the nature of bilingualism and bilingual practices. It insists that students be invited to foster, maintain, and develop their complex repertoires. It invites teachers to reject static views of Language A versus Language B kept separate and pristine. It urges them to engage thoughtfully and joyfully with the richness of multicompetence in children's lives.

We will learn much from this timely and significant book, and from the implementation of the *linguistically sustaining pedagogies* presented here. As these pedagogies are implemented, I predict that the field will engage in challenging and important conversations and debates about the theories and ideologies that are uniquely presented and problematized in this volume. As my class at Stanford makes enormously evident, our understanding of "bilingualism" has shifted in important ways. We now know more, and we now question many established views that had prevented us from seeing the complexity and potential of linguistic flexibility and range. In the case of my students, most of whom are deeply committed to social justice, making a difference in students' lives across their professional careers will require their constant examination and problematization of both established and current theories. It will also require, as Paris (2012) suggested, a clear change in *stance, terminology, and practice*. How we think, how we talk, and how we act matters. I applaud the authors for providing us with a guide for moving forward and sincerely thank them for their deep commitment to the complex, multicompetent voices of the children of the world.

Guadalupe Valdés
Palo Alto, California

Preface

If you have chosen to read *The Translanguaging Classroom: Leveraging Student Bilingualism for Learning*, you are probably an educator—a teacher, a curriculum developer, a professional development provider, a school administrator, or other school personnel. And like most educators, you probably have students in your classrooms and schools who speak languages other than English (LOTE) and you are interested in how to further their education, including their English language and literacy development. This book is for you.

This book shows teachers, administrators, consultants, and researchers how **translanguaging**, a way of thinking about and acting on the language practices of bilingual people, may hold the key to successfully educating bilingual students. The translanguaging pedagogy that we put forward in this book is purposeful and strategic, and we demonstrate how teachers can use translanguaging to

1. Support students as they engage with and comprehend complex content and texts
2. Provide opportunities for students to develop linguistic practices for academic contexts
3. Make space for students' bilingualism and ways of knowing
4. Support students' socioemotional development and bilingual identities

These four purposes frame the translanguaging pedagogy, and they work together to advance the primary purpose of translanguaging—social justice—ensuring that bilingual students, especially those who come from language minority groups, are instructed and assessed in ways that provide them with equal educational opportunities.

Translanguaging classrooms are aligned with the global and local realities of the 21st century. These dynamic classrooms advance the kinds of practices that college and career-readiness standards demand, as they enhance bilingual students' critical thinking and creativity. Teachers learn to expand and localize their teaching in ways that address all content and language standards, and integrate home, school, community, and societal practices and understanding. Translanguaging classrooms also allow teachers to carry out the mandates of the growing number of states that are adopting seals of biliteracy to reward students' bilingual abilities. At the time of this writing, 14 states have adopted seals of biliteracy.

WHO SHOULD READ THIS BOOK?

This book has been written specifically with bilingual students in 4th–12th grades in mind. Teachers and other educational leaders can use this book to guide teaching, instructional programming, and action-oriented research in any context.

Our primary audience is teachers. Any teacher, whether monolingual or bilingual, and whether involved in a program officially designated as English-medium[1] or bilingual education, can create a translanguaging classroom. You could be a specialized language teacher or professional—a teacher of English as an additional language, bilingual education, home language literacy, or world language[2]—a general education teacher of either children or adolescents, or of a specific content-area at the secondary level, or even the principal of a school. Teachers and administrators are capable of building instructional spaces that go beyond our traditional understanding about programs for bilingual students.

Many, if not most, classrooms are multilingual, with students who speak languages in addition to English. Some of these students are highly bilingual and biliterate (**experienced bilinguals**), whereas others' bilingualism and biliteracy is emerging (**emergent bilinguals**). Some of these bilingual learners have developed strong academic foundations through quality school systems, while others may have experienced limited formal schooling. Regardless of where your students fall within bilingual or educational progressions, this book demonstrates innovative ways of educating them.

Because of the important place of bilingual Latino students in U.S. education, this book emphasizes the context of Latino students—in English-medium and bilingual instructional settings—to help you understand translanguaging classrooms.[3] Because we know that translanguaging is not limited to Spanish–English bilingualism, we also draw on examples from English-medium classrooms that include bilingual students from linguistically and culturally diverse backgrounds. Whether your students are speakers of Spanish, Mandarin, Korean, Karen, Pular, or any other language, the principles for translanguaging in the classroom are the same.

Research and practice on bilingualism at U.S. schools has focused narrowly on English language learners' content and language learning, generally in English-medium classrooms, and reflecting a language-as-problem or deficit orientation. In contrast, *The Translanguaging Classroom: Leveraging Student Bilingualism for Learning* takes a much broader approach. We focus on all bilingual students, including those who are emergent bilinguals, as well as those who are seen by the academic mainstream as English speakers but speak languages other than English at home. We show teachers how to identify and build on the varied bilingual performances of all bilingual students, regardless of whether or not they perform well academically in English or another language, and regardless of whether they are learning in English-medium, bilingual, or LOTE classrooms.

We bring the translanguaging pedagogy to life through vignettes from three very different classrooms:

- A 4th-grade dual-language bilingual education classroom of students who speak English, Spanish, or both at home, taught by a bilingual (Spanish–English) teacher in Albuquerque, New Mexico
- An 11th-grade English-medium social studies classroom of students who speak English, Spanish, or both at home, taught by a monolingual teacher in New York City

---

[1]English-medium classes and programs officially use English for instructional purposes, and they aim for academic achievement and language development in English. Bilingual education classes and programs use two or more languages for instructional purposes, and they aim for biliteracy and academic performance in two languages.

[2]In the United States, world language refers to a class focused on the teaching of a LOTE as a subject to language majority students, whereas home language literacy classes teach that language to bilingual students as a subject. English as an additional language teachers could teach only the subject (English literacy) or be classroom teachers of all subjects. Bilingual teachers are classroom teachers teaching subjects through two languages.

[3]We use Latino not as a "Spanish" word with an "o" inflection, but simply as a word that is inclusive of all gender identities and all persons of Latin American heritage who are Spanish speakers.

- 7th-grade English-medium math and science classes that include emergent bilinguals who speak Spanish, Cantonese, Mandarin, French, Tagalog, Vietnamese, Korean, Mandingo, and Pular (Fula) at home, co-taught by a math and science teacher and an ESL teacher in Los Angeles, California

These rich and varied cases clearly demonstrate how teachers can adapt the translanguaging pedagogy that we introduce in this book for all students, whatever their bilingualism looks like, in whatever instructional context.

WHAT ARE THE KEY COMPONENTS OF A TRANSLANGUAGING PEDAGOGY?

The central innovative concept in this book for teachers is *translanguaging*, which García (2009) describes as "an approach to bilingualism that is centered not on languages, as has been often the case, but on the practices of bilinguals that are readily observable" (p. 45). This book builds on that approach in three important ways. First, we describe the **translanguaging corriente**,[4] the natural flow of students' bilingualism through the classroom. Second, we propose the **dynamic translanguaging progressions**, which is a flexible model that allows teachers to look holistically at bilingual students' language performances in specific classroom tasks from different perspectives at different times. Third, we introduce a **translanguaging pedagogy** for instruction and assessment that teachers can use to purposefully and strategically **leverage** the translanguaging corriente produced by students.

Translanguaging classrooms have two important dimensions. First, teachers observe students' languaging performances, and then describe and assess their complex language practices. Then teachers adapt and use the translanguaging pedagogy for instruction and assessment to leverage the translanguaging corriente for learning. Our work revolves around three principles:

1. Bilinguals use their linguistic repertoires as resources for learning, and as identity markers that point to their innovative ways of knowing, being, and communicating.
2. Bilinguals learn language through their interaction with others within their home, social, and cultural environments.
3. Translanguaging is fluid language use that is part of bilinguals' sense-making processes.

Translanguaging Corriente

We suggest that the translanguaging corriente, produced and driven by the positive energy of students' bilingualism, flows throughout all classrooms. Metaphorically, we think about the translanguaging corriente as a river current that you can't always see or feel, but that is always present, always moving, and responsible for changes in the (classroom) landscape. Sometimes the translanguaging corriente flows gently under the surface, for example, in classrooms where teachers do not generally tap into students' home language practices for learning. At other times the translanguaging corriente is much stronger, for example, in bilingual classrooms or English-medium classrooms that do draw on students' home language practices.

---

[4] We use the Spanish word *corriente*, which is a cognate with the English word *current*. Throughout the book we use other Spanish terms to reflect our own language practices. Because Spanish constitutes the language practices of over three fourths of U.S. bilingual students, this book pays special attention to the Latino population. However, educators working with other language groups might want to use terms in other languages that maintain the spirit of these terms.

To feel the translanguaging corriente, all you have to do is take a step back from your daily routine and listen and look. Listen hard to what your students say to you and their peers, inside the classroom, hallways, and cafeteria, and on the playground. If you listen hard enough you might be able to perceive their intrapersonal voices (the unvoiced dialogues they have in their heads with themselves or friends). Listen also to the conversations that take place when their families and peers are present; try to hear what is being said and how it is said, as well as what is not being said and why. Listening in this way allows you to hear your students' voices anew, and puts you in touch with the translanguaging corriente, even if it is not obviously at the surface of your classroom.

In this book the translanguaging corriente runs through the content it communicates and also through the ways that we have chosen to use words in Spanish in this predominately English-language text, without any italics. We do this to indicate that, for us, the Spanish features we use are not alien or foreign; they are simply part of our narrative, always present and part of us, even when we are writing in English. We translate some documents in the Appendix into Spanish because, as we said earlier, this is the largest population of U.S. bilingual students and in the classrooms featured in this book. However, you can translate the English text in these documents to any of the languages in your classroom as one means of strengthening the translanguaging corriente in your classroom.

Dynamic Translanguaging Progressions

The notion of the translanguaging corriente moves us from the concept of linguistic *proficiency*, which is assumed to develop along a relatively linear path in more or less the same way for all bilingual learners, to one of linguistic *performance*. The dynamic translanguaging progressions enable teachers to do the following:

- Gauge the students' different bilingual performances on different tasks from different perspectives
- Distinguish between **general linguistic performance** (bilingual students' ways of performing academic tasks—e.g., express complex thoughts effectively, explain things, persuade, argue, compare and contrast, recount events, tell jokes—without regard to the language used to express these tasks) and **language-specific performance** (bilingual students' use of features corresponding to what society considers a specific language or variety)
- Leverage the translanguaging corriente for learning in their classes

Teachers in translanguaging classrooms use the dynamic translanguaging progressions to document their students' language performances on specific classroom-based tasks—in any language.

Translanguaging Stance, Design, and Shifts

The translanguaging pedagogy in this book encompasses both instruction and assessment, and is structured into three interrelated strands: the **translanguaging stance**, **design**, and **shifts**.

A stance refers to the philosophical, ideological, or belief system that teachers draw from to develop their pedagogical framework. Teachers with a translanguaging stance believe that bilingual students' many different language practices work **juntos**/together, not separately, as if they belonged to different realms. Thus, the teacher believes that the classroom space must promote collaboration across content; languages; people; and home, school, and community. A translanguaging stance sees the bilingual child's complex **language repertoire** as a resource, never as a deficit.

Designing translanguaging instruction and assessment involves integrating home, school, and community language and cultural practices. The movement is created by the interaction between the translanguaging corriente and the teacher and students' joint actions, which enable bilingual students to integrate their home and school practices. Designing translanguaging instruction also means planning carefully (e.g., the grouping of students; elements of planning—essential ideas, questions, and texts; content, language, and translanguaging objectives; culminating projects; design cycle; pedagogical strategies). The translanguaging design is a flexible framework that teachers in English-medium and bilingual classrooms can use to develop curricular units of instruction, lesson plans, and classroom activities. The flexible design is the pedagogical core of the translanguaging classroom, and it allows teachers and students to address all content and language standards and objectives in equitable ways for all students, particularly bilingual students who are often marginalized in mainstream classrooms and schools. Designing assessment to set the course of the translanguaging corriente means including the voices of others, taking into account the difference between content and language, and between general linguistic and language-specific performances, and giving students opportunities to perform tasks with assistance from other people and resources, when needed.

Because the translanguaging corriente is always present in classrooms, it is not enough to simply have a stance that recognizes it and a design that leverages it. At times it is also important to follow the dynamic movement of the translanguaging corriente. The translanguaging shifts are the many moment-by-moment decisions that teachers make all the time. They reflect the teacher's flexibility and willingness to change the course of the lesson and assessment, as well as the language use planned for it, to release and support students' voices. The shifts are related to the stance, for it takes a teacher willing to keep meaning-making and learning at the center of all instruction and assessment to go with the flow of the translanguaging corriente.

USING THIS BOOK

We have three purposes for this book. First, we want educators and researchers to see a clearly articulated translanguaging pedagogy in practice. The examples from three very different classrooms stimulate concrete thinking about students, classrooms, programs, schools, practices, and research in different bi/multilingual communities. Second, we want to guide teachers' efforts to adapt the translanguaging pedagogy put forth in this book to any translanguaging context. Third, we provide the foundation for teachers and researchers to gather empirical evidence in translanguaging classrooms, which will help refine theory and strengthen practice.

We provide templates and examples from our focal bilingual and English-medium classrooms to assist you in designing instructional units, lessons, and assessments that identify and build on the translanguaging corriente in your classroom, school, and community context. When teachers enact a translanguaging stance, implement a translanguaging design for instruction and assessment, and intentionally shift their practices in response to student learning, they help fight the English-only current of much U.S. educational policy and practice and advance social justice.

We have divided the book into three parts:

Part I: Dynamic Bilingualism at School
   This part of the book focuses on the "what" and "why" of translanguaging
Part II: Translanguaging Pedagogy
   This part of the book focuses on how to create a translanguaging pedagogy
Part III: Reimagining Teaching and Learning through Translanguaging
   This part of the book focuses on how a translanguaging pedagogy works to enhance students' performances in different standards and literacy, develop their socioemotional identity, and advance social justice.

We divide each chapter into three parts. Learning objectives lay out what readers will learn and be able to do with chapter material. This is then followed by the core of the chapter—vignettes from classroom practices, tools, templates, or frameworks. Each chapter ends with questions and activities that pre-service and practicing teachers can use to reflect on aspects of translanguaging classrooms, as well as "take action" in their contexts. As a whole, the taking action questions guide educators to develop a translanguaging pedagogy in specific contexts. They also assist practitioners in developing, implementing, monitoring, and evaluating their translanguaging pedagogy in practice. We encourage you to work through these questions and activities with a close community of educators so that you can support one another as you explore and take up the translanguaging corriente in your classroom.

We invite you now to become a reflective practitioner and let yourself be swept up by the translanguaging corriente, as we explore its meaning in instruction and how to teach by capitalizing on its ebbs and flows. We hope that together we will

- See and hear the translanguaging corriente that already exists in classrooms and schools
- Learn how to intentionally, purposefully, and strategically navigate the translanguaging corriente in both instruction and assessment by applying the translanguaging stance, design, and shifts
- Demonstrate ways that bilingual students and teachers leverage the translanguaging corriente to learn content, develop language, make space for bilingual ways of knowing, and foster more secure socio-emotional identities
- Become more critical as we take up the stance of reflective practitioner and/or critical researcher and work toward social justice
- Show the kinds of challenges educators may face in translanguaging classrooms and reflect on how to overcome them
- Launch an action-oriented, social justice agenda to strengthen translanguaging pedagogy, practice, and research in diverse multilingual contexts.

ACKNOWLEDGEMENTS

This book was the result of much negotiation among ourselves and with our editor, Rebecca Field. Although the process was difficult at times, Rebecca pushed our thinking, our words, and the manuscript itself. What we never told you when things were difficult—gracias, Rebecca.

We also want to acknowledge the insights gained from Kathy Escamilla, Jamie Schissel, Guadalupe Valdés, and other reviewers. García also acknowledges a summer 2015 Visiting Appointment at the University of Cologne, and her colleague, Julie Panagiotopoulou, for the space given to her to revise this manuscript.

Contents

CHAPTER 9

Content-Area Literacy in the Translanguaging Classroom   129

CHAPTER 10

Biliteracy in the Translanguaging Classroom   142

CHAPTER 11

Socioemotional Well-Being and Social Justice   156

THE TRANSLANGUAGING CLASSROOM

PART I

DYNAMIC BILINGUALISM AT SCHOOL

CHAPTER 1

Translanguaging Classrooms: Contexts and Purposes

LEARNING OBJECTIVES

- Define translanguaging
- Explain how translanguaging can be used by teachers in different types of classroom contexts
- Summarize the four purposes of translanguaging and how they serve the overarching purpose of social justice
- Give concrete examples to illustrate translanguaging purposes in practice
- Begin to profile your classroom

One of the best ways to understand translanguaging is to see and hear it in action. Many of the teachers we have worked with have "aha moments" when they stop and listen to the ways students use language in their classrooms. For example, two students negotiate in Spanish over a math problem posed to them in English. One student with more experience in English quietly explains the directions to a newly arrived student from China. A group of students joke with one another using word play and English/Spanish puns. Once you take up this new lens for observing your bilingual students, you will notice new and exciting things about the way they language, which can guide the ways you plan, teach, assess, and advocate for their needs. Our use of the verb "to language" (e.g., "languaging," "translanguaging") reflects our understanding of language use as a dynamic communicative practice.

A translanguaging classroom is any classroom in which students may deploy their full linguistic repertoires, and not just the particular language(s) that are officially used for instructional purposes in that space. These classrooms can be developed anywhere we find students who are, or are becoming, bilingual. This includes classrooms that only use English as the official language for instruction (i.e., English-medium classrooms, including English as a second language [ESL] classrooms, whether **pull-out**, **push-in**, or **structured English immersion** programs), as well as bilingual (i.e., dual language, transitional) and world language or heritage language classrooms. We refer to the

1

students in translanguaging classrooms as *bilingual students,* by which we mean **emergent bilinguals** who are at the early stages of bilingual development, as well as more **experienced bilinguals** who can use two or more languages with relative ease, although their performances vary according to task, modality, and language. Our use of the term *emergent bilingual* in this book includes students who are officially designated by schools as "English language learners ("ELLs")," as well as English speakers who are learning other languages (e.g., Spanish, Arabic, Mandarin). We do not use the term *ELL* because it renders the languages other than English (LOTE) in the emergent bilinguals' developing linguistic repertoires invisible. We do, however, use this term when it refers to the official school designation.

TRANSLANGUAGING CLASSROOMS

A **translanguaging classroom** is a space built collaboratively by the teacher and bilingual students as they use their different language practices to teach and learn in deeply creative and critical ways. The term **translanguaging** comes from the Welsh *trawsieithu* and was coined by a Welsh educator, Cen Williams (1994, 2002), who developed a *bilingual* pedagogy in which students were asked to alternate languages for the purposes of receptive or productive use. For example, students might be asked to read in English and write in Welsh and vice versa to deepen and extend their bilingualism.

Since Colin Baker translated the Welsh term to English in 2001, translanguaging has been extended by many scholars to refer to both the complex language practices of bilingual and multilingual individuals and communities, as well as the pedagogical approaches that draw on those practices.[1] García (2009) explains that translanguaging "is an approach to bilingualism that is centered not on languages as has been often the case, but on the practices of bilinguals that are readily observable" (p. 45). From a linguistics perspective, Otheguy, García, and Reid (2015) define translanguaging as "the deployment of a speaker's full linguistic repertoire without regard for watchful adherence to the socially and politically defined boundaries of named languages" (p. 281). According to Flores and Schissel (2014, pp. 461–462):

> Translanguaging can be understood on two different levels. From a sociolinguistic perspective it describes the fluid language practices of bilingual communities. From a pedagogical perspective it describes a pedagogical approach whereby teachers build bridges from these language practices and the language practices desired in formal school settings.

Our focus in this book is on pedagogy, by which we mean the art, science, method, and practice of teaching.

Bilingualism is the norm in translanguaging classrooms—regardless of the official language of instruction of the class. We put forward a translanguaging pedagogy that shows educators how to **leverage**, or use to maximum advantage, the language practices of their bilingual students and communities while addressing core content and language development standards. We illustrate this pedagogy in action with three particular cases that together represent the kinds of diversity we find among students, teachers, language policies, program types, and grade levels in schools. As you read we encourage you to think about the actual language practices of your students relative to the official language policy of your school.

---

[1]For more on translanguaging, see García and Li Wei, 2014. See also Lewis, Jones, and Baker, 2012a, 2012b.

Carla's Elementary Dual-Language Bilingual Classroom

Carla teaches a 4th-grade dual-language bilingual[2] class in Albuquerque, New Mexico, where all of the students are from Spanish-speaking homes. This elementary school program aims for bilingualism, biliteracy, and academic achievement in two languages. Carla was born in Puebla, Mexico, and she came to New Mexico at the age of 10 with her family. She is bilingual and studied Spanish in high school and at college as she pursued her bilingual education certification.

Most of Carla's students are Spanish-speaking bilinguals, though their individual profiles are very different. *Moisés,* for example, emigrated from Mexico to the United States two years ago, and is considered a newcomer. Moisés is officially designated as an ELL, but we refer to him as an emergent bilingual. Though Moisés is developing his Spanish and English practices in Carla's classroom, he prefers speaking Spanish. *Ricardo*, like Moisés, is considered a newcomer, and is officially designated ELL. Ricardo is in the process of learning English. At home he speaks Spanish and Mixteco, the language he spoke with his family and community in Mexico. At different points on the bilingual spectrum are *Erica* and *Jennifer*, who were both born in the United States. Erica prefers to speak English, though her family does speak some Spanish at home, while Jennifer, a more experienced bilingual, feels comfortable using both languages to carry out academic tasks. As we can see, not all of Carla's students are classified as ELLs or are, as we call them, emergent bilinguals. Her students' bilingual performances are varied and the students have a wide range of strengths within and across languages.

The Common Core State Standards (CCSS) have been adopted by the state of New Mexico, and New Mexico is, at the time of this writing, part of the Partnership for Assessment of Readiness for College and Career (PARCC) consortium. Carla's instruction must therefore be aligned with the CCSS and students must demonstrate proficiency on PARCC assessments. New Mexico is also a member of the WIDA consortium. Carla's instruction for emergent bilinguals who are officially designated as ELLs must therefore align with the WIDA English language development (ELD) standards, and these students must demonstrate English language proficiency on the test developed by WIDA, Assessing Comprehension and Communication in English State-to-State (ACCESS) for ELLs. At this time, New Mexico also gives their emergent bilinguals the LAS Link Español, a diagnostic assessment of Spanish language development. Furthermore, all students in the dual-language bilingual program must demonstrate learning relative to the goals of bilingualism and biliteracy. This school district uses the Developmental Reading Assessment (DRA) to assess reading in English and the Evaluación del desarrollo de la lectura (EDL) to assess reading in Spanish.

Although Carla was always comfortable translanguaging and saw its value in intercultural communication, she was taught never to use it for instruction.

---

[2]We use the term **dual-language bilingual education** intentionally. In New Mexico, this type of bilingual program is often referred to as **one-way dual language education**. In some education districts, this type of program is referred to as a developmental bilingual education program, or as a developmental-maintenance bilingual education program. We do not use the term "one-way" because in practice we find tremendous variation in the ways that emergent and experienced bilingual students from the "same" language background use languages in their everyday lives. We also include the word *bilingual*, which has largely disappeared from discussions about dual language education in response to the backlash against bilingualism and bilingual education. In fact, it is not uncommon to hear bilingual educators say that dual language education is not bilingual education, a stance with which we disagree. Our use of bilingual emphasizes that dual language education is bilingual education.

Her teacher education program in bilingual education advocated that unless there was a clear and separate space for Spanish, English would take over instruction and Spanish would not be maintained. In studying the dual language model she was told that teachers were never to put the different language practices alongside each other. She was taught to make sure that writing in English and Spanish never appeared together, dedicating different parts of the room to the two languages. At the beginning of her career, she taught strictly in Spanish in the morning and in English in the afternoon, and corrected students when they spoke the "wrong" language at the "wrong" time. She never brought multilingual resources into the classroom—she used Spanish resources during Spanish time and English resources during English time.

When Carla discovered the concept of a translanguaging pedagogy for the first time, she questioned and resisted it. However, she quickly realized that despite all her strict rules about English here and Spanish there, her students were always using features from Spanish and English to make meaning, albeit surreptitiously. For example, during English time, they often whispered to each other in Spanish, and when Carla approached, the discussion would simply stop. Carla decided to bring the students' language practices to the forefront and build on them in the classroom. Instead of "policing" which language was used where, she encouraged students to use their entire **language repertoires** to learn and demonstrate what they had learned. Though she maintained an official space for English and an official space for Spanish to provide the appropriate opportunities for language development, she now allowed some flexibility in student language use.

At the center of Carla's literacy and language instruction during her (bi)-literacy block is the sharing of human experiences, and especially those of the neighborhood and land, el barrio y la tierra, which she sees as interrelated. The experiences of the New Mexico barrio where Carla's school is located are deeply connected to the tierra because many of her students' parents are farm workers. Carla introduced a translanguaging space into her dual-language bilingual classroom through what she called "Cuéntame algo," which she describes as a time for bilingual storytelling when a translanguaging literacy activity takes center stage. Her instructional unit, *Cuentos de la tierra y del barrio*, focuses on stories of how students, families, and the local community are tied to their land and, by extension, to their traditions. Students discuss cuentos written by Latino bilingual authors about land and traditions, as well as those told to them by family and community members, including abuelitos and abuelitas, grandparents whom Carla invites to her classroom. They also discuss the video clips that they watch, as well as their own experiences, and those of barrio residents, with the land.

Stephanie's High-School Social Studies Class

Stephanie is an 11th-grade social studies teacher in New York City, and English is the official language used for instructional purposes in her classroom. Thus, Stephanie's classroom provides an example of a translanguaging classroom in an English-medium context. She is of Polish descent and, though she knows some Spanish words that she has learned from her students, she does not consider herself bilingual. Stephanie was trained as a history teacher but found that once she entered the classroom she also had to teach content-area literacy.

The linguistic diversity in Stephanie's English-medium classroom is rich. Most, though not all, of Stephanie's students are Spanish-speaking Latinos who perform differently in language and literacy in Spanish and English. A few of her students are officially designated as ELLs. Some of these emergent bilinguals (to use our preferred term), like **Noemí**, are newcomers with solid educational backgrounds and strong oracy and literacy in Spanish. Other newcomers, like *Luis*, have had interrupted or poor schooling in the countries they came from and struggle with literacy and numeracy in any language. Other emergent bilinguals, like *Mariana*, have received most or all of their education in the United States but were labeled as ELLs when entering school and have yet to test out of this status. Although Mariana is now classified as a **long-term English language learner (LTELL)**, she generally uses English at school; in fact, many of her teachers do not even realize she is still officially considered an ELL.

It is important to emphasize that we also find considerable linguistic diversity among Stephanie's "English-speaking" students. Most of her students are bilingual Latinos, but because they are not designated as ELLs their bilingualism tends to go unnoticed. Stephanie, however, knows that these students have a wide range of experiences with oral and written Spanish and English. Some, like *Eddy* and *Teresita* were born in the United States and have different degrees of comfort with using Spanish. The few students who are not Latinos in her class are African Americans, some from the Anglophone Caribbean, and their English also includes features that are not always considered standard or appropriate for academic purposes.

In 2010, New York State adopted what it called the P–12 Common Core Learning Standards (CCLS) for English Language Arts and Literacy in History/ Social Studies, Science and Technical Subjects, and for Mathematics. These are based on the CCSS, with a few additions. This means that Stephanie's instruction must be aligned with New York's CCLS and that all students in her class have to demonstrate proficiency on assessments aligned to the CCLS. In addition, New York State has standards for science and social studies in place. Academic achievement tests for graduation (the Regents Exams) are translated into the five most common languages of students—Chinese, Haitian Creole, Korean, Russian, and Spanish—although students also have to pass the English Regents exam. Furthermore, all students who are designated as ELLs in New York State must demonstrate English language proficiency on the New York State English as a Second Language Achievement Test (NYSESLAT).

New York launched the Bilingual Common Core Initiative (BCCI) in 2012, which is intended to help all teachers differentiate CCLS language arts instruction and assessment for the bilingual students in their schools. At the heart of this initiative are the New Language Arts Progressions (NLAP) and Home Language Arts Progressions (HLAP). Unlike the English language proficiency and development frameworks used by other states, the BCCI explicitly acknowledges that students' home languages are a valuable resource to draw on and that the new and home languages are inextricably related in learning. These progressions are flexible and can be used by teachers as a first step toward understanding how students use their new and home languages to learn. In fact, emergent bilinguals at the early stages of ELD are allowed to demonstrate their understanding of content in their home languages. Teachers can use formative assessments to approximate the new and home language development levels of their students along these progressions (Velasco & Johnson, 2014).

When she first started teaching, Stephanie realized quickly that her students were capable of thinking critically and understanding deeply. But she also knew that the English language through which the content was taught was a real challenge for some of her students. How could she work with the students' strengths and creativity *and* make the content comprehensible? When she learned about translanguaging, she realized that she could use translanguaging strategies with her students to leverage the many different language resources in her class. Without knowing it, she had already set up her classroom in ways that made it possible to capitalize on translanguaging. She had always organized students into groups that had mixed strengths so they could help each other in the project-based activities of her thematic, often interdisciplinary, units. In these groupings she noticed that peers helped each other using Spanish as well as English. She realized she could encourage this kind of translanguaging interaction to enable all students to engage with the learning activity.

Since learning about translanguaging, Stephanie has made a strong effort to build a robust **multilingual ecology** in which all her students can thrive. For example, although her classroom is not officially bilingual, Stephanie works with bilingual staff members and student volunteers to translate and create multilingual materials and actively seeks out Spanish language resources. Stephanie also has a shelf full of bilingual dictionaries and picture dictionaries that students can use at any point in the lesson. She has been successful in securing iPads, which newcomers use frequently to access the Spanish version of their history textbook, and she also uses apps like Google Translate.

Stephanie is passionate about helping her students see connections across different content areas. While schools separate topics into categories like social studies or science, Stephanie believes that one cannot be understood without the other. Thus, many of Stephanie's units focus on history but bring in interdisciplinary connections. For example, one of Stephanie's interdisciplinary units, *Environmentalism: Then and Now,* is a historical study of the U.S. environmental movement. Students learn about the history of this social movement by reading their textbooks and many supplemental readings from websites, newspapers, and magazines. They also listen to podcasts and radio interviews, watch clips from documentaries, and look at visual art. Stephanie also invites in community experts, for example the 11th-grade science teacher and the leader of a local nonprofit.

Though the textbook does not focus heavily on the environmental movement, Stephanie places this movement within a larger historical context, from its beginnings during industrialization, to social action campaigns in the 1960s and 1970s, to today's political conversation on climate change. Because she knows that her students excel when their understanding is "brought home," the unit culminates in students designing a plan of action that would make the school or local community more environmentally sound and/or sustainable.

Justin's Role as a Middle-School English as a Second Language Teacher

Justin provides push-in ESL services in English-medium middle-school math and science classrooms in Los Angeles, California. Justin speaks English and Mandarin Chinese (following two years of studying Chinese in Shanghai). His students are speakers of many languages, including Spanish, Cantonese Chinese, Mandarin Chinese, Korean, Mandingo, Tagalog, Vietnamese, and Pular (Fula). The students who speak Fula and Mandingo also speak French, the colonial language of West Africa. Because there are multiple speakers of Spanish, Cantonese, Mandarin, French, Tagalog and Vietnamese in this classroom, Justin groups students according to their home languages and mixed English language abilities. But there is only one Korean student in the class, *Jeehyae.*

Although most students in Justin's class have at least one other student with whom they can collaborate to make meaning of the texts, there is great diversity among students, even among those with the same language background. For example, *Yi-Sheng* arrived recently from Taiwan. Unlike some of the other students from mainland China, Yi-Sheng has not received any instruction in using Latin script, so she needs lots of writing practice. *Pablo* came not from Mexico, the country of origin of most of the Latino students in the class, but from Argentina, and attended private English after-school classes before coming to Los Angeles. *Fatoumata* came from Guinea not long ago.

She had only gone to school irregularly in Africa, so she struggles with literacy in French, the language of instruction in Guinea. She is not the only Pular-speaking student in Justin's classroom, although West African children in the class often speak to each other in French, the colonial language.

California has adopted the CCSS, and is a member of the Smarter Balanced consortium as of this writing, which means that Justin's instruction needs to align with the CCSS and that all of his students need to demonstrate proficiency on the Smarter Balanced assessments. California has also developed the Common Core en Español, which is a translation of the CCSS from English into Spanish that also addresses concepts that are specific to Spanish language and literacy. All students in California who are officially designated as English learners (ELs) have to demonstrate proficiency on the state-developed California English Language Development Test (CELDT), based on the California ELD Standards.

Justin's role in the content classrooms has been to support the students so that they could meet the demands of the California CCSS and the California ELD Standards. He often obtains supplementary written material in the languages of the students and brings it to class. He uses Google Translate to write worksheet instructions in the students' languages. Justin also encourages students to use iPads to look up words and translate passages, and he often uses the iPad to make himself understood in students' languages. Because Jeehyae is the only Korean student in the class, Justin spends lots of time using Google Translate, trying to make the material accessible to her. He also makes sure to help her translanguage on her own, telling her to use her intrapersonal inner-speech to brainstorm, and he encourages her to prewrite and annotate texts in Korean. Though Justin won't understand what Jeehyae writes, he makes it clear that the language she brings with her is useful and necessary to her learning and her development of English. Justin also often seeks help from other Korean-speaking students in the school. Because students in this classroom often write in their home languages, Jeehyae has discovered that she knows some of the Chinese characters the Cantonese and Mandarin speakers use because she learned some of them in her Korean school.

Although these three teachers' classrooms are different with respect to their students' language practices, the official language policy in their classes, and the different state-mandated standards, they all use translanguaging in their classrooms.

It is important to remember that translanguaging classrooms can be of any type—bilingual (whether dual language or transitional) or English-medium (whether ESL programs or mainstream classrooms). Translanguaging also can be used by any teacher, whether bilingual or monolingual; whether an elementary, middle school, or high school teacher; whether officially a language teacher (English or a language other than English) or a content teacher.

PURPOSES FOR TRANSLANGUAGING

The translanguaging pedagogy we put forward in this book is purposeful and strategic. We identify four primary translanguaging purposes:

1. Supporting students as they engage with and comprehend complex content and texts
2. Providing opportunities for students to develop linguistic practices for academic contexts
3. Making space for students' bilingualism and ways of knowing
4. Supporting students' bilingual identities and socioemotional development

These four translanguaging purposes work together to advance social justice. That is, when teachers effectively leverage students' bilingualism for learning, they help level the playing field for bilingual students at school.

Supporting Student Engagement with Complex Content and Texts

When we make space for students to use all the linguistic resources they have developed to maneuver and navigate their way through complex content, myriad learning opportunities open up. Rather than watering down our instruction, which risks oversimplification and robs students of opportunities to engage in productive grappling with texts and content, translanguaging better enables us to teach complex content, which in turn helps students learn more successfully.

Moll (2013) describes the importance of working with bilingual students in what he calls the **bilingual zone of proximal development**, in which assistance is offered to students bilingually to mediate their learning and stretch their performance. As we will see, there are many ways of doing this. Students can work in home language groups to solve difficult problems or analyze a complex text. They can talk to one another about content using their own language practices in ways that help them better understand that content. Because learners develop knowledge *interpersonally,* it is important for them to enter into relationships with others whose language repertoires overlap with theirs so that they can deeply understand the classroom texts. Knowledge is also developed *intrapersonally,* as students try out new concepts and new languaging in internal dialogue and private speech. Because bilingual students have a voice that includes their home languages, they need to be encouraged to draw on all of the resources for learning in their linguistic repertoires.

Unfortunately, we don't often find LOTE being used as resources for learning challenging content and engaging with complex texts in U.S. classrooms serving bilingual students. Instead, teachers generally tell students to only use English; bilingual students (and particularly emergent bilingual students) often learn that only English counts. This is especially the case for Spanish-speaking students who are told: "speak English," "don't speak Spanish"; "think in English," "don't think in Spanish." As a result, Latino students often learn to see Latino cultural and linguistic practices only as home and community practices that are not to be used in academic environments. In so doing, bilingual Latino students are often silenced, using only part of their linguistic repertoires and accessing only a small portion of the adults, peers, and texts that are important to them in acquiring content knowledge. Leveraging translanguaging interpersonally and intrapersonally can help bilingual students overcome this silence and engage with and understand complex content and texts.

Schools need to find ways of ensuring that all students, not just those whose language practices align with those used in school, understand challenging content and texts. Translanguaging enables educators to more equitably provide opportunities for students to engage with complex material, regardless of language practices. In this way, translanguaging at school is inextricably linked with social justice.

For example, in a lesson from the *Environmentalism: Then and Now* unit plan that Stephanie designed for her 11th-grade English-medium class, students were asked to analyze some statistics about air pollution and asthma, issues that disproportionately affect Latinos and other residents of urban areas, as well as make a connection to the previous day's lesson on the Clean Air Act of 1970. Stephanie included statistics about asthma rates among Latinos, as well as the map in Figure 1.1 that illustrated which counties did not meet standards for air pollutants.

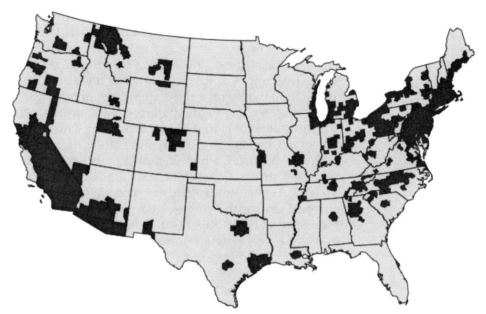

Figure 1.1   Counties that do not meet standards for air pollutants, based on U.S. Environmental Protection Agency data. (Retrieved from http://www.nrdc.org/health/effects/latino/english/latino_en.pdf)

After analyzing the two different forms of data, Stephanie asked students, organized into small groups, to come up with some kind of connection—how did these two sets of data tell a story about the issue? Although the official language of instruction was English, Stephanie told students that they could discuss the statistics, the map, and the answers to her question in English and/or Spanish and could write their responses in English and/or Spanish. She also told students they were expected to share with the whole class. This vignette shows us what happened next:

After examining the map and discussing it with his group, Luis, who recently came to the United States from El Salvador, shared in Spanish with the whole class that "las áreas oscuras están cerca de ciudades como Nueva York y Los Ángeles. Muchos Latinos viven en esas ciudades." [The dark areas are near cities like New York and Los Angeles. A lot of Latinos live in those cities.] Mariana, who was in Luis' group, eagerly added: "Yes, Latinos live in the dark areas on the map. Like in New York and Los Angeles." Some students nodded and others wrote down the comment in Spanish or English next to their own in their notebooks. Eddy added in English that "cities have more pollution than other places." Stephanie then summed up the two comments in English, restating, "It sounds like what you're saying is that if most Latinos live in cities, and cities have more air pollution than rural or suburban areas, that this might be a cause of increased asthma in Latinos." Students nodded and voiced their agreement.

The kind of linguistic flexibility we see here—using both languages to discuss, negotiate, and finally write down connections; sharing out their learning in both languages—helped all of the students in Stephanie's classroom engage with English texts, synthesize a complex issue, and demonstrate their learning. As we can see from Luis', Mariana's, and Eddy's comments, the translanguaging they had done in groups allowed them to access the content, despite the fact that, for example, Luis was a less experienced English user than Eddy. Without translanguaging, which was both an explicit part of Stephanie's instructional design and a naturally occurring phenomenon among students in their small groups, this kind of intellectually rich conversation would not have taken place.

Carla also uses translanguaging to engage her bilingual students with complex content and texts. However, because an important goal of Carla's instruction is biliteracy, translanguaging in her classroom looks quite different from what we saw in Stephanie's class. During Cuéntame algo, students engage in studies of Latino bilingual authors who translanguage to make experiences and characters come to life. Students are encouraged to use all their language practices, which include English and Spanish, to discuss and evaluate these stories. Sometimes texts are chosen with English as the main language but other times Spanish is the main language of the text. Besides reading and discussing, students are encouraged to design texts (orally and in writing) that reflect the dynamic bilingual language use of communities, both when they communicate among themselves and when they communicate with others who may not share their language practices.

For example, in a lesson from her unit on *Cuentos de la tierra y del barrio*, Carla and her students used the Cuéntame algo space to do a read-aloud and shared reading of *Three Wise Guys: Un cuento de Navidad* by Sandra Cisneros:

Carla read en voz alta:

> The big box came marked *do not open till xmas*, but the mamá said not until the Day of the Three Kings. Not until Día de los Reyes, the sixth of January, do you hear? That is what the mamá said exactly, only she said it all in Spanish. Because in Mexico where she was raised, it is the custom for boys and girls to receive their presents on January sixth, and not Christmas, even though they were living on the Texas side of the river now. Not until the sixth of January.

Carla engaged students in telling her about *el Día de los Reyes*. Some of the students did so in English, some in Spanish, and some in both languages.

To get students to engage with the text in a deeper, more nuanced way, she set forth the following activity:

Carla took [a] large sheet of chart paper and drew la corriente del Río Grande. On one side she wrote a sentence the author had written in English. She then asked the groups to translate into Spanish what the author would have said if she were on the Mexican side of the Río Grande. While they worked, one group grew louder. Carla asked what was the matter and one of them said: "Maestra, es que mi familia on the other side also speaks English. And on this side también hablamos español." A whole class discussion then ensued about bilingual language practices in the borderlands and when and how to use them.

Rather than stop with simple comprehension of the story, the shared reading of this class was the jumping-off point for students' engagement in Cisneros' book. Carla's explicit focus on the language of the book, and how different contexts and characters use different language practices, helped students connect with the story on a much deeper level. Carla also tapped into students' bilingualism, asking them to translate sentences from the book from one language to the other. This not only helps students with the close reading of a text; it also helps them to learn new vocabulary and make connections between their languages. Carla encourages students not to produce a literal translation, but to transform the text as they render it in the other language.

When students came to the realization that their familia on both sides of the border spoke both languages, they began a larger, critical conversation about language practices in borderlands like Texas. This connection and intellectual exchange would not have been possible without the translanguaging that students experienced in the Cuéntame algo space. Similar to Stephanie's lesson, Carla's explicit use of translanguaging helped her students engage more deeply with a text.

Providing Opportunities for Students to Develop Linguistic Practices for Academic Contexts

"Academic language" is a term we encounter over and over again. Following Valdés (2017), we wish to reframe this term, imagining that what some call academic language is simply one of many forms of languaging that students must take up to be successful in school. Translanguaging can help us teach the types of linguistic practices that are deemed appropriate for academic contexts. For example, translanguaging supports bilingual students' ability to use language to gather, comprehend, evaluate, synthesize, and report on information and ideas, using text-based evidence, as the CCSS (or any other 21st-century standards) require. Translanguaging also helps students develop the ability to use language to persuade, explain, and convey real or imaginary experience. Because translanguaging requires collaboration, it also bolsters students' ability to use language socially through cooperative tasks, another language requirement of the CCSS.

Encouraging students to use all the features of their language repertoires, including lexical (words), syntactic (grammar), and discourse (larger chunks of text that hang together as a unit) features, gives them something on which to "hang" new linguistic features—what García has called translanguaging "hooks." When learning a new language, translanguaging can help students make connections and comparisons, ask deep questions, and practice and play with language. Translanguaging can also demystify what some call academic language, showing students that using the highly valued language practices for academic purposes is actually just adding another set of **language features** and practices to their growing repertoires.

When translanguaging is not allowed in schools, bilingual students are placed at a disadvantage because they are assessed on only a portion of their linguistic repertoires and are taught in ways that do not fully leverage their language resources. Furthermore, the new language features that bilingual students learn at school do not always become part of their own linguistic repertoires, continuing to represent a "second" language that belongs to others. Thus, this translanguaging purpose is also linked to social justice because it creates the space for fair educational and assessment practices for bilingual students—without the linguistic prejudice that accompanies accepting only the linguistic features of standard English—the language of power.

The following example from Stephanie's lesson on air pollution illustrates how she and her students use translanguaging to strengthen students' linguistic practices for academic purposes. The focus is on the asthma rates among Latinos, specifically Puerto Ricans.

Stephanie projected the following statistics up on the SMART Board and asked one student to read through them aloud:

- Puerto Rican Americans have twice the asthma rate as compared to the overall Hispanic population.
- Hispanics are 30 percent more likely to visit the hospital for asthma, as compared to non-Hispanic Whites.

- Puerto Rican children are 3.2 times more likely to have asthma, as compared to non-Hispanic Whites.
- Hispanic children are 40 percent more likely to die from asthma, as compared to non-Hispanic Whites.

After the student read the statistics, Stephanie checked the class' comprehension of the English used. Luis said: "Maestra no entiendo" (and pointed to the phrase "more likely"). Stephanie asked students to translate it for Luis, and this turned into a heated discussion. Some translated it as "más me gusta" [I like it more]. Others as "más como" [more like]. Finally, Stephanie asked Luis to use the translating app on a class iPad, and he immediately came back with "más probable." Stephanie annotated the text on the SMART Board with this Spanish phrase. Now all students in the class knew not only what it meant in English, but also how to say it in Spanish.

This simple classroom vignette illustrates two important points. First, bilingual students may think they know the meanings of a word or phrase (e.g., more likely) in an academic text because they know each of the words in other contexts, but this is not always the case. This vignette also illustrates ways that students' existing language practices are valued and channeled into learning new practices, such as those deemed important in academic contexts. Because Stephanie is not a Spanish speaker, she encourages her students to help one another and to use resources such as translation apps to better understand this and other texts in English. By annotating an English text with a Spanish phrase, Stephanie is also helping students grow as bilingual and biliterate people, even if she herself is not bilingual and this is not a "bilingual" class.

Furthermore, Stephanie encourages her African American students to think about differences between ways they use language among their friends and at school. She often discusses language in hip hop and compares it to written social studies texts that students have to read. Stephanie observes that her African American students are also picking up some Spanish words, while her Latino students are learning about features of African American English and of, for example, Jamaican Creole, spoken by some of the Anglophone Caribbean students in the class. Stephanie's time and focus on language in her content-area classroom demonstrates her belief that teaching students to use language in academic contexts is as important as learning social studies content.

Making Space for Students' Bilingualism and Ways of Knowing

In addition to improving teaching and learning, translanguaging contributes to the creation of a new kind of classroom, one that takes bilingualism and the bilingual understanding of language as the norm, putting bilingual people at the center. Shifting focus like this makes space for students to learn and make choices about language that help them traverse the uneven waters of communication in our society. Rather than viewing languages according to rigid power hierarchies, translanguaging can help our students understand languages as practices that are used in different social contexts for different purposes.

This kind of bilingual lens fosters **critical metalinguistic awareness**—an understanding that there are social, political, and ideological aspects of language (Fairclough, 1995). Students learn that language use is not neutral, but regulated by different social groups for their own purposes. This space—the intentional moment when teachers allow students to use their entire language repertoires—can help all students become more aware of their expressive potential and how and why we make choices about language. When students gain this kind of awareness they can challenge linguistic hierarchies and rules and tap into seeing the world through their creative and critical bilingual or multilingual perspective.

Thus, translanguaging makes possible the educational inclusion of bilingual students' ways of knowing and languaging. In giving expression to other ways of being and knowing, translanguaging has the potential to build a more socially just world. For example, during a different day's Cuéntame algo, Carla and her students read *Lluvia de plata* by Sara Poot Herrera, a story about Mariana, a young woman who visits the Tarahumara region in Chihuahua, Mexico and experiences a cultural and language transformation. To help them better comprehend the story, Carla had students place illustrations onto a backdrop that she created of la Barranca del Cobre [Copper Canyon] overlooking la sierra Tarahumara.

Moisés placed his illustration card on to the backdrop and shared the following:

> Esta parte que leí me gusta porque los trabajadores que construyeron el ferrocarril le llamaban al tren que venía de Kansas a Chihuahua "si te cansas." Yo creo que no sabían cómo decir Kansas, entonces para recordar cómo decirlo solamente mencionaban "si te cansas." [This part that I read I liked because the workers that built the railroad would call the train coming from Kansas to Chihuahua "si te cansas" ("if you get tired"). I think they did not know how to say Kansas, so to remember how to say it they would mention "si te cansas"].

[Everyone starts laughing.] Moisés explained how railroad workers adapted the word Kansas [/kǽnzəs/] to a Spanish word that was similar in pronunciation, cansas [/kansas/]. Although other students laughed, some immediately joined in: "En mi casa nosotros usamos este tipo de palabra. . . ." [We use this type of word at home.] And another, "Sí es cierto; he oído algo así también en mi casa." [Yes, it's true; I've heard this also at home.] Some students acknowledged that at home Spanish was often used to remember the sounds of English words. The teacher asked how this was so. The students then shared that, for example, the Spanish word gel [pronounced "hel"] for hair gel was used to remember how to pronounce the English word help. The Spanish word flor [flower] was used to help recall the pronunciation of the English word floor.[3]

The play-on-word jokes or chistes that emerge from words that sound nearly the same in Spanish and English are more than just entertaining; to find a word that creates a chiste takes linguistic and cultural knowledge *across* languages and cultures. The students found the translanguaging moment amusing, yet the humorous moment reflected the complexity of their understanding of language use across contexts and languages. Further, Carla invited this complex understanding into the classroom as a strength and asset on which her students could draw. By using a text that is culturally and linguistically relevant and that builds on students' translanguaging practices, Carla's students could hear and see themselves and their communities in the text and feel safe enough to experiment with and explore translanguaging.

Our earlier discussion of Carla and her class' shared reading of *Three Wise Guys: Un cuento de Navidad* illustrated how a focus on bilingualism and bilingual language practices can foster students' critical metalinguistic awareness. In the next vignette, we see how Carla's focus on the author Sandra Cisneros' translanguaging helped students engage with a complex text by drawing on their own bilingualism and ways of knowing.

---

[3]This example is developed further in Johnson and Meyer, 2014.

Students continued to read the story in guided reading groups beyond what Carla had read out loud, and Carla asked them to pay careful attention to the words Cisneros had chosen to include in Spanish—chicharras (insects), urracas (black/white birds), comadre (woman relative). In their groups, they reflected on and discussed why these words and not others were rendered in Spanish and why the author might have made these choices. Carla then instructed the students to select other words they would have rendered in Spanish if they had been the author.

As bilingual people, Carla and her students have the ability to discuss Cisneros' translanguaged text in a more nuanced, complex way. By drawing their attention to the author's language choices, Carla helps her students grow more critical about language, which in turn helps them grow as bilingual thinkers and writers themselves. The students commented that comadre was probably rendered in Spanish because it is a word from their own culture and community. A discussion ensued about why Cisneros had used urraca and chicharras. One student immediately said: "Because of the beautiful rolling double r." They then explored other words in Spanish that had a double r. They looked through the text to see if there were other words in English that would have an equivalent in Spanish that had a double r. This kind of critical metalinguistic analysis of a translanguaged text also demonstrates to students that bilingual languaging is rich and intentional, not messy or impure. When they discussed Cisneros' translanguaging, Carla and her class were also reaffirming their own translanguaging and drawing on their bilingualism to understand a complex text.

Supporting Students' Bilingual Identities and Socioemotional Development

Translanguaging fosters bilingual students' identities and socioemotional development, which promotes social justice. First, translanguaging enables all bilingual students to participate actively in daily classroom life. For many students whose ways of languaging differ from the status quo ideal of those considered "native speakers," classroom learning can be difficult and alienating. By making space for students to language on their own terms and participate fully in academic conversations and work, we are modeling the kind of active participation needed for the creation of a more just world. Second, translanguaging helps students to see themselves and their linguistic and cultural practices as valuable, rather than as lacking. By teaching students to see their languages as part of a whole, contingent, and ever-changing performance, we are challenging a monolingual version of society and breaking the socially constructed fronteras that stand between languages and create hierarchies of power.

We return to Stephanie's *Environmentalism: Then and Now* unit to see this translanguaging purpose in action. To help students build background on the topic of air pollution, Stephanie started the day's lesson by showing students a public service announcement (PSA) about asthma. The PSA, which ran about 30 seconds, depicted a young Latino male suffering from an asthma attack. Stephanie played the clip twice, once in English and once in Spanish, and asked students to share any questions or connections they had regarding the video clip:

Eddy shared in English that his brother had really bad asthma and has had to go to the hospital several times. Luis jumped in saying, "Me too! My brother. . .él. . .in El Salvador. . ." Sensing that Luis was having trouble continuing in English, Stephanie asked him to finish his sentence in Spanish. Luis continued in Spanish, explaining that his brother, who still lives in El Salvador, worked construction and that the dust from the worksite gave him asthma attacks. Stephanie listened, and when Luis was finished, she asked another student in Luis' group, Mariana, to translate what Luis said. Though Mariana understands Spanish, she has told Stephanie that she feels more comfortable speaking English. However, she is a very competent translator, a skill for which, as Stephanie knows, she is often praised by her family.

In this short excerpt, we interpret Stephanie's comfort with linguistic flexibility and translanguaging as an act of social justice and a way of supporting her students' socioemotional growth. To understand what we mean, we only have to put forth a different image, one we have seen in far too many English-medium classrooms: Luis, stymied by his emerging English practice, gets frustrated and falls silent, putting his head down on his desk. Other students who are not comfortable sharing in English stare out the window, doodle, whisper to one another, and sneak looks at their phones underneath their desks. Instead of this image, Stephanie's classroom is one of engagement and shared learning. All students are encouraged to use all their languages to share their ideas, which helps Stephanie understand what they know and can do. In addition, students' out-of-school lives—their stories and skills, such as Mariana's experience as a translator—are honored and drawn on to learn new content. Translanguaging, then, becomes a way of working against the kind of classroom experiences that render many students mute. By enabling them to use all their languages, they are able to be themselves, help one another, and succeed academically.

The few African American students in Stephanie's class also relate well to the PSA. Many join in the discussion and share their families' struggles with asthma. Together, the African American and Latino students in Stephanie's class become aware of the toxins in the neighborhoods where they live. They start questioning why. This is not only the beginning of a research project on environmental toxins where students worked through English and Spanish, but also of a letter-writing campaign to their elected officials where students used their voices in both English and Spanish.

Meanwhile, after reading the story *Three Wise Guys: Un cuento de Navidad* in Carla's bilingual class, she asks students to work on translating a piece of the story from English into Spanish: "The mother in the story doesn't speak English. Write the story in a way that the mother would understand." Once student groups had worked together on translating, Carla told them to

Reflect on the language practices of the characters in the story—the Spanish-speaking mother; the bilingual children, Rubén and Rosalinda; and the father who speaks English but cannot read it. As you discuss, feel free to use features from both English and Spanish to recapture the bilingual voice of the family in the story and to integrate your own language practices, as the narrator of the story has done.

Through the translation activity and the ensuing discussion, Carla encourages bilingual students' use of translanguaging to make meaning, to develop a bilingual voice in writing, and to deepen their understanding about how all their language practices work together. To this end, Carla has students analyze the ways in which English and Spanish are used in a literary piece written primarily in English, and she has her students practice translation. Through these activities, students learn how translanguaging and translating are transformative acts, changing not only the text but also the text's ability to engage others and give them voice. The students' translation of part of the text into Spanish was not merely an academic exercise; it enabled the students to imagine and hear the Spanish-language voice of the mother who cannot say anything in the story itself. Thus, translanguaging allows us to hear voices that may have been excluded. It gives students an understanding of how language use is tied to power, how its use is often employed to produce and reproduce social inequalities, and how bilingual students can rewrite texts to include diverse contributions and perspectives.

CONCLUSION

A translanguaging classroom is purposeful and strategic, not chaotic and messy. Of course, the ways that teachers design their translanguaging pedagogy will vary according to their own bilingual experiences and relative to the school and community context in which they work. Translanguaging classrooms are powerful, equitable learning environments for bilingual students that enable these learners to (1) engage with complex content and texts, (2) strengthen linguistic practices for academic contexts, (3) draw on their bilingualism and ways of knowing, and (4) develop socioemotionally with strong bilingual identities. When teachers effectively leverage students' bilingualism for learning, they can level the playing field and advance social justice.

QUESTIONS AND ACTIVITIES

1. What are the challenges that translanguaging presents to your understanding of bilingualism or how bilingual students are taught?
2. Compare and contrast Carla's and Stephanie's uses of translanguaging. Why do you think those differences occurred? You might think about their personal backgrounds, the grade levels they teach, and their classroom contexts.

TAKING ACTION

1. Begin a preliminary profile of a translanguaging classroom. This can be your own classroom or it can be one that you are focusing on for action-oriented classroom research. Use the profiles from Carla's, Stephanie's, and Justin's classes as models.
   - Who are your bilingual students? Choose several bilingual students that together reflect the range of linguistic variation in your class. Describe each of their sociolinguistic histories/practices.
   - Who is the teacher? Describe his or her sociolinguistic history and practices.
   - What language(s) are used for instructional purpose in the class?
   - What are the content, language, and literacy goals for the instructional program serving these bilingual students?
2. Investigate the type of program for emergent bilinguals implemented in your context. (You can find definitions of different types of programs in the glossary.)
   - What is the official language policy?
   - What content and language development standards are used?
   - Who are the target populations?
   - What are the goals of the program?
   - How is the program structured to meet those goals?
   - How are students performing relative to those goals?

CHAPTER 2

Language Practices and the Translanguaging Classroom Framework

LEARNING OBJECTIVES

- Explain what it means for a bilingual student to draw on the full features of his or her linguistic repertoire
- Compare and contrast the notions of dynamic bilingualism and additive bilingualism
- Define the translanguaging corriente
- Use the translanguaging classroom framework to explain how the translanguaging corriente sets learning and teaching in motion
- Begin to identify evidence of the translanguaging corriente in your focal classroom

This chapter introduces the translanguaging classroom framework, which educators can use to understand **translanguaging classrooms** like *Carla's*, *Stephanie's*, and *Justin's*. First, however, we must think about how language is used by different speakers in context. When we look closely at the actual language practices of bilinguals, we see variation, dynamism, and complexity. The flow of students' bilingual practices, what we call the **translanguaging corriente**, is at work in all aspects of classroom life. When bilingual students engage with texts, they do so while drawing on all their linguistic resources, even if those texts are rendered only in English or only in Spanish or another language. When bilingual students write or create something new, they may filter certain features of their linguistic repertoires to create the *product*, but the *process* will always be bilingual.

When we view students' bilingualism in this way—as a fluid, ever present current that they tap into to make meaning—we see bilingual students differently. This shift in perspective opens new possibilities for teaching and assessing bilingual students. The translanguaging classroom framework that we propose helps teachers imagine a translanguaging pedagogy that **leverages** students' **dynamic bilingualism** for learning.

REFLECTING ON THE MEANINGS AND USES OF LANGUAGE

As school practitioners we often think of language solely as the standardized variety that is present in textbooks or used in assessments. We think we teach in "English," or "Spanish" or "Chinese" or "Korean" or "Russian." But the reality of language is a lot more complex than names of languages indicate.

Think, for example, of how we use language when we are speaking, reading, talking to a family member, disciplining a child, teaching a class, or working with an individual student. The ways we use language are different, and the features (the words, sounds, word order, etc.) of "English" or "Spanish" or "Chinese" vary depending on the context of use.

Think also of the language practices of different 6-year-old students, or of high school students with diverse experiences. Their so-called "English" or "Spanish" or "Russian" would vary, even among students in the same age group. Students use language differently, depending on who they are, what they are doing, what they are feeling, and with whom they are interacting. Now think of how different groups of English speakers (e.g., African American, British, Texan) or Spanish speakers (e.g., Mexican, Cuban, Puerto Rican) use the "same" language. Their so-called "English" or "Spanish" would also be very different, reflecting the language practices used in their communities. It is important to remember that monolingual English speakers and monolingual Spanish speakers, or those considered monolingual speakers of any language, are in fact multidialectal because they can use more than one variety of the "same" language.

If we cannot say that there is a single English or Spanish or Arabic for those who are monolingual, we can imagine how much more complex it is to think about the languages of bilinguals. So, we start with the question, How do bilinguals use language?

Bilingual speakers use language differently from multidialectal, monolingual speakers. Although all speakers use language differently, bilinguals have more choices to make because their **language repertoires** include many more language features. **Language features** include, for example, phonemes (sounds), words, morphemes (word forms), nouns, verbs, adjectives, tense systems, pronoun systems, case distinctions, gender distinctions, syntactic rules, and discourse markers (e.g., marking transitions, information structure). Though from a societal point of view bilinguals are said to speak two languages, from their own perspective bilingual speakers have *one language repertoire—their own*. This language repertoire includes linguistic features that are associated *socially* and *politically* with one language or another and are named as English, Spanish, Chinese, Russian, and the rest.

One Bilingual Repertoire vs. Two Monolinguals in One

Recall the students that we met in Carla's dual-language bilingual elementary classroom and in Stephanie's English-medium high school classroom. *Jennifer*, a student in Carla's class, and *Eddy*, a student in Stephanie's class, were born in the United States, and they speak a variety of Spanish that includes different features than that of *Luis* (Stephanie's class), recently arrived from El Salvador, or *Ricardo* and *Moisés* (Carla's class), recently arrived from Mexico. The variety of Spanish that Jennifer and Eddy speak has features of "English," whereas the variety that Ricardo speaks has features of "Mixteco," an indigenous language spoken in Mexico and in Ricardo's home.

In Carla's class, Jennifer and Moisés are asked what they like about the school playground. Jennifer replies: "Me encanta por los swings." [I love it because of the swings]. In contrast, Moisés answers: "Me encanta por los columpios." [I love it because of the swings]. For Jennifer, the word "swings" is neither English (although for dictionaries and nations it may be) nor Spanish. It is simply part of her language repertoire, the word she uses to communicate with the other bilingual Latino children with whom she plays on the playground. Jennifer has one language repertoire, as illustrated in Figure 2.1 (upper box), with entwined linguistic features (Fn) that she often uses to make meaning, but that countries, schools, dictionaries, and grammar books classify as different languages (Spanish and English in the lower boxes of Fig. 2.1). School (and other monolingual contexts) would want her to use only Spanish, or only English, as if she were two monolinguals in one. However, as Grosjean (1982) emphasized, the notion of two monolinguals in one is impossible.

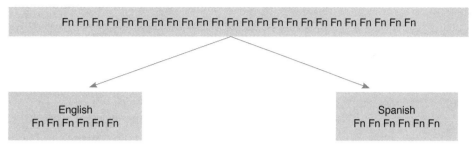

Figure 2.1   Language repertoire of bilinguals. Fn, (linguistic) features.

Although Jennifer has learned to distinguish which linguistic features of her repertoire to use in different communicative settings (i.e., when she uses English and when she uses Spanish), she is also capable of languaging with all the features of her repertoire. This occurs often when she speaks in bilingual contexts with her family. We can then say that Jennifer has one linguistic repertoire. However, that repertoire, seen from an external social perspective, is divided into two named languages. In school, for example, she is expected to perform according to standard definitions of language, and she has to select only those features in her repertoire associated with English during "English time," Spanish during "Spanish time," and suppress the rest. But when she plays and speaks with her bilingual friends, she is free to use all her linguistic repertoire. Seeing bilingualism in this way is very different from traditional concepts of bilingualism.[1]

Dynamic Bilingualism vs. Additive Bilingualism

Traditionally bilingualism has been described from a monolingual external perspective simply as the addition of a language. Figure 2.2 presents this traditional conceptualization of **additive bilingualism**, in which a first language (L1) is added to a second language (L2), each with its own autonomous and bounded linguistic features.

But Jennifer's bilingualism is not just additive; it is *dynamic*, the linguistic features of what are considered two languages function in interrelationship and adapt to the communicative circumstance at hand (see García, 2009). Jennifer deploys all the features of her entire language repertoire to communicate and make meaning, thus transgressing traditional societal and national definitions of what language should be and the ways in which language should be used.

Furthermore, Jennifer's bilingualism cannot be understood simply in terms of L1 or L2 languages. Jennifer learned to speak Spanish first because her grandmother raised her and spoke to her in Spanish, but her mother also spoke English to her as she was growing up. Although Jennifer can say that she learned Spanish first, Spanish is not her L1 because she feels more confident in English, uses it more, and identifies with it first. Jennifer's bilingualism is not made up of the simple addition of L1 + L2, but of the dynamic interaction of language features that she uses to communicate appropriately in different situations.

García (2009) conceptualizes students' dynamic bilingualism with the image of a banyan tree, with features that are always interdependent (Cummins, 1979) and that together form one intricate communicative repertoire that bilinguals learn to adapt to monolingual contexts whenever they occur. García (2009) also uses the image of the all-terrain vehicle to explain how

---

[1]See García and Li Wei, 2014 for further discussion.

Figure 2.2 Traditional bilingualism as the sum of two monolingualisms. F1, features of first language; F2, features of second language; L1, first language; L2, second language.

bilinguals use the features of their language repertoires to adapt to different communicative situations. This is in contrast to the traditional view of bilingualism, seen as two wheels of a bicycle that are always balanced and move in the same direction.

Rather than thinking about languages as fixed entities with strict boundaries between English and the students' other languages, the translanguaging classroom invites us to think about how to use the multiple language practices of bilingual students strategically. Such thinking supports these students as they engage with complex content and texts and develop new language practices, including those practices that are appropriate in academic contexts.

Translanguaging vs. Code-Switching

Translanguaging refers to both the complex language practices of multilingual individuals and communities and to the pedagogical approaches that draw on them to build the language practices desired in formal school settings. From a sociolinguistic perspective, translanguaging differs from two concepts we have heard in relation to bilingual students: code-switching, and in the case of bilingual Latinos, "Spanglish."

Code-switching refers to switching back and forth between language codes that are regarded as separate and autonomous. It considers language only from an *external perspective* that looks at bilinguals' language behavior as if they were two monolinguals in one. Code-switching is often considered a violation and a disruption of monolingual language use, and is frequently stigmatized.

Translanguaging, however, refers to the ways that bilinguals use their language repertoires, *from their own perspectives*, and not from the perspective of national or standard languages. The language repertoires of bilingual speakers are made up of features that dictionaries, grammar books, and schools put into two categories, in the case of Latino students, English and Spanish. Of course bilinguals learn to use the appropriate features according to the context in which they communicate. However, what is important is to realize that from the speaker's (i.e., *internal*) perspective, what he or she has is one linguistic repertoire.

Whereas the term code-switching focuses on alternation of named languages, translanguaging refers to the languaging of people who at times have to suppress features of their repertoires. Unlike code-switching, which is considered a simple alternation of language codes, translanguaging goes *beyond* named languages (Li Wei, 2011). The act of translanguaging is in itself transformative, having the potential to infuse creative bilingual meanings into utterances. We've seen several examples of this transformative creativity in Carla's classroom in Chapter 1—Cisneros' use of the word "comadre," breathing Latino life into an English language text; and students in Carla's class relating how their parents use the Spanish homonym "gel" to remind them of the English word "help." We'll see many more examples of this transformative creativity throughout this book.

The term "Spanglish" is often used to demean and stigmatize the Spanish of U.S. Latinos as "corrupted" Spanish (Otheguy & Stern, 2011). Translanguaging refers instead to bilingual speakers' creative and critical construction and use of interrelated language features that can be used for learning, and that teachers can leverage, regardless of the quality of students' performances in one or another national language. Furthermore, translanguaging can also be used to acquire and to learn how to use features that are considered part of standard language practices, which have *real and material consequences* for all learners.

TRANSLANGUAGING CORRIENTE

We use the metaphor of the translanguaging corriente to refer to the current or flow of students' dynamic bilingualism that runs through our classrooms and schools. Bilingual students make use of the translanguaging corriente, either overtly or covertly, to learn content and language in school and to make sense of their complex worlds and identities. When bilingual students work together to carry out an academic task, they negotiate and make meaning by pooling all of their linguistic resources.

A current in a body of water is not static; it runs a changeable course depending on features of the landscape. Likewise, the translanguaging corriente refers to the dynamic and continuous movement of language features that change the static linguistic landscape of the classroom that is described and defined from a monolingual perspective. Figure 2.3 represents the translanguaging corriente flowing and changing terrain that is traditionally considered "English" or "home language" territory and connecting them. From the surface, we see two separate riverbanks, with each side showing distinct features. Depending on the current, however, the riverbanks shift and their features change. And at the river bottom, the terrain is one; the river and its two banks are in fact one integrated whole.

As the translanguaging corriente forms an integrated whole, it allows bilingual students to combine social spaces with language codes that are usually practiced separately. For example, it is often said that Latino students use Spanish at home and English in school. In reality, however, language use is more fluid. In Latino homes, some families may speak Spanish; others may speak English; and most speak both. Spanish might be spoken or used while

Figure 2.3 A metaphor for the translanguaging corriente. (Retrieved from https://www.flickr.com/photos/79666107@N00/4120780342/)

listening to the radio, while English might be used for reading or watching television.

Fluid Language Practices in the Classroom

We find the translanguaging corriente in every classroom that includes bilingual students; of course, the quality of the corriente varies. The characteristics of the translanguaging corriente in any particular classroom reflect the language repertoires of the bilingual students and their teachers. Therefore, teachers like Carla, Stephanie, and Justin experience the translanguaging corriente differently because their linguistic repertoires and those of their students are diverse. Moreover, the implicit and explicit language policies in bilingual and English-medium classes are different. The corriente is stronger (and more visible) in the bilingual classroom, where the language other than English (LOTE) is also the language of instruction and the ability to use it is an explicit goal and expected student outcome.

Teachers also experience and respond to the translanguaging corriente differently. For example, Carla is bilingual and, like her students, has experienced what it means to suppress some of the features in her linguistic repertoire in academic contexts. She was trained in the traditional dual-language bilingual model, which rigidly separates the two languages used for instructional purposes. When Carla learned about the translanguaging corriente, she at first questioned and resisted it. Only later, when she realized that students used their languages flexibly despite her "language policing," did she embrace the corriente and leverage it with great success. Stephanie, on the other hand, speaks a relatively standard variety of English and the features of her language repertoire, with few exceptions, have rarely been called into question socially or academically. Stephanie does not consider herself bilingual; yet she responded to her students' bilingualism and translanguaging positively from the start. She saw that her students were already using all their linguistic resources to make meaning of the complex social studies content, so she began explicitly building this kind of translanguaging into her instruction. Despite their different experiences with languages and their different contexts, both Carla and Stephanie make use of the translanguaging corriente in instruction and assessment.

In school the lesson might be in English, but Latino students often speak Spanish to each other, and language features that are considered Spanish may populate their inner speech as they write, read, talk, and think. Because it is always moving, the translanguaging corriente changes the static linguistic landscape that establishes limits on when one language or the other is used and transforms the traditional concept of "a language."

Creative Potential of the Translanguaging Corriente

The translanguaging corriente produces *new* language practices. For example, in Latin American countries, Spanish is constrained by governmental edicts and official discourses that reflect national histories, with Spanish used in monolingual and monocultural ways. (Although, of course, there are variations in the language features associated with Spanish in different countries.) But in the United States, bilingual Latinos experience the Spanish language in interaction with English and its histories. Thus, the Spanish used in different U.S. communities includes features of the varieties of Spanish (e.g., Cuban, Mexican, Argentinian, Puerto Rican) used by the bilingual Latinos in those communities—interwoven with features of the standard and vernacular English used in them. Likewise, English in the United States, in the speech, minds, and hearts of bilingual Latinos, acquires the intentions of speakers with different histories and ideologies.

Thus, U.S. Latinos, as well as other bilinguals, experience "language" and histories constructed through one or another named "language" as an integrated system of linguistic and cultural practices. The translanguaging corriente generates the creative energy and produces the speaker's way of interacting with others and other texts, rather than responding to restrictions imposed by the officially accepted way of using language. It involves, as Li Wei (2011) has said, going both *between* different linguistic structures, systems, and modalities, and going *beyond* them. For Li Wei, translanguaging "creates a social space for the multilingual user by bringing together different dimensions of their personal history, experience, and environment; their attitude, belief, and ideology; [and] their cognitive and physical capacity into one coordinated and meaningful performance" (p. 1223). In short, the translanguaging corriente is generated by the students' bilingualism, and it sets in motion learning and teaching in the translanguaging classroom.

TRANSCENDING TRADITIONAL NOTIONS OF MONOLINGUAL AND BILINGUAL CLASSROOMS

Now that we are more familiar with dynamic bilingualism and the translanguaging corriente, what would it mean to use these concepts to reimagine how bilingual students are educated? U.S. classrooms are said to be either monolingual or bilingual; there does not seem to be anything in between. But classrooms today are never just monolingual or bilingual. If we look closer, there is much more diversity, and much more dynamic language use in classrooms, than what we hear and see at the surface level.

Limitations of Traditional Models

In any "monolingual" classroom we find children who speak LOTE, even if they also speak English. By ignoring linguistic practices other than those that are regarded as "legitmate school English," schools are ignoring the potential to build on a child's entire linguistic repertoire and rendering other ways of speaking invisible.

Furthermore, despite the existence of many bilingual classrooms, **bilingual education** often suffers from a **monoglossic ideology**. That is, bilingualism is often understood as simply "double monolingualism" (Grosjean 1982; Heller, 1999). Both major types of bilingual education classrooms—transitional bilingual and dual-language bilingual—conceptualize the two languages as separate. Transitional bilingual classrooms transition children who are acquiring English (those we call **emergent bilinguals** and others call English language learners [ELLs] or limited English proficient) to English-only instruction. In **early-exit** programs the transition is as soon as possible. In **late-exit** programs, students do not exit until they finish the program of instruction. The proportion of English used for instruction increases as the use of the other language decreases. English language development, then, never benefits from its interrelationship with the existing language features of the student's language repertoire. And Spanish development is not supported over time.

Most **dual-language bilingual education** (DLBE) classrooms also suffer from the same monoglossic ideology (García, 2009; Martínez, Hikida, & Durán, 2015), that is, the idea that the two languages are to be used only in monolingual ways. Echoing this idea, Fitts (2006) demonstrates how language separation in DLBE programs is a mechanism that "authorizes the use of standard forms of English and Spanish in separate spaces, and illegitimizes the use of vernaculars" (p. 339). The prototypical dual language model (which we refer to as dual-language bilingual education) requires that English and the partner language always remain separate (for critiques of the language separation approach, see Gort, 2015; Gort & Sembiante, 2015; Palmer & Henderson, 2016; Palmer, Martinez, Mateus, & Henderson, 2014). Furthermore, **two-way dual language bilingual programs** (or two-way immersion as they are sometimes called) insist on balanced numbers of English-speaking children and speakers of the other language.

In the case of English/Spanish DLBE classrooms, students are generally recognized as either "English dominant" or "Spanish dominant," but rarely both. Teachers in these programs teach in either English or Spanish, but never both. The language use in these classrooms seldom reflects the language use of the community, whose members speak English or Spanish, but mostly both. In many DLBE classrooms, bilingual language use is generally not overtly recognized, and teachers talk about students as either ELLs or English as a second language (ESL) speakers, or Spanish language learners or Spanish as a second language speakers (Lee, Hill-Bonnet, & Gillispie, 2008; Palmer & Martínez, 2013). This dichotomous conceptualization prevents bilingual identities from emerging. For example, an Anglophone child is socialized in the classroom as English speaking and a Hispanophone child as Spanish speaking, with little leveraging of their bilingualism and ways of knowing, which would strengthen their identities as U.S. bilinguals.

Imagining Translanguaging Classrooms

Translanguaging classrooms transcend traditional definitions of monolingual and bilingual education and build on the linguistic complexity of language practices used by multilingual speakers. Translanguaging classrooms could be either officially monolingual (like Stephanie's and Justin's classrooms) or bilingual (like Carla's classroom). The vision of translanguaging classrooms shifts us from the deficit view of "así no se dice" [this is not how it's said] or "no se dice aquí" [we don't say it here] that is so prevalent in both monolingual and bilingual classrooms to a more inclusive one of "también así se dice" [this is also how it's said] or "también aquí se dice" [it is also said here] and "¿qué más se dice?" [what else is said?].

If bilingual students constantly make meaning bilingually, how can we assess them solely in one language? If students' intrapersonal voices are bilingual, how can we tell them to "think in English?" If students' identities and ways of knowing are formed by deploying features from complex, multiple linguistic and cultural repertoires, how can we provide them with texts and academic experiences that present the world as static and monolingual? The answer to these questions is—we simply cannot. If we want bilingual students, and especially Latino students, to be successful U.S. citizens, we must provide them with educational spaces—with translanguaging classrooms— where all the features of their language repertoires are valued and leveraged in ways that support and strengthen learning.

THE TWO DIMENSIONS OF THE TRANSLANGUAGING CLASSROOM

The direct participants in all education activities in school are the students and the educators. The translanguaging classroom framework focuses on both dimensions, and pays attention to who the students are and what they can do with language, as well as to how teachers draw on the translanguaging corriente to teach and assess those students.

Translanguaging classrooms are not chaotic; students and teachers do not just do as they please. On the contrary, they are constructed based on planned and structured activities by the teacher in interaction with students, families, and communities, ensuring that students' entire linguistic repertoires are used. Regardless of whether the classroom is officially an English-medium classroom

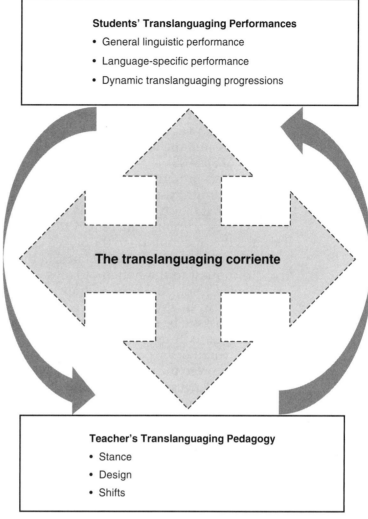

Students' Translanguaging Performances
- General linguistic performance
- Language-specific performance
- Dynamic translanguaging progressions

The translanguaging corriente

Teacher's Translanguaging Pedagogy
- Stance
- Design
- Shifts

Figure 2.4   The translanguaging classroom framework.

or a bilingual classroom, teachers in translanguaging classrooms design their instructional units and their assessment systems purposefully and strategically to mobilize all features of their bilingual students' linguistic repertoires, accelerate their content learning and language development, encourage their bilingualism and ways of knowing, strengthen their socioemotional development and bilingual identities, and advance social justice.

A translanguaging classroom, then, is built by weaving together the two dimensions—the students' linguistic performances and the teacher's pedagogy, as we illustrate in Figure 2.4. It is the translanguaging corriente that creates the dynamic flow, the movimiento, between these two dimensions. The students' linguistic performances shift the instruction and assessment, and the teacher's instruction and assessment shift the students' linguistic performances.

Students' Translanguaging Performances

The first dimension of a translanguaging classroom revolves around the students' translanguaging performances. The flow of the translanguaging corriente moves us from the concept of linguistic *proficiency*, which is assumed to develop along a relatively linear path that is more or less the same for all bilingual learners, to one of linguistic *performance* in situated practice, that is, according to the task at hand.

Both Haugen (1953) and Weinreich (1979), pioneers in the study of bilingualism in the United States, considered even minimal proficiency in two languages as a sign of bilingualism. The range of bilingual performances of today's students, however, is broader and more complex. Bilinguals today acquire and use many different linguistic features because mobility and technology have given them more opportunities to interact with texts and speakers whose repertoires differ from their own. In bilingual communities and homes speakers do not shy away from using all their linguistic features to communicate. In most schools, however, bilingual students are often required to suppress half of the features of their language repertoires to perform only in English or Spanish.

Teachers in translanguaging classrooms view students' linguistic performances holistically. They look at the students' performances while taking into account what they (the teachers) know about the translanguaging corriente in their classes. Students' linguistic performances are valued not only when the features they use conform to the official language used for school purposes, but also when they leverage the full range of their linguistic repertoires to learn.

In contrast to the notion of language proficiency as demonstrated on a standardized test, the focus in translanguaging classrooms is on task-based performances in situated practice. It is possible for the performance level on some tasks to be emergent and more experienced on others. For example, in immigrant settings where not much attention is paid to bilingualism in schools, youth oracy performances in a home language may be more experienced. However, the same students may not have experience with literacy in their home language and, thus, the literacy dimension might be more emergent. A Deaf bilingual child may have different degrees of signacy, literacy, and even oracy. All bilinguals are emergent bilinguals in some aspect or another, in certain situations and with different interlocutors. Students' linguistic performances shift in very dynamic and creative ways depending on different contexts and factors and cannot simply be captured by a one-time proficiency score.

To view students' translanguaging performances, teachers pay attention to two elements—the *dynamic* nature of students' bilingualism (which we have discussed) and the difference between their *general linguistic* and *language-specific performances*.

General linguistic performance refers to an oral, written, or signed performance that draws on a bilingual speaker's entire language repertoire to demonstrate what that speaker knows and can do with content and language (e.g., to explain, persuade, argue, compare and contrast, or evaluate). When bilingual speakers draw on the full features of their language repertoires, they are not required to suppress specific linguistic features (of the LOTE, of the vernacular variety of a language, etc.).

Language-specific performance refers to an oral, written, or signed performance that only draws on those features associated with a specific language; here we focus on standard language features associated with school contexts. Bilingual speakers, to demonstrate what they know and can do, deploy only the features in their language repertoires that correspond to the language of the content-specific task, and produce only what schools consider to be standard language features. Regardless of the specific language he or she may be using, a bilingual speaker always leverages his or her entire language repertoire to make meaning, even when only using features of one specific language.

Teachers can view students' translanguaging performances through what we call the *dynamic translanguaging progressions,* which will be further discussed in Chapter 3. The **dynamic translanguaging progressions** is a flexible model or construct that teachers can use to look holistically at a bilingual student's general linguistic and language-specific performances on different tasks at different times from different perspectives. These progressions are *dynamic* because they provide evidence of how a bilingual student's bilingualism ebbs and flows with experiences and opportunities. The dynamic translanguaging progressions model stands in contrast to traditional language models that see language development as a relatively linear, unidirectional, stage-like process.

As we will see in Chapter 3, the dynamism of students' translanguaging performances makes it clear that bilingualism is not static; it is not attainable; it is not something that one purely "has." On the contrary, one needs to "do" bilingualism—work with it, use it, perform it in different ways, whether through oracy, literacy, or signacy (for Deaf populations)—or any combination thereof. Bilingual students also need to understand the potential of their linguistic performances when they are allowed to use all the features of their language repertoires, that is, when schools also legitimize their translanguaging performances.

Teachers' Translanguaging Pedagogy

The second dimension of the translanguaging classroom framework focuses attention on the teacher's instruction and assessment, which adapt to, and leverage, the students' translanguaging performances. The translanguaging pedagogy we propose, and that will be developed in Part II, includes the teacher's general stance toward the students' dynamic bilingualism, the intentional ways that teachers design curricular units of instruction and assessments to build on what students can do with the full features of their language repertoires, and the moment-to-moment shifts that teachers make in response to their observation of student participation in language-mediated classroom activities.

Although some teachers understand the power of translanguaging and are able to give students this flexibility so that they can translanguage moment-by-moment in their classes, it takes thoughtful, effective planning. That is, it is not enough to go with flow of the translanguaging corriente. A teacher needs to have a **translanguaging stance**, build a **translanguaging design**, and make **translanguaging shifts**—the three strands of the **translanguaging pedagogy**.

We explain how to develop these strands in both instruction and assessment in later chapters. Here we simply introduce them.

Stance

A stance refers to the philosophical, ideological, or belief system that teachers draw from to develop their pedagogical framework. Teachers cannot leverage the translanguaging corriente without the firm belief that by bringing forth bilingual students' entire language repertoires they can transcend the language practices that schools traditionally have valued. Clearly, teachers with a translanguaging stance have a firm belief that their students' language practices are both a resource and a right (Ruiz, 1984). But beyond these orientations to language, teachers with a translanguaging stance believe that the many different language practices of bilingual students work **juntos**/together, not separately as if they belonged to different realms. Thus, the teacher believes that the classroom space must be used creatively to promote language collaboration. A translanguaging stance always sees the bilingual child's complex language repertoire as a resource, never as a deficit.

We see the influence of this translanguaging stance in educators' actions. Our planned actions as teachers in translanguaging classrooms are what we term the translanguaging design.

Design

Teachers in translanguaging classrooms must design units, lessons, and instruction and assessments that build connections between, as Flores and Schissel (2014) say, "[community] language practices and the language practices desired in formal school settings" (p. 462). The translanguaging instructional and assessment design does not simply direct the translanguaging corriente toward the school and away from the home or simply construct a bridge across the two banks (home and school) of the river. Instead, teachers purposefully design instruction and assessment opportunities that integrate home and school language and cultural practices. Learning is created by the translanguaging corriente that teachers and students jointly navigate to reduce the distance between home and school practices.

This translanguaging design is what prevents learners from being swept away by different currents—those created by school language practices that are beyond their reach or those of home language practices that, without blending with those of the school, do not lead to academic success. But the translanguaging design is not a simple scaffold for the kinds of languaging and understanding that the school deems valuable. Instead, students' bilingual practices and ways of knowing are seen as both informing *and* informed by classroom instruction.

The design is the pedagogical core of the translanguaging classroom. But to open ourselves and our students to constructing this flexible design together, we need to make room for translanguaging shifts.

Shifts

Because the translanguaging corriente is always present in classrooms, it is not enough to simply have a stance that recognizes translanguaging performances and a design that directs it. At times it is also important to follow el movimiento de la corriente. The translanguaging shifts refer to the many moment-by-moment decisions that teachers make in the classroom. They reflect the teacher's flexibility and willingness to change the course of the lesson, as well as the language use planned in instruction and assessment, to release and support students' voices. The translanguaging shifts are related to the translanguaging stance, for it takes a teacher willing to keep meaning-making and learning at the center of all instruction and assessment to go with the flow of the corriente.

Teachers can use the translanguaging pedagogy to leverage the translanguaging corriente that runs through their classes. This translanguaging pedagogy encompasses both instruction and assessment, and can be used to mobilize students' bilingualism and accelerate their content and language learning. The strands of the translanguaging pedagogy are interrelated and form a sturdy but flexible rope that strengthens the learning and teaching of both language and content, as shown in Figure 2.5.

These interrelated strands enable the translanguaging corriente to flow through the daily life of the classroom—planning lessons, facilitating conversations about content, strengthening of students' general linguistic and

Figure 2.5 The translanguaging pedagogy strands.

Stance

Design

Shifts

language-specific performances, and assessing student growth along the dynamic translanguaging progressions. These strands also weave together the four translanguaging purposes:

1. To support student engagement with complex content and texts
2. To provide opportunities for students to develop linguistic practices for academic contexts
3. To make space for students' bilingualism and ways of knowing
4. To support students' socioemotional development and bilingual identities

Together the strands of this pedagogy secure not only these educational purposes, but also connect the educational project to a higher goal—constructing a more just world, especially for minority students.

CONCLUSION

This chapter has encouraged our reflections on language use through the movimiento of the translanguaging corriente, and especially the language use of bilingual students. In so doing, we questioned notions of additive bilingualism and took up the concept of dynamic bilingualism. We then explored the concepts of translanguaging and the translanguaging corriente. We introduced the two dimensions of the translanguaging classroom framework—the students' translanguaging performances and the teacher's translanguaging pedagogy. We also identified the three strands that make up the translanguaging pedagogy for instruction and assessment—the stance, design, and shifts.

QUESTIONS AND ACTIVITIES

1. Have you ever experienced or felt the translanguaging corriente? Where and why? How did it make you feel?

2. How does the concept of bilingual students' translanguaging performances differ from traditional concepts of language proficiency?

3. What are the challenges that translanguaging poses for you? Identify and talk through with other educators the challenges posed by each of the three strands—the stance, design, and shifts.

TAKING ACTION

1. Visit the bilingual community of your choice. Listen to the ways that language is used in the street, in the stores, and in the restaurants. What do you hear? Look for signs written by store owners and others. What can you conclude about the ways that bilingualism is used in this community? How does it adjust (or not) to the concept of dynamic bilingualism discussed here?

2. What evidence of the translanguaging corriente can you see and hear in your focal classroom? Take notes on the ways that your bilingual students draw on all of the features of their linguistic repertoire orally and in writing in different communicative activities at school.

CHAPTER 3

Documenting Students' Dynamic Bilingualism

LEARNING OBJECTIVES

- Identify strategies that educators can use to build a robust multilingual ecology at school and encourage bilingual families to share their bilingualism
- Identify and profile each bilingual student in the class and then develop a classroom bilingual profile
- Describe the construct of dynamic translanguaging progressions and explain how teachers can use them to evaluate student performances on different tasks, at different times, from different perspectives
- Explain how the dynamic translanguaging progressions complement and extend the language development standards/progressions that states use to assess bilingual students

This chapter helps teachers compile a holistic, dynamic view of their students' bilingualism. First, we explain how teachers and administrators can build a robust **multilingual ecology** in their schools—one that encourages parents and students to share their bilingualism; breaks down boundaries between home, school, and communities; and allows the **translanguaging corriente** to flow. We also show teachers how to gather different types of data to identify and profile each bilingual student in their class (not just those labeled as English language learners [ELLs]), and from there to develop a classroom bilingual profile that they can use to plan their translanguaging pedagogy. The second part of the chapter introduces the construct of the **dynamic translanguaging progressions**, with attention to how it is compatible with, and goes beyond, state-sanctioned language development standards and assessments. The tools that we provide in this chapter prepare teachers to **leverage** the myriad linguistic performances of bilingual students in ways that effectively support student learning at school.

BUILDING A ROBUST MULTILINGUAL ECOLOGY AT SCHOOL

Parents/guardians who register their children for school fill out a home language survey. However, many family members do not identify their children's bilingualism for fear that this will be a stigma. Although every school is required to administer a home language survey to the parents/guardians of every child, the information gleaned from this survey is used mostly to identify students who could be classified as "limited English proficient" or as "ELLs." When schools determine that students have command of English, not much is done with the information on the home language survey. Thus, bilingual students are not properly identified and their bilingualism is generally ignored.

The first step toward appropriately identifying bilingual students, especially when they are deemed English proficient, is to encourage families and students to self-identify as bilingual. To facilitate this effort, the school can build an ecology of multilingualism, enabling every family member and student to feel that their languages are appreciated and valued, and to see that their languages make important contributions to learning in the school. We have developed the Promoting an Ecology of Multilingualism Checklist (Appendix A.3.1) to help school administrators and teachers identify and build on the bilingual language practices of all of their students. This checklist includes actions that school leaders can take to encourage families and students to share their bilingual use, thus allowing the translanguaging corriente to flow. For example, the school can have multilingual welcome signs and multilingual resources for parents who are registering their students in school. Teachers can request that they be given access to the information on the home language surveys or conduct their own inquiries. Teachers can also engage students in sharing their bilingualism, especially through personal stories, language biographies or testimonios, and discussions. This checklist provides a vehicle for educators to engage the parent/guardian and student in the identification of multilingualism as an asset in the school.

DEVELOPING BILINGUAL PROFILES

If we encouraged families and students to share their bilingualism, we would see that almost all classrooms have bilingual students. We also would learn that children's range of abilities with their bilingual repertoires differs greatly. In the United States most bilingual students are Spanish speaking, and most will be categorized as English speakers. However, depending on where we teach, the level we teach, and the type of class we teach, the bilingual students in our classrooms will have very different characteristics. We see examples of such variation when we look within and across *Carla's* dual-language bilingual elementary classroom in Albuquerque, New Mexico, *Stephanie's* English-medium high-school social studies classroom in New York City, and *Justin's* role as a **push-in English as a second language (ESL)** teacher in middle-school math and science classrooms in Los Angeles, California. When teachers and administrators work together to build a robust multilingual ecology, they can strengthen the translanguaging corriente in their classrooms. This is the first step in developing a translanguaging pedagogy.

Student Bilingual Profiles

U.S. schools categorize children as ELLs, former ELLs, and fully English proficient. Teachers are generally not encouraged to think about bilingual students beyond these categories, and they do not usually gather valuable data about the language and literacy practices of the bilingual students in their classes—not even of those who are classified as ELLs or who are learning through two languages in bilingual programs. Educators may talk about the importance of culturally responsive pedagogy, but how are teachers to enact such pedagogy if they do not systematically collect information about who their students are, the languages they speak, their cultural practices, their experiences, and the worlds that they know? We have developed the Bilingual Student Identification and Profile (Appendix A.3.2) that teachers can adapt and use to address this gap.

Part 1 of this form is the Bilingual Student Identification Checklist, which includes five questions that teachers can use to start conversations with students about their bilingualism. The checklist includes a range of topics—bilingual use at home, bilingual friends, bilingual exposure, education, and literacy in language(s) other than English (LOTE) used at home. Teachers tally the points for each area they identify for bilingualism. In the case of very young students, teachers can fill out this part of the form with parents or guardians. If the student has been identified as being potentially bilingual (i.e., if he or she has received a *score of 2 or more* on Part 1 of the form), then the teacher proceeds to Part 2, Bilingual Student Profile.

Notice that the Bilingual Student Profile does not make a distinction between **emergent bilinguals** (those that schools classify as ELLs) and more **experienced bilinguals** (the category of bilingual students who speak English and whose bilingualism is generally ignored at school). We encourage teachers to think of each of their student's bilingualism holistically and to inquire about how, when, where, and why they have become bilingual. The focus is on identifying each student's bilingual experiences, not solely their performances in English.

The Bilingual Student Profile starts with questions about the languages the child speaks or is exposed to consistently at home, as well as the countries in which he or she has lived and gone to school. The profile asks questions about where students were born and the years they have lived in the United States, as well as where they have studied English and where they have used or studied LOTE. The form also includes space for other information on the students' languaging performances.

Why is this understanding of students' bilingualism important? Sociolinguistic, socioeducational, and socioeconomic factors influence the language practices of bilingual students, and all teachers can use the answers to the questions on the bilingual profile to work more effectively with their students. For instance, the language the student speaks can give teachers information about the possible cognates the student might be able to identify in English, whether the home language is written or not, and what kind of script is used for writing the home language. When teachers know that a newcomer has been schooled in a language that does not use a Roman script, they can expect this student to need explicit attention when developing script for English. When teachers know that an emergent bilingual student has studied English in his or her country of origin, they can expect that student to be able to use English for academic purposes more quickly than a student who is being exposed to English for the first time. When teachers know that their students go to after-school and supplementary schools that are developing their literacy in other languages, they can leverage those literacy practices and understanding, even when teaching in English-medium classrooms. Using the Bilingual Student Identification and Profile (see Appendix A.3.2), teachers can begin to explore the linguistic realities of their bilingual students, especially at home, to leverage their bilingualism at school. This form can be filled out by the teacher, in consultation with the student or family member.

Classroom Bilingual Profiles

Just as teachers need to be mindful of individual bilingual students' profiles, they also have to find ways to make the classroom bilingual profile visible. We have developed the Classroom Bilingual Profile, which you can see in its generic form in Appendix A.3.3, for this purpose. Teachers are encouraged to observe and record the students' languaging performances, noticing especially what students know and can do in each of the two languages.

We use Carla's classroom to describe how she adapts the Classroom Bilingual Profile to her **dual-language bilingual education (DLBE)** classroom in New Mexico. As Table 3.1 shows, Carla fills in the languages used at home (column 2) with information she collected on the Bilingual Student Identification and Profile that we discussed in the previous section. Carla now knows that *Moisés* and *Ricardo* use more Spanish at home than her other students, an asset she can draw on in her DLBE classroom. Carla also indicates students'

TABLE 3.1   **Classroom Bilingual Profile**

Students	Languages Used at Home	ELL Status	English Language Proficiency Score (ACCESS for ELLs)	Spanish Language Proficiency Score (LAS Links)	Spanish Reading Level (EDL2)	English Reading Level (DRA2)
Erica	Mostly English, some Spanish	No	NA	3	30	40
	Erica can answer opinion questions with details.					
Jennifer	Mostly English; but also Spanish	No	NA	4	40	50
	Jennifer can summarize information from multiple texts.					
Moisés	Spanish with parents, English with siblings	Yes Newcomer	3	4	40	30
	Moisés can explain strategies in solving problems across content area.					
Ricardo	Spanish and Mixteco with parents, Spanish and English with siblings	Yes Newcomer	3	4	30	20
	Ricardo can interpret oral information and apply to new context.					

ACCESS, Assessing Comprehension and Communication in English State-to-State; DRA2, Developmental Reading Assessment; EDL2, Evaluación del desarrollo de la lectura; ELL, English language learner; LAS, Language Assessment Scale.

Adapted to Carla's classroom.

ELL status, which all U.S. schools are required to monitor, in column 3; she writes *no* for each student who is not officially designated as an ELL and *yes* for each student who is. For these emergent bilinguals, Carla distinguishes among (1) newcomers, who have arrived in the United States in the last six years; (2) **long-term English language learners (LTELLs),** who have been classified as ELL for more than six years[1]; and (3) **students with incomplete/interrupted formal education (SIFE).**

Subsequent columns capture data on language performance in English and in the LOTE, orally and in writing, in as much detail as possible, leaving space for the teacher to write statements about what each student can do. We find considerable variation in the kinds of data that teachers, programs, schools, districts, and states collect and report. Teachers will therefore need to adapt this form to accommodate the data they draw on in their context.

In the beginning of the year, Carla compiles the standardized test scores that are mandated in her state and district. Recall that Carla teaches in Albuquerque, New Mexico, which is part of the WIDA consortium that has developed standards and assessments for ELLs. In column 4 of Table 3.1, Carla records her students' composite levels (1–5) on the Assessing Comprehension and Communication in English State-to-State (ACCESS) for ELLs English Language Proficiency test that WIDA administers. WIDA also reports data according to the domains of listening, speaking, reading, and writing, so Carla could adapt this form to accommodate the levels for each domain.

Carla teaches in a DLBE program, and she collects home language data for all her students by using the Language Assessment Scale (LAS) Links for Spanish. This instrument indicates the students' performance according to five levels, which you see in column 5 of the table. Carla's school district also requires that all students in DLBE programs be given a formative literacy

---

[1]Districts and states will vary in terms of how many years they consider students to be newcomers, and whether and when they begin to label students as LTELLs or identify them as SIFE.

assessment in Spanish and English—the Evaluación del desarrollo de la lectura 2 (EDL2) and the Development Reading Assessment 2 (DRA2), respectively. The EDL2 and the DRA2 scores are arranged by lexiles—30 (3rd-grade level), 40 (4th-grade level), 50 (5th-grade level), and 60 (6th-grade level). Carla indicates the scores for her students' reading levels in Spanish (column 6) and English (column 7).

This classroom bilingual profile provides an easy way for Carla to see at a glance what her students can do in Spanish and English according to the data sources they draw on in the DLBE program at her school. This inclusive approach transcends traditional categorizations of bilingual students in the United States that render the bilingualism of most bilingual students invisible. It also allows Carla to begin to see and hear the linguistic assets that her students bring with them to school.

Reflecting on State-Mandated English Language Proficiency and Development Systems

Although the student and classroom bilingual profiles provide an important foundation for teachers' understanding of their students' bilingualism, teachers need to look critically at the data that states and districts require. Under current policy, all states must adopt English language development (ELD) or proficiency standards and assessment systems, and all schools must report their ELLs' progress in learning English. States either join consortia (e.g., WIDA, ELPA21) or, in the cases of New York, California, and Texas, develop their own language development standards and assessment systems. The concept of monitoring emergent bilinguals' development toward *commanding* or *bridging* levels is important for Carla, Stephanie, and Justin because they need to understand and document their students' language development.

Let's briefly consider similarities and differences within and across systems to identify their strengths and limitations. First, each system divides language development into progression stages or developmental levels in reading, writing, listening, and speaking. For example, New York, WIDA, and ELPA21 have adopted a five point progression for emergent bilinguals—*entering, emerging, developing* or *transitioning, expanding,* and *bridging* or *commanding*—whereas California has a three point progression—*emerging, expanding,* and *bridging*. Each system has created performance indicators or Can-Do descriptors that teachers can use to understand what emergent bilinguals are likely to be able to do with language at each level of development in reading, writing, listening, and speaking. Teachers can use these Can-Do descriptors or performance indicators to guide their efforts to differentiate instruction and assessment for emergent bilinguals along the continuum of language development.

The systems also differ in important ways, reflecting the theories of language that underlie them. For example,

- WIDA's ELD system is the one currently being used by most states. The WIDA consortium provides Can-Do descriptors and model performance indicators that make explicit the continuum of language development in reading, writing, listening, and speaking for emergent bilinguals in grades preK–12 relative to five ELD standards: (1) social and instructional language, (2) the language of language arts, (3) the language of math, (4) the language of science, and (5) the language of social studies. WIDA has also created Spanish language development standards and Can-Do descriptors.
- New York State has developed the Bilingual Common Core Initiative with New and Home Language Arts Progressions that correspond to each of the New York Learning Standards at every grade level (see Velasco & Johnson, 2014). Each set of progressions is organized around student performance

indicators that describe what students can be expected to do with their new and home languages at each of the five stages used in this system.

- ELPA21 includes ten English language proficiency standards that are organized in relation to content-area language practices, particularly those called for by college and career-readiness standards in English language arts and literacy, mathematics, and science. For example, Standard 1 expects students to construct meaning from oral presentations and literary and informational text through grade-appropriate listening, reading, and viewing. Standard 5 expects students to conduct research and evaluate and communicate findings to answer questions or solve problems.

Although each of these systems is state-mandated, their differences reflect varying assumptions about (1) the number of standards to include in the system, (2) the relation of the language development standards to the content-area standards, (3) the content areas addressed by the standards, and (4) the role and relationship of the home language to the new language. Teachers from different states (e.g., CA, TX) and consortia (e.g., ELPA21) are encouraged to learn about the language development system used in their states, use the extensive resources that each system offers, and look critically at those systems in terms of what data are (or are not) collected and how those data are used.

An important limitation of all of these systems is that they reflect an assumption of a relatively linear, stage-like, unidirectional process of language development. For example, a student would proceed from the *entering, beginning,* or *emerging* levels of language development through each level, in order, until they reach "proficiency." As we see in the next section, bilingual students' language practices are actually much more complex than these state-mandated English language proficiency and development systems can capture.

DYNAMIC TRANSLANGUAGING PROGRESSIONS

The **dynamic translanguaging progressions** help teachers understand and document the complexity of each student's bilingual practices. They are a flexible model or construct that teachers can use to look holistically at the differentiated **dynamic bilingualism** of each bilingual student in their classes. The model takes into account the *dynamic* nature of students' bilingualism, as well as the difference between two types of linguistic performances, *general linguistic* and *language-specific.* We discuss both these elements, starting with the dynamic nature of the model, which provides evidence of how a student's bilingualism can ebb and flow with experience and opportunities. Bilingualism is not static or attainable ("had"); it has to be "done" (performed).

Evaluating Bilingual Performances on Different Tasks from Different Perspectives

The dynamism of the translanguaging progressions comes from the perspective that bilingual performances have to be evaluated differently, depending on the task or context in which the speaker is involved and the perspective of the evaluator.

For example, at home it is possible that parents will evaluate their child's biliteracy performances as relatively experienced as the child reads, translates, and helps complete health insurance forms in English for her Spanish-speaking parents; helps younger siblings write an essay in English as she speaks to them in English; reads from the Spanish-language bible at church where the service is bilingual; and writes in a personal journal and texts her friends in both languages. By *commanding* performances, we mean performances in which language is used with relative ease—although the specific performances may vary

Entering ◄————————————————————————————————————► Commanding

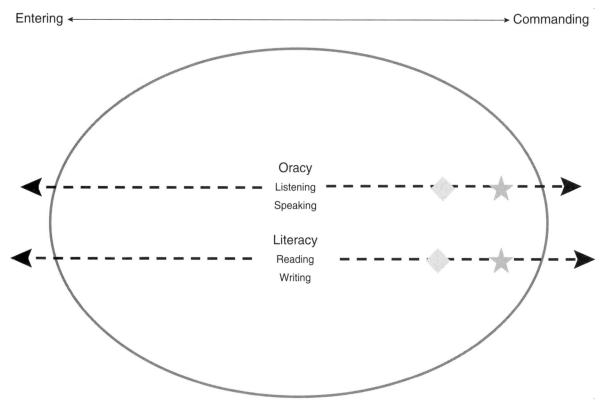

Figure 3.1   Noemí's translanguaging progression, as evaluated by her parents at home.
◆ Language-specific performance in English
★ Language-specific performance in Spanish

according to task and modality (e.g., whether the child is reading, speaking, or texting). In school, however, teachers wouldn't necessarily have an opportunity to see these kinds of experienced literacy practices. Teachers would likely evaluate the same child's bilingualism differently.

This is precisely the case of **Noemí**, an 11th grader in Stephanie's classroom who came to the United States from Ecuador three years ago. Noemí is officially classified as an ELL; she now uses English orally with relative ease.

Figure 3.1 illustrates how Noemí's parents placed her bilingual performances in Spanish and English more toward the experienced end of the axis.[2] After all, her biliteracy was stronger than that of her parents who relied on her at all times to fill out applications and translate for them at the doctor´s office and in school. Her parents realized that her Spanish (represented by the star) was stronger than her English (represented by the diamond), but they evaluated Noemí's bilingual performances in both languages as quite experienced.

In contrast, Noemí's teacher (Stephanie) thinks of her bilingualism quite differently. Stephanie draws on a range of data sources to inform how she evaluates Noemí's performances. She consults Noemí's Bilingual Identification and Profile. She has scores from the New York State English as a Second Language Assessment Test (NYSESLAT) given to ELLs and from the English language arts test. Stephanie is also a keen observer of the ways that Noemí

---

[2]We use the terms *entering* and *commanding* on either end of each axis of the translanguaging progressions in Figures 3.1 and 3.2 because they closely resemble the terms used on state language-development standards and assessments. Teachers are encouraged to use the terms that make the most sense in their contexts (e.g., those that align with the levels used for their state language development standards and assessments or new terms that teachers in a district agree work better for their purposes).

uses English and Spanish for different school-based tasks in her class, and she makes notes of her observations on her bilingual profile. But because this is not a bilingual class, Stephanie does not have standardized test scores for Noemí in Spanish. Because she does not speak Spanish, Stephanie consults with her bilingual colleagues for their perspectives on Noemí's oracy and literacy performances in Spanish. Stephanie's evaluation of Noemí's bilingualism on the dynamic translanguaging progressions is shown in Figure 3.2.

Stephanie evaluates Noemí's oracy performances in English as more experienced than her literacy performances in English. Based on her discussion with her bilingual colleagues, Stephanie represents Noemí's oracy performances in Spanish as more experienced than her literacy performances in Spanish. Comparing Figures 3.1 and 3.2 shows us that Stephanie constructs a different profile of Noemí's bilingual performances than her parents, who see their daughter as a more experienced bilingual, especially in literacy.

Teachers can also include students' perspectives on their bilingualism, whether they speak the languages of those students or not. For example, Justin works with emergent bilinguals from diverse language backgrounds in middle-school math and science classes. Like Stephanie, Justin does not speak the home languages of most of his students. However, he knows that his role as an ESL teacher includes helping the content-area teachers at his school see bilingual students holistically. This, in turn, will not only help him develop students' English; it will help *all* teachers to design instruction that is tailored to bilingual students.

Like Stephanie, Justin draws on data from the Bilingual Student Identification and Profile, standardized test scores, and his own in-class observations. He also sits with each of his emergent bilingual students and asks them about

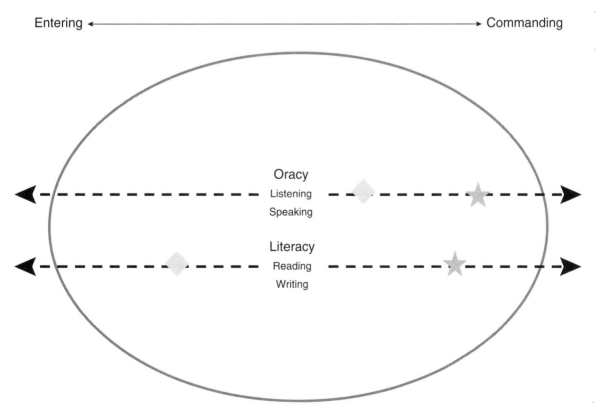

Figure 3.2   Noemí's translanguaging progression, as evaluated by her teachers in school.
◆ Language-specific performance in English
★ Language-specific performance in Spanish

their perceptions of their performances in both English and their home languages. For example, using both English and Mandarin, Justin learns that **Yi-Sheng**, the recently arrived student from Taiwan, was one of the top students in her class there, and even won an award for her writing. However, she has little knowledge of Latin script. For this reason, Justin and Yi-Sheng together decide that while her literacy performances in Mandarin are very experienced, her performances in English are much more emergent. Regarding oracy, Yi-Sheng tells Justin in English that though she is nervous to speak in class, she often uses English to help her parents with errands and other elements of daily life in Los Angeles. Keeping this in mind, and combining it with other data, Justin and Yi-Sheng rate her oracy performances in English as *developing*. Justin records this and Yi-Sheng's perspective on her bilingualism, as seen in Figure 3.3.

Teachers can always find creative ways to gather information about their students' bilingualism. Even students in English-medium contexts who are just beginning to use English can share information about their experiences and expertise in oral and written LOTE. Teachers can use the blank Dynamic Translanguaging Progressions form in Appendix A.3.4 to document their students' specific bilingual performances on different tasks, at different times, from different perspectives using all of their linguistic repertoires. The dynamic translanguaging progressions can be used by different constituents to observe and document students' bilingualism in ways that allow teachers to obtain a holistic view of each student's bilingualism over time. (Appendix A.3.4 includes a reference to general linguistic performance, which is discussed in the next section.)

State-sanctioned English language proficiency and development systems have clearly articulated performance indicators of what students can do with

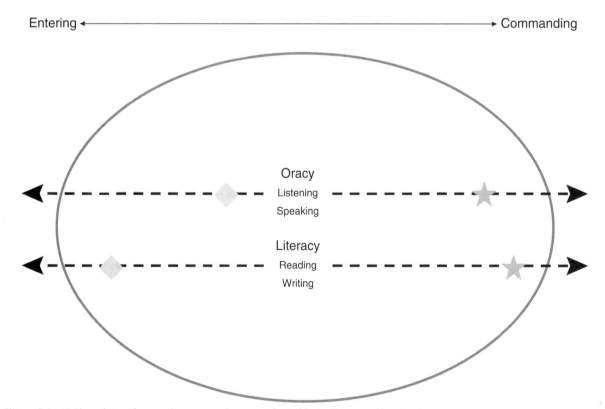

Figure 3.3   Yi-Sheng's translanguaging progression, as evaluated by Yi-Sheng and her teacher.
◆ Language-specific performance in English
★ Language-specific performance in Mandarin

language as defined, categorized, and scored by those systems (e.g., interactive, productive, interpretive; reading, writing, listening, speaking) at a specific moment in time on standardized tests. In contrast, bilingual students' translanguaging performances consist of dynamic, fluid practices that vary depending on the task (e.g., writing in a personal journal in Spanish and English at home or writing an essay that includes specific textual evidence to support conclusions drawn from the text in English at school) and on the evaluators' perspective (e.g., by the parents at home on a familiar task or by the teacher at school on a new type of task).

It is important to emphasize that bilingual students' movements along the dynamic translanguaging progressions are not always linear. That is, their bilingual performances don't *always* move toward the experienced side of the progressions. Often, we see shifts occurring as bilingual students are given opportunities to use language for different purposes at different times in their lives. For example, teachers' evaluations of a bilingual student's performances in Spanish literacy are likely to move *away* from the experienced side of the translanguaging progressions as that student moves from a bilingual elementary school to an English-medium middle school and uses more English and less Spanish for academic purposes. Later, when that same bilingual student goes to high school and takes a Spanish for Spanish speakers class that focuses on Spanish literacy, teachers are likely to evaluate the student's Spanish literacy performances as moving *toward* the experienced end of the progressions, again showing how the dynamic translanguaging progressions allow us to capture the ebb and flow of students' bilingualism in different contexts over time. Thus, they allow us to understand and document the complex nature of bilingual students' language practices.

Distinguishing between General Linguistic and Language-Specific Performances

The Common Core State Standards (CCSS) assume that standards have to be met in English and in what have been defined as the standard features of English. State-sanctioned language development standards and progressions make the same assumption, although some systems (like the one in New York State) make room for the use of the students' home language as a scaffold in beginning levels. But when you put translanguaging into the progressions mix, the possibilities of linguistic achievements go beyond simple monolingual performances using only standard features.

When we evaluate bilingual students' language practices using the dynamic translanguaging progressions, we understand that language does not simply develop or progress along a linear, unidirectional path in relatively fixed levels or stages. Instead we understand language performance to include different dimensions that must be viewed separately. The two dimensions of language performance are the following:

1. **General linguistic performance**. Bilingual speakers, to show what they can do, deploy any of the features in their entire **language repertoires** to accomplish language and content-specific tasks.
2. **Language-specific performance**. Bilingual speakers, to show what they know and can do, deploy only the features in their language repertoires that correspond to the language of the content-specific task, and produce only standard **language features**—although they leverage their entire language repertoires in the process.

Translanguaging classrooms show us that bilingual students perform better with *targeted* language features when they have been given ample opportunities to perform tasks using the full features of their *entire* linguistic repertoires first.

The general linguistic performance dimension understands that a bilingual speaker has one linguistic repertoire with full features; thus, the construct of "national language" or "standard language" is irrelevant. General linguistic performance has to do with the ability to express complex thoughts effectively, explain things, persuade, argue, compare and contrast, give directions, recount events, tell jokes, and so forth, without regard to the language features used to accomplish these linguistic tasks. Thus, general linguistic performance addresses the most important part of the standards. In reading, it means being able to provide text evidence of key ideas, make inferences and identify main ideas and relationships in complex texts, recognize the text's craft and structure (chronology, comparison, cause/effect), and associate knowledge and ideas from multiple sources and texts. In writing, general linguistic performance refers to producing text types (e.g., opinion, informative, explanatory, and narrative pieces) for various purposes. The standards in listening and speaking that refer to comprehending knowledge and ideas and presenting them collaboratively are also part of general linguistic performance. Because teachers in translanguaging classrooms are concerned with developing bilingual students' general linguistic performances on these types of academic tasks, and with assessing their general linguistic performances relative to this dimension of the dynamic translanguaging progressions, they encourage students to draw on the full features of their linguistic repertoires.

The language-specific performance dimension acknowledges that schools expect students to perform using features of standard languages. For example, educators must target certain features if they want their students to perform well on standardized tests or to demonstrate competence on standard academic essays or in formal presentations using only one language. Thus, these features cannot simply be ignored; they must also be the target of instruction. Of course, students in English-medium and bilingual classrooms must also learn to perform as fluent users of a named "standard" language. But this performance with standard language features—grammar, usage, vocabulary, and interactional routines—must be assessed independently of general linguistic performance. These language-specific performances also demand that any student whose language repertoire has features that are not school-sanctioned—not only bilingual students but also bidialectal students (e.g., those who speak with features described as African American English, Appalachian English, Chicano English, Hawaiian Creole)—learn to suppress those linguistic features at times, although they continue to draw from the entire language repertoire to process the information.

Leveraging Language-Specific and General Linguistic Performances to Accelerate Learning

The dynamic translanguaging progressions also differ from the standards by which students are traditionally evaluated because even the language-specific performances *leverage the process of translanguaging*. That is, even when students are evaluated on their abilities to use standard English only or standard Spanish only, instruction and performance do not start there. Instead, instruction starts with encouraging students to use all the features in their repertoires to perform linguistically, and then they are taught to perform linguistic tasks with only part of their language repertoires. We illustrate this point by looking again at Stephanie's evaluation of Noemí's oracy and literacy performances in her class. Figure 3.4 shows that Stephanie has placed Noemí's general linguistic performance as slightly more experienced than her performance in Spanish (her stronger language). As we will see, understanding Noemí's general linguistic and language-specific performances is very important for instruction.

Entering ← ─────────────────────────────────────── → Commanding

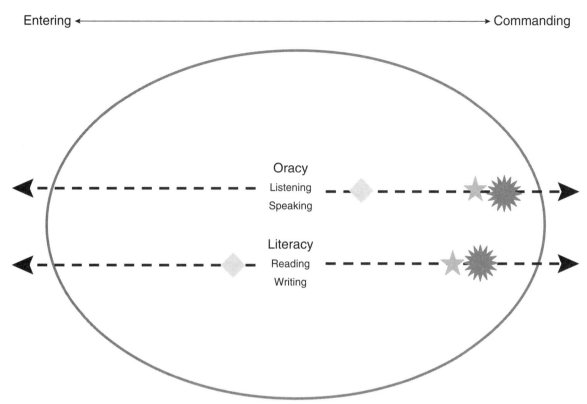

Figure 3.4 Noemí's general linguistic and language-specific performances, as evaluated by her teacher at school.
◈ Language-specific performance in English
★ Language-specific performance in Spanish
✳ General linguistic performance using the full features of her linguistic repertoire

A culminating project in Stephanie's *Environmentalism: Then and Now* unit is for students to write a persuasive public service announcement (PSA) in English. Noemí's language-specific performance writing a persuasive PSA in English would be toward the *entering* end of the progressions if she were asked to complete this literacy task using only English (see Fig. 3.2). However, Stephanie uses translanguaging to leverage Noemí's general linguistic performance and her language-specific performance in Spanish so that she can perform much better on this writing task in English.

What translanguaging pedagogical strategies did Stephanie use? At the beginning of the unit Stephanie showed the class a short video clip in Spanish about an effect of air pollution (asthma) on human beings, specifically on Latinos. Then she asked the students to discuss the video using the full features of their language repertoires. After the students had discussed the PSA using Spanish and English, Stephanie asked the students to describe in English the persuasive features from the PSA video that they saw and heard in Spanish. Noemí's performance on this task in English is more toward the experienced end of the translanguaging progressions because this is a relatively concrete task where Noemí can draw on her comprehension of the videos in Spanish and on her conversations with her peers using the full features of her repertoire to strengthen her performance in oral English.

However, writing a persuasive essay in English is a much more complex task than describing persuasive features seen in a video in Spanish. When Stephanie asks students to write a persuasive PSA in English, she purposefully draws on Noemí's oracy and literacy expertise in Spanish (i.e., her performances in her stronger language) to propel her performance forward on this more advanced literacy task in English (i.e., with only part of her linguistic repertoire in her less experienced language). Thus, translanguaging allows Noemí to give a more experienced performance in English than if she were required to suppress her Spanish and exclusively use English.

We emphasize that teachers in translanguaging classrooms *are* concerned with developing bilingual students' performances in the specific language(s) of school because this is very important for academic success. But because teachers in translanguaging classrooms understand dynamic bilingualism and the interrelationship of language features that form a bilingual's linguistic repertoire, they differentiate between the bilingual student's language-specific and general linguistic performances. Teachers know that bilingual students who can express complex thoughts through the use of their entire language repertoires will be able to develop the specific features that they need to express those same complex thoughts in English or another language using school-sanctioned linguistic features.

Furthermore, giving bilingual children opportunities to draw on the full features of their linguistic repertoires in school can lead to greater linguistic confidence because children lose the fear of expression that is often the result of artificial linguistic boundaries in schools—which in turn can result in strengthened academic performance. For example, one of the authors of this book (Johnson) has been involved in evaluating bilingual students' work toward the Seal of Biliteracy in a high school in New Mexico. To obtain the seal on their high school diplomas, students are required to present a portfolio about their academics, their personal accomplishments (including interests, hobbies, and community service), a self-reflection, and a language reflection. The teachers at this high school have opened up a space for students to organize their presentations, drawing on Spanish and English as needed. One student began his presentation by explaining his math coursework in English and concluded the presentation by explaining what he had learned in math in Spanish, and used both languages fluidly throughout the presentation. For this part of the portfolio presentation, the evaluators were focused on assessing the students' content-area knowledge in *math*, without concerning themselves with how much time was spent in English or Spanish or which features were being used.

Translanguaging involves the bilingual speakers' deployment of their entire language repertoires, which we can productively understand in terms of general linguistic and language-specific performances. A translanguaging perspective liberates bilingual speakers from *always* having to filter and suppress some of the features of their linguistic repertoires (e.g., languages other than the dominant one or vernacular varieties) to fit the particular communicative situation in which they find themselves. By focusing on their general linguistic performances, bilingual students are on par with students who come from homes that use more-or-less standard features of the official school language, and who therefore do not have to suppress parts of their linguistic repertoires. Thus, besides encouraging virtuoso linguistic achievement, attention to the general linguistic performance dimension is a way of acting on the potential of translanguaging for social justice by leveling the linguistic playing field for bilingual students.

Viewing translanguaging in this way, and pointing out the inaccuracy of measuring a bilingual's language proficiency by forbidding translanguaging, Otheguy, García and Reid (2015) argue the following:

> Accuracy of measurement is a bedrock value in the context of educational testing. Yet forbidding bilinguals to translanguage, or assessing it negatively, produces an inaccurate measure of their language proficiency. If proficiency assessment is to be accurate and informative, it must adopt the *inside* perspective that will reveal the linguistic condition of the individual student's idiolect, irrespective of the social

rules that qualify or disqualify some or all of the idiolect as belonging to a particular named language (p. 299, italics added for emphasis).

As such, adopting translanguaging for students' language progressions recognizes that language performances are not flat; that is, they do not occur on neutral ground or on monolingual territory. Rather, language performances are carried out on territory that has peaks and valleys that are shaped by language ideologies surrounding a particular speech event and by the interlocutors in that event. Educators can therefore use the dynamic translanguaging progressions to reduce the monolingual bias we find in most assessment practices, and to paint a more holistic portrait of what students can do with content, language, and literacy at school.

It is translanguaging that leverages the students' linguistic resources to propel them toward deeper understanding of complex content and texts; more advanced linguistic performances for academic contexts; and greater learning, creativity, and criticality. Translanguaging is the impetus for the sophisticated general linguistic performance, raising it to greater heights on any new task (e.g., using language to explain, compare, contrast, and synthesize). Translanguaging also enhances students' ability to use language in ways that conform to standardized conventions at school. We turn to an example from Carla's 4th-grade DLBE classroom to illustrate this point.

VIEWING STANDARDIZED SYSTEMS THROUGH THE DYNAMIC TRANSLANGUAGING PROGRESSIONS LENS

Recall that Carla has designed an instructional unit, *Cuentos de la tierra y del barrio,* which focuses on how students, families, and the local community are tied to their land, and by extension to their traditions. One of the CCSS for English language arts that is addressed in Carla's unit plan is Reading Literature: Standard 1 for Grade 4, which states, "Refer to details and examples in a text when explaining what the text says explicitly and when drawing inferences from the text." To leverage her students' entire linguistic repertoires, Carla plans biliteracy activities that support students' efforts to meet this and other standards by

- Providing Spanish, English, and bilingual texts to preview specific textual evidence of the local farming practices in New Mexico
- Accessing YouTube, TED Talks, and other media sites in Spanish and English to find specific textual evidence of local farming practices in New Mexico
- Making available community resources (e.g., bilingual guest speakers and local farming sites) to review specific textual evidence of local farming practices in New Mexico

Carla began with a read-aloud of *Lluvia de plata* by Sara Poot Herrera, which is written in Spanish, using necessary scaffolding and support to engage all of her students with the text. Next, students worked in groups to explain what the text said using specific textual evidence, examples, and details to support their points and make inferences. Carla provided the students with a note-taking guide to scaffold the group work. Each student was required to write a short response in Spanish to a question that demonstrated an understanding of the text, the ability to make inferences, and the use of text-based evidence to support their points. The final task in this activity was a narrative essay to be written independently in Spanish.

Carla drew on information she had gathered on her students' individual bilingual profiles to place them into heterogeneous groups. She wanted to make sure that the groups included students with strong literacy practices in Spanish who could then assist the group with their narrative essay written in Spanish. During group work to find specific text-based evidence, Carla gave students the freedom to use all the features of their linguistic repertoires to support their academic conversations about the Spanish-language text.

Carla closely observed her students' participation in these tasks, and she was able to see the degree to which they could use language as they provided evidence from the text for the inferences they made. At this point in her unit of instruction, Carla was not looking to see whether students used features of Spanish or English. Rather, she was focusing on whether students could make inferences and provide evidence from the text using the full features of their linguistic repertoires. Carla also looked to see how her students drew on their general linguistic performances in collaboration with each other to perform concrete tasks that met or exceeded the academic demands of the Reading Literature: Standard 1. By assessing these general linguistic performances, Carla was then able to adapt her teaching to ensure that those students who needed assistance in finding evidence and inferring were supported, regardless of whether they could perform with the linguistic features expected in one specific language or another.

Carla also made sure to communicate to her students that they were going to have to write the short answers and their essay in Spanish. Thus, Carla demonstrated that she valued students' performances in a standard language, in this case their performance with targeted features of written Spanish. Regardless of the language in which Carla expected the *product*, she ensured that students knew to leverage all their bilingual resources in the *process* of writing. In sum, Carla expected all her students to perform and meet grade-level standards for language and literacy, leveraging their entire language repertoires to do so.

Let's focus on **Erica**, a student in Carla's class, to illustrate this point. Erica's parents are Puerto Rican but she was born in New Mexico and grew up speaking mostly English at home, although Spanish was also spoken. Because Erica was not officially designated as an ELL she was simply seen as an English speaker, and the Spanish she brought with her to school went unnoticed. After attending an English-medium kindergarten, Erica's parents requested that Erica be placed in the DLBE program so she would develop her bilingualism and biliteracy. Erica is now in Carla's 4th-grade class and her literacy performances are at grade level in English, and almost at grade level in Spanish. In terms of speaking, Erica prefers to communicate with her friends in class and during recess in English. In class, Carla notices that Erica is hesitant to speak Spanish. Carla also has noticed that since she allowed Erica to use both languages during Cuéntame algo, Erica has further developed her comfort with using Spanish. Figure 3.5 presents Erica's translanguaging progression relative to the performance tasks required during the activities surrounding the reading of *Lluvia de plata,* as evaluated by Carla.

Carla evaluates Erica's oracy performances in English as much more experienced than her oracy performances in Spanish on these types of tasks. However, her literacy performance in Spanish is nearly as experienced as her literacy performance in English. Carla then knows that she can leverage Erica's strong oracy and literacy in English, and her relatively strong literacy in Spanish, in ways that enable Erica to produce more *commanding* oracy performances in Spanish on these tasks. Carla also expects that Erica's interactions with group members with stronger Spanish oracy and literacy will propel her performances in Spanish oracy forward on this task.

If Carla had asked Erica to read *Lluvia de plata* in Spanish, discuss it in Spanish, and write an independent essay in Spanish that included textual evidence to support the inferences she made, Erica's oracy and literacy performances in Spanish for this activity series would likely have looked much less

Entering ←————————————————————————————————→ Commanding

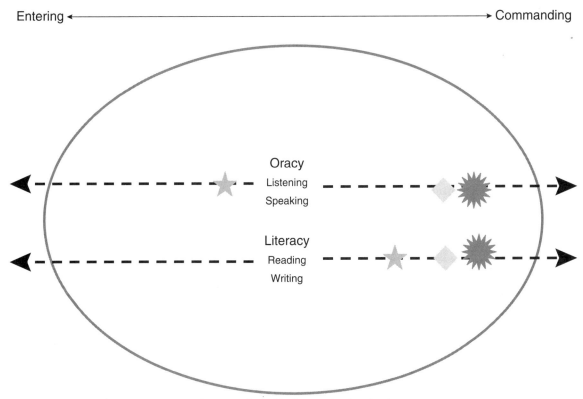

Figure 3.5   Erica's translanguaging progression, as evaluated by her teacher in school.
◆ Language-specific performance in English
★ Language-specific performance in Spanish
✳ General linguistic performance

Student: Erica
Text: *Lluvia de plata* by Sara Poot Herrera
Standard: Reading Literature, grade 4. Refer to details and examples in a text when explaining what the text says explicitly and when drawing inferences from the text.

Performance tasks
• Reading in Spanish
• Discussing reading with peers using a guide to compile textual evidence (details, examples) to support text summary and inferences.
• Independent writing task in Spanish that summarizes the reading text and makes inferences from that text using examples and details from the text.

experienced. However, when not limited to the use of one language, Erica's general linguistic performances on the types of tasks in this particular activity series (e.g., reading for information, participating in evidence-based conversations around text, summarizing a reading and making inferences, using examples and details from the text) are stronger than her performances in English only or Spanish only would be. For example, Carla noted that Erica's participation in the discussion about evidence from the text was richer than if she had asked Erica to speak only in Spanish.

Carla observed that translanguaging leveraged *all* students' performances in ways that propelled them forward to greater learning and more advanced linguistic performances. For example, *Jennifer* was able to identify text-based evidence easily, but in Spanish only she would not have been engaged with the group. In contrast, although Ricardo speaks Spanish fluently, he has not had much practice finding text-based evidence. Jennifer supported Ricardo in finding evidence; in turn, Ricardo supported Jennifer's spoken Spanish as they collaborated using Spanish. Carla also observed that after the rich unfettered discussion, students were able to put their thoughts in written Spanish with relative ease.

The construct of the dynamic translanguaging progressions allows us to see students' linguistic performances not as static scores, but as dynamic and imbricated with the context in which they are performed, and in interaction with the teacher's pedagogy. When teachers apply the translanguaging progressions to understand what their students can do using the full features of their linguistic repertoires, and in interaction with other students in the class, teachers can leverage students' linguistic resources, propelling them to greater heights in content learning, linguistic performances, creativity, and criticality.

In short, teachers in translanguaging classrooms not only develop student profiles that help inform instruction in *a* language (i.e., *one* language, whether English or Spanish), *they start from a different place*. They start by ensuring that they develop and assess the *holistic linguistic performance* of children, including their general linguistic and language-specific performances. In so doing, they

TABLE 3.2 **Performances along the Dynamic Translanguaging Progressions**

Student _____*Erica*_____

Reading Literature: Grade 4

Common Core Anchor Standard	**Main Academic Demand**
Read closely to determine what the text says explicitly and to make logical inferences from it; cite specific textual evidence when writing or speaking to support conclusions drawn from the text.	Draw inferences using evidence from the text
Common Core Grade Standard	**Grade-Level Academic Demand**
Refer to details and examples in a text when explaining what the text says explicitly and when drawing inferences from the text.	Refer to text detail to explain and draw inferences

	Oracy	Literacy
Commanding	Refers to ample details and examples in a text that explain what the text says and can draw substantial inferences from the details and examples **General linguistic**	Refers to ample details and examples in a text that explain what the text says and can draw substantial inferences from the details and examples **General linguistic**
Expanding	Refers to many details and examples in a text that explain what the text says and can draw appropriate inferences from the details and examples **English oracy**	Refers to many details and examples in a text that explain what the text says and can draw appropriate inferences from the details and examples **Spanish literacy** **English literacy**
Developing	Refers to multiple details and examples in a text that explain what the text says and can draw relevant inferences from the details and examples **Spanish oracy**	Refers to multiple details and examples in a text that explain what the text says and can draw relevant inferences from the details and examples
Emerging	Refers to several details and examples in a text that explain what the text says and can draw vague inferences from the details and examples	Refers to several details and examples in a text that explain what the text says and can draw vague inferences from the details and examples
Entering	Refers to very minimum details and examples in a text that explain what the text says. Details and examples cited may not be appropriate.	Refers to very minimum details and examples in a text that explain what the text says. Details and examples cited may not be appropriate.

Translanguaging: Bilinguals from all levels can refer to details and examples in a text and draw inferences from details and examples by previewing, viewing, and reviewing the texts in multiple languages, discussing orally/ signing and/or exploring in writing and responding orally using their *entire language repertoire*s, with freedom to select linguistic features *or with language-specific features.*

Carla's assessment of Erica's type of performance on each of the progressions is indicated in **bold**.

offer children more practice with language, instead of silencing them or making them feel self-conscious when performing solely in one language or another.

As we have seen, Carla adapted traditional progression categories to gauge her bilingual students' placement along the dynamic translanguaging progressions for particular standards. As noted, the standard on Reading Literature states: "Refer to details and examples in a text when explaining what the text says explicitly and when drawing inferences from the text." Carla has been observing Erica as she works in her group and independently. She notes that Erica's oracy in Spanish is at the *developing* stage because Erica never initiates conversation in Spanish but does respond when others speak it. Yet, her Spanish literacy is more advanced, as is her English literacy, a sign of her ability to read and write school texts well. Thus, when Erica is allowed to use all her resources, her performance in both oracy and literacy is what Carla calls "stellar." Erica is convincing as she brings up rich examples and details from the text to make her points, and she makes excellent inferences.

Table 3.2 shows how Carla placed Erica along the progressions (indicated in bold in the table). She adapted standard progressions (WIDA ELD standards) to gauge Erica's placement in the dynamic translanguaging progressions for this specific task.

The table shows that Carla substitutes the term *commanding* (used in New York State) on the experienced end of the progressions for *bridging* (used by WIDA). But she uses *developing* (WIDA's term) rather than *transitioning* (New York State's term) because of her bilingual developmental stance. It is important to note that, just as students at times are given the liberty to select different features of their repertoires, teachers who work with the dynamic translanguaging progressions also are given the freedom to adapt aspects of their state systems developed only for ELLs to make them useful for all bilingual students.

Because teachers need a way of recording their observations and data regarding where their bilingual students stand on task-based performances using different aspects of their linguistic repertoires, we include the checklist in Appendix A.3.5. This is a useful form that teachers can reproduce to see at a glance what individual students can do with all or some of their linguistic features, which in turn provides a foundation for instruction.

CONCLUSION

This chapter has explored how teachers can acknowledge, validate, document, and build on the linguistic performances of bilingual students in classrooms and schools. If we want to design appropriate instruction for bilingual students, we must understand their bilingualism. Because data about bilingualism is not generally gathered in schools, educators have to make a special effort to gather this kind of information. The chapter introduces tools that educators can use to connect with bilingual students and their families, explore students' experiences with language and education, and document students' bilingualism.

The dynamic translanguaging progressions that we propose in this chapter offer a different approach to language development than we have seen in state-sanctioned English language proficiency standards and assessment systems. For example, rather than focus exclusively on the ELD of students who are officially designated as ELLs, teachers can use the dynamic translanguaging progressions with *all* bilingual students, including those who schools may simply see as English speakers. In contrast to a view of language development as a relatively linear, stage-like, and unidirectional process, the dynamic translanguaging progressions allow teachers to capture the complexity of students' holistic bilingual performances on different tasks, at different times, from different perspectives. Instead of viewing the home language of an emergent bilingual as an important scaffold for learning at the beginning stages of ELD, teachers see translanguaging as appropriate to demonstrate skilled linguistic performance.

If we are interested in gauging what students can do with language to accomplish content-specific tasks, and if we understand translanguaging as characteristic of linguistic performances of all bilinguals, then translanguaging has to be considered a valid way of demonstrating linguistic virtuosity and content understanding. Teachers can use the dynamic translanguaging progressions to evaluate bilingual students' performances in different academic tasks at school over time. Over the longer term, the dynamic translanguaging progressions can be used to gather empirical evidence that illustrates how translanguaging works in different multilingual settings, and to document the degree to which translanguaging can mobilize and accelerate learning.

QUESTIONS AND ACTIVITIES

1. What are some steps that you could take to encourage students and their families to share their bilingualism with you?

2. What are the differences between the state and consortia systems of ELD and the construct of the dynamic translanguaging progressions? How can you use the translanguaging progressions to build on what your state is doing?

3. Select any standard and choose three bilingual students in your classroom. Evaluate generally (more specific assessment instruments will be discussed in the chapter on assessment) these students' general linguistic and language-specific performances. Fill out the form in Appendix A.3.5. What can you say about the differences?

TAKING ACTION

1. Ask your school administrator and a teacher in your school to try out the Promoting an Ecology of Multilingualism Checklist (see Appendix A.3.1). Interview these educators afterward and find out what they learned about their students as a result.

2. Use the Bilingual Student Identification and Profile Form (see Appendix A.3.2) with ten of your students. What did you learn about them? How were you able to gather the information?

PART II

TRANSLANGUAGING PEDAGOGY

CHAPTER 4

Translanguaging Stance

LEARNING OBJECTIVES

- Describe the importance of the first strand of the translanguaging pedagogy—the stance
- Identify the three core beliefs of the translanguaging stance
- Explain how the stance is reflected at the classroom and societal levels in English-medium and bilingual programs
- Describe how a teacher's stance is enacted in practice
- Articulate your own stance toward your students' dynamic bilingualism

---

Creating a translanguaging classroom is not easy. It runs contrary to what has traditionally been taught in teacher education and what some may consider common sense. General education teachers are usually taught that their role is to teach content in English only, and that all students should know how to use English to learn. **English as a second language (ESL)** teachers are often told that the **emergent bilinguals** they teach in **push-in, pull-out,** or **structured English immersion programs** are "limited" or just "English learners." **Transitional bilingual education** teachers are frequently encouraged to transition students to English as quickly as possible, often without providing students with opportunities to learn to use Spanish or English for complex academic purposes. Dual-language bilingual teachers are usually taught to keep the two languages separate for instructional purposes, and to protect Spanish (or the other language) from the encroachment of English. All teachers are taught to emphasize English to prepare students for what is often seen as most important—the state assessments.

In this chapter, we challenge these beliefs about educating bilingual students and open ourselves to other perspectives that are brought to our classrooms by the **translanguaging corriente**, or the constant flow of students' **dynamic bilingualism** in a classroom. We focus here on the *translanguaging stance*, which is the first strand of the translanguaging pedagogy. The **translanguaging stance** refers to a teacher's belief that a bilingual student has one holistic language repertoire that he or she draws on at school as teachers address the four purposes for translanguaging:

1. To support students as they engage with and comprehend complex content and texts
2. To provide opportunities for students to develop linguistic practices for academic contexts
3. To make space for students' bilingualism and ways of knowing
4. To support students' socioemotional development and bilingual identities

Teachers with a translanguaging stance have a strong social justice orientation, and they assume that effective instruction and assessment for bilingual students requires drawing on or leveraging students' bilingualism for learning.

JUNTOS/TOGETHER

We all remember a teacher who strongly influenced our learning or the trajectory of our lives. Many of us have been saved, inspired, changed, or given renewed hope by educators who took the time to help us become the best versions of ourselves. These kinds of memorable teachers bring with them more than just good teaching strategies or a deep understanding of content. (Though they bring those too!) They also act on the belief that who their students are, what they know, and where they come from matters and that they have the potential to do great things with their lives. While all students deserve teachers like these, they are especially important for those young people who have been historically marginalized and underserved by schools. Though teachers alone cannot solve the difficult economic, political, and social realities faced by many students and their families, we can make a powerful, *local* impact by putting our students' languages, cultures, interests, and ways of knowing at the center of our classrooms.

The translanguaging stance refers to the philosophical orientation that teachers draw on to construct a **translanguaging classroom**. It is a necessary mindset or framework for educating bilingual students that informs everything from the way we view students and their dynamic bilingual performances and cultural practices to the way we plan instruction and assessment. We use the term **juntos**, the Spanish word for together, to describe this stance. The juntos stance is informed by three beliefs of joint collaboration:

1. Students' language practices and cultural understanding encompass those they bring from home and communities, as well as those they take up in schools. These practices and understanding work juntos and enrich each other.
2. Students' families and communities are valuable sources of knowledge and must be involved in the education process juntos.
3. The classroom is a democratic space where teachers and students juntos co-create knowledge, challenge traditional hierarchies, and work toward a more just society.

Taking up a translanguaging stance is one step toward Cummins' (2010) simple, yet powerful, call to action: *"If you want students to emerge from schooling after 12 years as intelligent, imaginative, and linguistically talented, then treat them as intelligent, imaginative, and linguistically talented from the first day they arrive at school"* (p. ix, italics in original).

This is the stance that our teachers—*Carla*, *Stephanie*, and *Justin*—hold and that many of us share. Of course, how the translanguaging classroom framework is implemented will differ for educators in different contexts.

ENACTING A TRANSLANGUAGING STANCE IN BILINGUAL AND ENGLISH-MEDIUM PROGRAMS

Though we mostly explore the translanguaging stance at the classroom level, it is important to emphasize that at the larger societal level, taking up a translanguaging stance is an act of social justice. The discourse around many bilingual students, especially Latino bilinguals, is often that of deficiency and failure. The increasingly large number of Latino students in U.S. schools is not reflected in the mostly white, English-speaking teaching force. We can see deficit-thinking and prejudice, even among the most well-meaning educators, and sometimes even among teachers who share linguistic and cultural characteristics with students.

Furthermore, in response to increasing numbers of Latinos and other minority groups, we have seen harsh immigration, antibilingual education, and antiethnic studies legislation in states like California, Massachusetts, and Arizona. Such measures make the lives of Latino and other immigrant students and their families difficult, at times dangerous. Thus, teachers of bilinguals, and especially Latino bilinguals, can understand their translanguaging stance as influential beyond the local, classroom level. In a very real way, the kind of philosophically informed pedagogy that we advocate has the power to make changes at the larger societal level.

For this reason, taking up a translanguaging stance cannot be limited to bilingual teachers. In reality, *every* teacher of bilingual youth can take up a translanguaging stance, no matter their language background or program type. To explain this further, we look briefly at how our three very different teachers, Carla, Stephanie, and Justin, enact a translanguaging stance through their practices.

Carla: A Spanish–English Bilingual Teacher in a Dual-Language Bilingual Education Program

Carla, born in Puebla, Mexico, immigrated to New Mexico when she was a young girl. Like her students, Carla understands and lives a borderlands existence, both culturally and linguistically. She and her family and friends speak with features of both Spanish and English that are specific to their New Mexican context. The translanguaging corriente is strong, and strict separation of languages is uncommon. Keeping her own language practices in mind, Carla teaches her **dual-language bilingual education (DLBE)** class in ways that push the boundaries of the program. Traditionally in these classrooms, students' languages are rigidly separated. There is time set aside for English and time set aside for Spanish, and students are discouraged from using the other language during those designated times. Though at first, Carla's practice was philosophically aligned with this more traditional approach, learning about translanguaging shifted her stance and helped her make space *within* that program for students' bilingual, bicultural voices.

Though she adheres to the macro-level language policy of her school, which sets out specific time and space for each language, Carla enacts her stance by making room for translanguaging in a variety of creative ways. Carla created in her class what she calls a Cuéntame algo space, where students actively bring together their language practices by reading translanguaged texts, engaging in activities and discussions that hone their metalinguistic awareness, and creating their own texts that include both English and Spanish. She also plans translanguaging instructional units that draw on students' experiences in their families and communities. Learning within these units is active, hands-on, and brings together/juntos students' languages, cultural understanding, family and community, and the school.

For example, part of Carla's *Cuentos de la tierra y del barrio* unit involved working in a garden run by members of the local community. Carla planned a series of lessons on preparing a jardín and invited **Sonia**, a bilingual herbalist in the community, to deepen students' understanding. She also invited some students' padres y abuelitos to accompany the class on a fieldtrip to the reclaimed plot of land where they would garden. Following is one small dialogue that ensues between Sonia and a student, **Erica**:

Sonia (S): ¿Qué pasa con nuestro jardín durante el invierno?

[What happens to our garden during the winter?]

Erica (E): El jardín se comienza a dormir. . . . Well it falls asleep, but not all of it.

[The garden starts to fall asleep. . .]

S: ¿Por qué no todo el jardín fall asleep?

[Why doesn't the entire garden fall asleep?]

E: Es que los perennials que son herbs, flowers, and shrubs, no todos se van a morir.

[It's because of the perennials that are herbs, flowers, and shrubs, not all will die]

S: Claro, muchos perennials regresan año tras año, y es por eso que tenemos que cortarlos once they completely go to seed.

[Of course, many perennials will come back year after year and this is why we have to cut them]

Carla believes that the linguistic and cultural practices that students bring from home and community must work juntos with those used in school to encourage deep understanding. That is why she never stops the dialogue and tells Sonia or the students, "Así no se dice," "English only, please," or "Spanish only, please." Carla's stance enables her to reject the notion that Sonia and the students speak "Spanglish," a stigmatized version of Spanish. And she also rejects the notion that these students have incomplete acquisition of English. Carla's stance encourages students to value their dynamic bilingualism, the way they speak with all the features of their **language repertoires**, and to continue developing language practices for academic purposes. This also makes it possible for Carla's students to develop strong bilingual identities. Carla's stance contributes to the students' socioemotional growth and academic learning.

Carla also involves students' families and communities to work juntos with the children, to teach and learn from the close relationship that she establishes among all of them. For Carla, teaching is also about co-learning (Li Wei, 2014) with her students and with the community and families. In the jardín, we often find Carla and her students, as well as community members like Sonia, planting juntos. According to Carla's stance, and echoing our third and fourth translanguaging purposes, school learning can only occur if students are able to **leverage** their ways of knowing and using language that they learn from those at home and in their communities, and if they are secure socioemotionally in their bilingual identities. Carla's stance enables her to make specific pedagogical choices to respond to students' bilingual practices and thus shift the ways in which bilingual students see themselves relative to the white monolingual students in their schools and in society.

In summary, Carla enacts her translanguaging stance in her DLBE classroom by

- Making space for translanguaging within the macro-level language policies of her school, which separate students' languages
- Planning units and activities and reading texts that connect with students' local understanding and their families' and communities' funds of knowledge (Moll, Amanti, Neff, & González, 1992)
- Partnering with students' families and community members to co-educate and nurture students, so that they can see their community reflected in school work
- Pursuing a holistic understanding of what bilingual students know and can do with content and language by assessing their **general linguistic performances** (e.g., using the full features of their linguistic repertoires to learn about and demonstrate their understanding of perennials and annuals) and their **language-specific performances** (using either Spanish or English appropriately to express their content learning)
- Placing students' performances in English and Spanish side by side on the **dynamic translanguaging progressions** and evaluating the relative strength of their general linguistic and language-specific performances in oracy and literacy
- Using translanguaging to leverage students' general linguistic performances in ways that deepen content-area understanding (e.g., to explain the difference between perennials and annuals without concern for specific **language features**) and then to further oracy and literacy development in language-specific performances.

We illustrated the last three bullet points in Chapter 3 when we saw how Carla uses state-sanctioned content and language development systems (i.e., Common Core State Standards and WIDA) to frame her placement of Erica along the dynamic translanguaging progressions, and to leverage Erica's *commanding* general linguistic performances in oracy and literacy to propel her oracy performances in Spanish forward.

Stephanie: An English-Speaking Teacher in an English-Medium Content-Area Classroom

Unlike Carla, Stephanie does not speak her students' home language, nor does she teach in a bilingual program. Furthermore, though most of her students are Latino, they have a wide range of experiences with Spanish. Some speak Spanish at home with their families and friends and feel comfortable using it for many purposes. Others hear Spanish from an abuela or a parent, but don't feel comfortable using it themselves. Still others use Spanish outside of school, but don't have experience using it for academic purposes. Adding another layer of complexity, some of Stephanie's students are African American and Caribbean, with language practices and varieties of English that are also marginalized in school. Informed by this complex linguistic and cultural landscape, as well as her own language background, Stephanie's translanguaging stance is enacted differently from Carla's.

Stephanie believes that all students must have access to all their linguistic resources at all times to make meaning of the complex content they encounter in her social studies class. As a monolingual English speaker, however, Stephanie must enact her stance through the use of other people and other resources, such as bilingual dictionaries, online translation tools, bilingual staff members, and, most importantly, the students themselves. Entering Stephanie's classroom, one can see how she utilizes the resources at her disposal to leverage the translanguaging corriente and enact her stance through her practice. For example, during her interdisciplinary unit *Environmentalism: Then and Now*, Stephanie asked students to use their textbooks and several short, supplemental readings in English to construct a timeline that illustrated the major events of the environmentalist movement. Students had access to the textbook in both English and Spanish and sat in heterogeneous groups comprised of students with diverse linguistic profiles. Because Stephanie could not find appropriate supplemental readings in Spanish, the readings she provided were in English, but at different levels of text complexity. The following vignette illustrates how Stephanie's planning and design, informed by her stance, made room for the translanguaging corriente to flow:

Stephanie circulates the classroom, listening to her students' conversations and checking their progress. One group, in which we find *Teresita* and *Luis*, is speaking Spanish, but writing its timelines in English. Luis has recently arrived from El Salvador and is just beginning to learn English, while Teresita is a strong reader and writer in both languages. The group uses Spanish to ensure that Luis can participate. Stephanie listens to their Spanish conversation for a moment, and then asks Teresita to tell her, in English, what they're talking about. Teresita fills her in; Stephanie contributes a few ideas that Teresita translates for Luis and Stephanie moves on.

Next to this table, there is another group working together. In this group *Noemí*, who emigrated from Ecuador and whose literacy performances are more experienced in Spanish than in English, and *James*, an African American student, are working together. James summarizes a piece of the reading in English, while Noemí listens and nods in understanding. Noemí asks a question in Spanish, and *Eddy* who is a more experienced bilingual translates it for her. James consults the English version of the textbook and Noemí consults the Spanish version and they collaboratively reach an agreement that answers Noemí's question. In the exchange, James learns the word "estereotipo" which he loves to repeat out loud, while Noemí adds the word "stereotype" to her repertoire. Noemí also notes that "stereotype" is missing an "e" at the beginning of the word and tries out pronouncing it in English with much group involvement. They return to their timeline.

Meanwhile, Luis, and *Carlos*, another recently arrived emergent bilingual, have gathered around the classroom computers and are using an online translation tool to find words in English to contribute to the timeline. As they find each new word in English, they write it above the Spanish word they had initially written on their timelines.

Several aspects of Stephanie's stance are visible in this snapshot from the daily life of her classroom. First, we see her comfort with linguistic flexibility. She does not police students' language, nor does she push them to use "English only," rather, she allows students to pool their linguistic resources to make meaning. We also see the many resources at work in Stephanie's classroom. Because she does not speak Spanish, Stephanie knows that she cannot be the only source of knowledge in the room. Instead, she has made available to students a whole host of resources that not only help them carry out an academic task, but also increase students' participation in, and responsibility for, their own learning. Lastly, the organization of her students into heterogeneous groups helps all students engage with the complex content and texts and eliminates the marginalization faced by so many emergent bilinguals in English-medium classrooms. Thus, to summarize, Stephanie enacts her translanguaging stance in her English-medium content-area classroom by

- Ceding some control and being comfortable with students' linguistic flexibility
- Providing students with access to other resources, such as bilingual dictionaries, online translation tools, a variety of written texts in both English and Spanish, and fellow bilingual students
- Organizing students into heterogeneous groups so that they can pool their linguistic resources and avoid marginalizing those who speak less English than others

Justin: A 7th-Grade English as a Second Language Teacher in a Multilingual, Multiethnic English-Medium Classroom

Like Stephanie, Justin does not speak all of his students' home languages. Though he is bilingual, speaking English and some Mandarin, the diverse students in his classes speak a variety of languages, such as Fula, Tagalog, and Cantonese. Some of his students' languages do not share any cognates or even a script with English, so drawing connections to English can be challenging. He also has one student who is the *only* Korean speaker in the classroom, which makes it difficult for her to consult with others to make meaning of new content. Because Justin often "pushes in" to his students' content-area classrooms, he is also charged with ensuring that students are academically *and* linguistically supported, without being "marked" among English speakers as less intelligent or competent because they have less experience with the new language.

Despite the numerous challenges present in Justin's context, he is resolute about his translanguaging stance. Like Stephanie, he believes that students must have access to all their linguistic resources at all times, even if he does not understand those languages himself. Also like Stephanie, Justin uses a variety of resources, such as online translation tools and more experienced bilinguals, to ensure that his translanguaging stance is enacted in practice. He also works with his co-teachers to ensure that lesson content is adapted to meet the linguistic needs of emergent bilinguals and bring their unique experiences to the surface. This last point is especially important. Because Justin is the ESL teacher in "mainstream" content-area classrooms, he thinks of himself as not only an educator, but an advocate and an ally. The following vignette of Justin co-planning with the 7th-grade science teacher illustrates this aspect of his stance:

As Justin and his co-teacher sat down to plan out the week's lessons, Justin made space for emergent bilinguals to use translanguaging to participate meaningfully in the instruction. The focus of the week was genetics, and the culminating design of the week was for students to carry out and write up a lab experiment. Originally, the science teacher had planned for the experiment to be carried out by students individually, but Justin suggested that he partner students who spoke the same home languages so that they could work together using all their linguistic resources. Justin also suggested that students build their background knowledge by prewriting and brainstorming on the topic of genetics. He explained how the teacher could use translanguaging with a traditional KWL chart, which asks students what they know, what they want to know, and what they have learned about a topic. Students would write what they know and what they wanted to know about genetics using all their linguistic resources, and then would share their ideas in English. They would also be able to take their own notes on what they learned in their home languages, but would share their new understanding in English. Later in the week, when they wrote up their findings, Justin and his co-teacher planned out lessons so that all students had sufficient academic and linguistic support and the flexibility and space to use all their linguistic resources to make meaning of content in English.

Taking up the role of advocate and ally for his emergent bilingual students meant that Justin often had to help his colleagues see and understand the translanguaging corriente. Rather than being relegated to the sidelines, as some **push-in ESL** teachers are, Justin positions himself as an instructional leader. He has gained the respect of his colleagues, which makes it easier to introduce new ideas that help emergent bilinguals learn. Justin's work with his co-teacher ensured that students would be provided with access to content and would be invited to share their prior knowledge and experiences with the topic. It also enabled all students to tap into their inner, intrapersonal translanguaging voice—even the student who did not have a partner or group of peers who spoke her home language—so that they could participate meaningfully. When his co-teacher worried that she wouldn't know how to assess her students if they spoke their home languages, Justin assured her that their **translanguaging design** would bring students' knowledge and understanding to the surface and that this would *help* rather than hinder their ability to assess their students.

THREE CORE BELIEFS

Although Carla, Stephanie, and Justin enacted their translanguaging stances differently because of their diverse experiences and contexts, each of their stances was informed by the three core beliefs introduced earlier in the chapter:

1. Students' language practices and cultural understanding encompass those they bring from home and communities and those they acquire in school. These practices and understanding work juntos and enrich each other.

Traditionally, schools have separated Latino students' "home language" (Spanish) from their "school language" (English), creating what Cummins (2008) calls "the two solitudes." This separation essentially takes from students a vital tool for communicating effectively, forming relationships, and fully engaging in the educational experience. Teachers in translanguaging classrooms embrace a flexible stance toward students' dynamic bilingualism. This does not mean that they do away with objectives and goals for students' language practices. On the contrary, teachers of bilingual students always think strategically about how they use language.

By embracing the translanguaging corriente, teachers make space for students to use their language practices in ways that lead to increased understanding and engagement. García uses the metaphor of "interlocking gears" to explain the necessity of this kind of flexible language use. Without students' home language practices, new language practices have nothing to lock into and, as such, cannot gain purchase. Recall our first and second purposes for translanguaging: *supporting students as they engage with and comprehend complex content and texts* and *providing opportunities for students to develop language practices for academic contexts*. Encouraging students to use their language practices in conversation facilitates the process of content and language learning juntos.

In addition to strengthening academic understanding and increasing classroom engagement, being open to the co-existence of English and other language practices can ease the tension that often occurs when one language is considered more valuable than another. When we tell students to speak only English and insist that they not use Spanish, we are telling them that Spanish—the language of their families, friends, and communities—is unwelcome in the classroom. When we think about times in our own lives when those we love or the places we are from have been denigrated or left out, we feel anger, frustration, shame, discouragement, and sadness. For example, Seltzer remembers the humiliation she felt when a teacher told her that her mother and father's intermarriage damaged the Jewish community. Ibarra Johnson remembers growing up in the borderlands of Mexico and the United States, where her relatives on the Mexican side of the border called her a "pochita" and the Tejas side called her a "pobrecita" because she spoke "ni inglés ni español bien" [neither English nor Spanish well]. And García has been told numerous times to "go back to her country," even though she considers the United States her country, as much as the Cuba she left for New York at the age of 11.

The emotions we feel when our lives, experiences, and understanding are not recognized or respected are not conducive to learning or to building a classroom community. When students feel they must choose between school and home, English and Spanish, being American or something else, academic success and being true to themselves, they are put in an impossible bind. Choosing the former in these dichotomies may feel like treachery. Choosing the latter may lead to abandoning school and discarding a chance at academic and economic success. Taking up a translanguaging stance means making a commitment to teaching students that these one-or-the-other choices are unnecessary—that, in fact, students can be successful in school *and* feel like authentic versions of themselves. Instead of asking students to be simply one or the other, we can emphasize places in our instruction that enable students to make connections from their own language practices and knowledge to those of the school's. This can help ease students out from between the proverbial rock and hard place that creates situations of antagonism, resistance, or failure and toward opportunities that support their socioemotional development and bilingual identities. For example, in Justin's situation, working as the students' advocate and ally by putting their needs and experiences at the center of the "mainstream" classroom ensured that their voices would be heard and that their bilingual and bicultural identities would be valued. Justin's stance was clearly one of affirming a sense of social justice in education.

2. Students' families and communities are valuable sources of knowledge and must be involved in the education process juntos.

Taking up a translanguaging stance means first, recognizing and rejecting negative discourses about minority students in mainstream schools and society. When we turn on the news, look at primetime television, go to the movies, or read popular magazines, we can see how minorities, especially Latinos, are viewed by our society. Popular media generally portray Latinos in a variety of crude stereotypes; we are much more likely to meet the gangster, the undocumented immigrant, or the teen mother than we are to find authentic, nuanced Latino stories. News programs report ad nauseam on poverty, crime, drugs, and school failure in the Latino community, but leave out its long history of activism and legacy of fighting for social justice. Worse yet are the xenophobic and racist policies and discourses that have pervaded the political and social landscape over the past few decades—harsh immigration laws, antibilingual education acts, and bans on ethnic studies. These discourses and policies limit educational opportunities for Latino youth to learn their own histories using their home language practices. Though we cannot change these realities, we can ensure that students walk away from our classrooms knowing that their families and communities are integral to—rather than a mark against—their success.

Taking up a translanguaging stance means countering these negative discourses and making space for students' families and communities to participate in their education. This is precisely what Carla did in her lesson on the jardín when she invited a community gardener, as well as the padres and abuelitos, to plantar with their children. The following vignettes from other translanguaging classrooms further demonstrate how adopting this kind of stance extends engagement with students' families and community members in ways that go beyond token gestures.

A monolingual, English-speaking ESL teacher in Port Chester, NY noticed that few parents and families came to see her at the first conference of the year. She spoke with a few of her students, who told her that their parents did not speak English and did not think that they could interact with her. The teacher spoke with her assistant principal, a Spanish-speaking Latina, about finding an innovative way of addressing the problem. They decided to purchase headsets that allowed for simultaneous translation, which meant that, with the help of the assistant principal, the teacher and parents could communicate without a delay so that more authentic and open conversations could occur.

Rather than take up the all-too-common tactic of blaming families for not attending school meetings, this teacher tapped into her translanguaging stance to make a positive change. This powerful scenario illustrates that taking up a translanguaging stance means challenging and talking back to the negative discourse around Latino families and communities by actively engaging them in the educational process. Here translanguaging itself becomes an act of *social justice*, uniting the school and the community.

Taking up a translanguaging stance might also involve using culturally relevant, local examples to teach academic content:

Cati de los Rios, a teacher and researcher in California, knew that many of her students and their families listened to corridos, Spanish-language ballads that tell stories of romance, oppression, revolution, and daily life. The teacher used corridos as a vehicle for teaching poetic elements like rhyme and metaphor and had students compare them with genres like hip hop and political speeches. The teacher brought in several members of the community to sing corridos and discuss their history and importance to the Chicano community.

This teacher tapped into her translanguaging stance to validate and leverage the resources present in her students' families and communities. With them, juntos, she was able to help her students better understand academic content, build their home language literacy, and see their culture represented in the classroom. This kind of instructional design, directly influenced by her stance, allowed the translanguaging corriente to flow freely and powerfully through both the classroom and students' communities. It also enabled students and their families *to draw on their bilingualism and ways of knowing* to better connect with classroom learning.

3. The classroom is a democratic space where teachers and students juntos create knowledge, challenge traditional hierarchies, and work toward a more just society.

Teachers who take up a translanguaging stance open themselves up to the idea that "traditional" classrooms do not always benefit, and may even harm, Latino bilingual students. Transforming a classroom into a translanguaging space means thinking differently about traditional notions of what it looks like to teach, assess, and learn. It means thinking about whose voices and stories are represented and heard, and whose are silenced. It means reviewing textbooks and curricular resources with a critical eye. It means opening up opportunities for students to use all of their language practices in every lesson and assessment. It means planning culturally sustaining units (Paris, 2012) that culminate not just in a standardized exam, but in relevant, action-oriented projects that challenge students to engage with the world outside the classroom walls. In sum, it means making the familiar classroom strange and taking steps to redesign it.

Imagining a more democratic classroom involves inviting students to actively participate and take a leading role in their own learning. This requires moving away from a banking model of education, where teachers deposit knowledge into passive students' empty heads, and embracing a dialogic, problem-posing model in which both students and teachers are actively engaged in the learning process (Freire, 1970). For bilingual students to engage in this way, they must be encouraged to use all their language practices to help them question, critique, and participate in important dialogues. Without access to their complete linguistic and cultural repertoires, students will be unable to participate in the kinds of conversations that lead to increased engagement and academic success. Bilinguals forced to learn content removed from their daily realities using only some of their language practices are also limited in their ability to grow a critical consciousness, what Freire (1970) calls concientização. A monolingual or bilingual monoglossic curriculum cannot engage Latino students in the kind of thinking and imagining that will make them the social actors and critical citizens that they can be.

The adoption of a translanguaging stance is a necessary ingredient for the transformation of the traditional classroom into what Gutiérrez (2008) calls a "third space." Gutiérrez defines third space as "a transformative space where the potential for an expanded form of learning and the development of new knowledge are heightened" (p.152). This necessarily calls for teachers to relinquish their traditionally hierarchical roles and embrace the idea that students bring with them knowledge and experiences that enrich and enhance learning. Thus, as we saw in Stephanie's classroom, teachers in a translanguaging third space are no longer the sole knowledge keepers, the only classroom experts, or the ideal language speakers. To help students engage in an "expanded form of learning," pupils need access to the language practices that help them *release* that knowledge. Without the ability to translanguage, students cannot tap into (and then expand) what they know.

NEGOTIATING A TRANSLANGUAGING STANCE

Valenzuela (1999) and others have written that Latino students are often subjected to a *subtractive* education that leads to the loss of home languages and cultural practices because bilingual students are pushed to learn English as quickly as possible so that they can achieve academically at school. In light of this fact, and coupled with Latino students' experiences of racism and discrimination in the United States, taking up a translanguaging stance can be challenging. Though we firmly believe that most educators want the best for their students, taking up a translanguaging stance may require us to confront those who do not value or refuse to see and hear the translanguaging corriente in classrooms.

In our own experiences talking about the translanguaging corriente with teachers, administrators, and policymakers around the country, we are sometimes met with skepticism, if not outright resistance. Some of these constituents hold tight to traditional notions of language acquisition and worry that students will never learn English if they continue to use what is considered "mixing" or "**code-switching**." Others compare their own or their family's immigrant narratives to those of our students, unable to understand why *these* students shouldn't just learn English like they or their families did. Still others stigmatize translanguaging, comparing it unfavorably to "Spanglish" and viewing it as inappropriate for academic contexts. Some are skeptical that translanguaging can actually sustain and develop minority languages, fearful that Spanish is not being protected from the encroachment of English. Adopting a translanguaging stance in the face of resistance like this is never easy. Translanguaging, as Flores (2014) reminds us, is a political act. It requires knowledge, confidence—and even *bravery*.

We cannot tell you exactly how to take up a translanguaging stance of your own when facing ideologies and practices that reinforce the monolingual status quo or even the traditional bilingual status quo. However, we recommend that you equip yourself with knowledge about the translanguaging corriente, learn to use tools and strategies that constitute the translanguaging pedagogy, and document your bilingual students' growth and success using the dynamic translanguaging progressions in your translanguaging classroom. Such knowledge, tools, and evidence will allow you to defend your stance and pedagogical choices.

Teaching for social justice means joining our students as they challenge deep-seated ideologies and power structures and working collaboratively toward changing the power hierarchies that legitimize national languages instead of the languaging of people. We believe that taking up a translanguaging stance is a powerful way of letting our bilingual students know that, like Carla, Stephanie, and Justin, we are their advocates and their allies, and that we will do everything in our power to give them the education they deserve.

CONCLUSION

This chapter has explored the first of the three interrelated strands of the translanguaging pedagogy, the translanguaging stance. We use the term juntos, the Spanish word for together, to describe the philosophical orientation that teachers who translanguage embrace and that informs everything from the way they view students and their language and cultural practices to the way they plan instruction and assessment. We have seen that bilingual education teachers (like Carla), English-medium content-area teachers (like Stephanie), and ESL teachers (like Justin) can all enact a translanguaging stance in their classes, although the particulars vary. This stance is what allows the translanguaging corriente, which is the basis for translanguaging for instruction and assessment, to flow in our classrooms.

QUESTIONS AND ACTIVITIES

1. What elements in the translanguaging stance do you see as easy to take up and which do you find difficult? Why?
2. Why is the translanguaging stance linked to the idea of juntos?
3. What sociopolitical and socioeducational factors affect some teachers' negative reactions toward translanguaging? How could you counteract such negativity?

TAKING ACTION

1. What elements make up *your* translanguaging stance? Write 3–5 beliefs that inform who you are and what you do as a teacher of bilingual students.
2. What evidence of a translanguaging stance can you find in your practice? Provide examples to illustrate your points.

CHAPTER 5

Translanguaging Design in Instruction

LEARNING OBJECTIVES

- Explain how teachers can design classroom spaces to encourage the translanguaging corriente to flow
- Describe the major components of the translanguaging instructional design
- Explain how and why Justin engages in translanguaging shifts
- Create a translanguaging unit of instruction for your class
- Anticipate some of the shifts you may need to make to go with the flow of the translanguaging corriente as you implement your translanguaging unit of instruction

Teachers in **translanguaging classrooms** must design instruction so that it responds to the **translanguaging corriente**, sets the right course for learning, and moves bilingual students along the **dynamic translanguaging progressions**. Recall that the translanguaging pedagogy consists of three interrelated strands: stance, design, and shifts. This chapter focuses on translanguaging in instruction, with attention to teachers' purposeful *design* and the moment-to-moment *shifts* they make to **leverage** students' bilingualism for learning.

Translanguaging design in instruction refers to how we strategically plan instruction to work within the translanguaging corriente. A strong design allows teachers to address the four purposes of translanguaging: to support students as they engage with complex content and texts, promote language practices for academic purposes, make space for students' bilingualism and ways of knowing, and support students' socioemotional development and bilingual identities. The design is flexible; it intentionally connects bilingual students' home and community language practices and identities to the language practices and identities deemed appropriate for school settings, while working to address social justice. Consider the following teachers' instructional designs in their translanguaging classrooms:

- *Carla*, our bilingual teacher, creates a Cuéntame algo space where she and her students collaboratively explore bilingual language use.
- *Stephanie*, our social studies teacher, encourages groups of students to use the internet to research information in English and in Spanish on the Clean Air Act.
- *Justin*, our **English as a second language (ESL)** teacher, creates collaborative groups that have common home languages so that students can discuss texts using their own language resources and look up translations and other support texts in their home languages.
- An English language arts teacher organizes a unit around authors and poets who use multiple languages in their writing.

- A bilingual teacher gives out a Spanish text and its English translation and asks students to compare and contrast the lexicon (words), syntax (word order), morphology (word formation), and discourse structure of the text.

The ways these teachers have designed different aspects of their instruction reflect their stance about teaching and learning. They believe, as we do, that a classroom's design—its physical design and the process of designing units, lessons, pedagogical practices, and assessments—must emerge "from the students up." Thus, when designing instruction in a translanguaging classroom, it is important to take stock of what students know and can do, how they learn, and what their needs are. That is, teachers must design instruction that responds to where students are along the dynamic translanguaging progressions.

We begin this chapter with the classroom space and focus on how teachers can encourage the translanguaging corriente to flow as they structure the learning environment for collaboration and to create a **multilingual ecology**. The majority of the chapter presents the translanguaging design for instruction that is at the core of the translanguaging pedagogy. We show teachers how to develop translanguaging unit plans, use the translanguaging instructional design cycle to implement their unit plans, and share pedagogical strategies that teachers can use throughout the design cycle to address the four purposes for translanguaging. We conclude the chapter with a discussion of the ways teachers can strategically shift their instruction to leverage students' bilingualism for learning.

DESIGNING THE CLASSROOM SPACE

Though we can't always choose the physical locations of our classrooms, we can usually make decisions about how we organize them. Whether we have our own classroom, share classrooms, or teach in multiple locations, we can all make design choices that reflect our translanguaging **juntos** stance. Though there are many different things you can do with classroom space to help your students succeed, we focus on two: designing space for collaboration and designing a multilingual ecology.

Fostering Collaboration

Vygotsky (1978) argues that learning is inherently social. By organizing opportunities for collaboration among students of different abilities, teachers create optimal scenarios for learning. Vygotsky calls the space between what students can do alone and what they can do with a "more knowledgeable other" the **zone of proximal development**. In this zone, students can learn and do *more* than they can on their own because of the "boost" they receive from their peers, some of whom know and can do more. When this collaboration includes the use of students' full **language repertoires**, students' performances are enhanced. Moll (2013) refers to the space between what students can do alone and what they can do bilingually as the **bilingual zone of proximal development**. The ideas proposed by Vygotsky and Moll are important for emergent bilingual students, who benefit from opportunities to learn from, and interact with, students who have more experience with the language that the **emergent bilinguals** are just learning (Celic, 2009; Walqui, 2006).

To maximize these learning opportunities, it is helpful to organize your classroom in ways that encourage effective group work, communication, and idea-sharing. You can do this in a number of ways:

- Switch out individual desks in rows for tables or desk clusters
- Organize tables or desk clusters so that students can see and communicate with other group members

- Create strategic groupings so that students are seated with peers who have different levels of **general linguistic** and **language-specific performances** and different levels of content knowledge, but who share a home language
- Plan activities and task-based projects that require communication and use different kinds of language and skills

While there will be times when homogenous groupings are necessary, it is beneficial for students to sit with, and learn from, peers at different levels of language performance and content knowledge. This also helps build classroom community and eliminates the stigma that can be attached to emergent bilinguals who are often isolated in their own groups and kept apart from the movimiento of the classroom.

Creating a Multilingual Ecology

Developing a robust multilingual ecology helps all students and their families feel that their languages are welcome in school. This in turn brings the translanguaging corriente closer to the surface, making students' **dynamic bilingualism** more visible and thus easier to leverage. We use the word *ecology* in this section to refer to how teachers shape the linguistic space of a classroom to interact with students, families, and communities.

To create a multilingual ecology at the classroom level, we must ensure that all students' language practices are present and visible in their learning environment. For example, teachers can

- Hang bilingual posters and signs
- Put up student work in English and in the students' home languages
- Create multilingual word walls or cognate charts
- Project or give out notes in English and in the students' home languages
- Include books/magazines/newspapers in all students' languages in the class library
- Use versions of a textbook in English and in the students' home languages
- Give students access to bilingual dictionaries, bilingual picture dictionaries, and iPads or laptops
- Encourage students to use both English and their home languages in conversation and in writing
- Set up a listening center where students can hear the content in both languages
- Encourage family and community members to come into class to tell a story in their home languages
- Use video clips with subtitles in English and in the students' home languages

Making students' languages visible (and audible) sends a clear message that they are valued and important to learning. However, it is not enough simply to hang posters or put bilingual dictionaries on bookshelves. Creating a multilingual ecology means *utilizing* these resources to help students tap into their entire linguistic repertoires for learning. In short, to make the most out of a collaborative multilingual space means designing rigorous and responsive instruction.

TRANSLANGUAGING DESIGN FOR INSTRUCTION

When teachers learn about translanguaging, many tell us that they have been doing it for years but haven't had a name for it. In fact, they'd been operating under the assumption that they were "cheating" or "breaking the rules" by allowing students to use both English and their home languages in the classroom at the same time. These teachers knew that the English-only rules they were being asked to follow did not fully serve them or their students, and they often transgressed these rules by using students' bilingualism quietly, behind closed doors. We hope that *naming* a design for instruction and assessment will enable educators and their students to translanguage en voz alta, with the doors wide open, in ways that lead to increased engagement, improved academic results, stronger relationships, more secure identities, and more social equality. Furthermore, as educators collect empirical evidence of their students' movement along the dynamic translanguaging progressions, they will be able to demonstrate the effectiveness of their translanguaging pedagogy.

Taking up a **translanguaging stance** and committing to a translanguaging design mean crafting instruction by listening to the voices that matter most—our own voices and our students' voices. The translanguaging design for instruction pushes teachers to put imagination and action into teaching bilingual students. Every unit of instruction is driven by students' specific, local knowledge and language practices and encourages students to take learning out into the real world and make it *do something*. We also see each step of this process coming alive through students' fluid language practices, which enable them to learn about and access a topic or theme in critical and creative ways.

We turn now to several short vignettes of Justin's unit planning with his colleague, a 7th-grade math teacher. Remember that Justin provides **push-in ESL** services in middle-school math and science classes, and that the emergent bilinguals he works with come from a wide range of linguistic and cultural backgrounds. These vignettes demonstrate how teachers can implement three components of designing instruction for the translanguaging classroom: the *translanguaging unit plan*, the *translanguaging instructional design cycle*, and *translanguaging pedagogical strategies*.

Translanguaging Unit Plan

Most of the planning elements of a translanguaging unit of instruction are the same as those necessary in monolingual instruction, and some of them (e.g., content and language objectives) are especially important in bilingual classrooms and for teaching emergent bilinguals in English-medium classrooms. But there are also elements that are specific to the translanguaging classroom (e.g., translanguaging objectives). The six elements in the translanguaging unit plan are essential questions, content standards, content and language objectives, translanguaging objectives, culminating projects and assessments, and texts.

We briefly describe each element of the plan and its importance to the translanguaging classroom. We also illustrate each element in action through excerpts from Justin's classroom, and we encourage you to think about how you might plan a translanguaging unit of instruction that leverages students' bilingualism for learning in your classroom. We provide a blank Translanguaging Unit Planning Template in Appendix A.5.1. But first let's look at Justin's translanguaging unit plan in its entirety; see Box 5.1.

Essential Questions

The translanguaging unit plan begins with essential questions that are used

> to stimulate thought, to provoke inquiry, and to spark more questions, including thoughtful student questions, not just pat answers. They are provocative and generative. By tackling such questions, learners are engaged in *uncovering* the depth and richness of a topic that might otherwise be obscured by simply *covering* it. (McTighe & Wiggins, 2013, p. 3)

BOX 5.1	JUSTIN'S TRANSLANGUAGING UNIT PLAN: GEOMETRY IN OUR WORLD	
Essential Questions	• Where do we see geometry at work in our lives? • How do we know how to measure? • Why it is important to understand the geometry of our world?	
Content Standards	• CCSS.MATH.CONTENT.7.G.B.4: Know the formulas for the area and circumference of a circle and use them to solve problems; give an informal derivation of the relationship between the circumference and area of a circle • CCSS.MATH.CONTENT.7.G.B.6: Solve real-world and mathematical problems involving area, volume, and surface area of two- and three-dimensional objects composed of triangles, quadrilaterals, polygons, cubes, and right prisms.	
Content and Language Objective(s)	*Content Objectives* Students will be able to • Use formulas for measuring area, volume, and surface area for different geometric objects. • Accurately draw geometric shapes. • Connect their mathematical understandings to real-world situations and problems.	*Language Performance Objectives** *General linguistic* Students will be able to • Summarize solutions to real-world math problems both orally and in writing • Synthesize their understanding of geometry into stories that are linguistically appropriate for elementary school students • Use nominalizations in English in their summaries and stories *Language-specific* Students will be able to • Explain their choices of measurement using appropriate content-area vocabulary in English • Use nominalization in their summaries and stories
Translanguaging Objective(s)	Students will be able to • Recognize and track math vocabulary cognates • Work in groups to solve math problems using both English and their home languages • Use both English and their home languages to write children's books about geometry • Explain their language choices in oral presentations (e.g., why certain words or problems were given in one language or the other; why a certain character used one language and not another) • Read their books to bilingual children, expanding on their ideas and asking younger students questions in both languages.	
Culminating Project and Assessments	*Culminating Project* In groups, students create *bilingual children's books* that explain a geometric concept using English and an additional language, as well as culturally relevant examples and connections. Students present their books to elementary school teachers and later read them to groups of elementary school students with whom they share a home language. Students are assessed on their understanding of math content as well as their creativity and strategic use of both languages.	*Other Assessments* *Teachers' Translanguaging Assessment*: Students are assessed on content understanding, intellectual curiosity, and language practices. Focus on whether the student can perform tasks, independently or with assistance, using the full features of their repertoires (general linguistic performance), as well as language-specific features. *Reading Math:* Students engage with a variety of readings from newspapers, magazines, and websites that connect geometry to the real world. Readings are in English and the students' home languages, when possible. Students discuss the readings in home language groups and work together to ask questions, make connections, summarize, and answer comprehension questions.

Box continued on following page

BOX 5.1 JUSTIN'S TRANSLANGUAGING UNIT PLAN (Continued)		
		Writing Math: Students create new geometry word problems using culturally relevant situations and translanguaging. Students are assessed on their creativity, use of language, and comprehension of math content. Students are also assessed on *why* they made the linguistic and content choices they made via short process papers.
		Student Translanguaging Self-Assessment: Throughout the unit, students provide feedback and self-assessment via questions about their own learning, language development, and content understanding.
Texts	*In the Home Language(s)* • Readings about geometry from websites, newspapers, and magazines • Children's books	*In English* • Math textbook • Readings about geometry from websites, newspapers, and magazines • Children's books

*Differentiated according to students' performances along the dynamic translanguaging progressions.

Let's look at the essential questions that Justin and his 7th-grade math co-teacher develop for a geometry unit of instruction.

Justin and his co-teacher wanted students to make connections between the content and their own diverse experiences with that content. Drawing on what he knew about the students' bilingual profiles and cultural backgrounds, he and his co-teacher came up with the following essential questions:

- Where do we see geometry at work in our lives?
- How do we know how to measure?
- Why it is important to understand the geometry of our world?

In the translanguaging classroom, essential questions help students make connections between their own lived experiences, including their language and cultural practices, and academic content.

Content Standards

Standards are guidelines for language and content that help us organize our instruction and promote student learning. When standards are *expanded* and *localized*, meaning that they *expand* past monolingual, monocultural understanding so that they connect with students' own *local* language practices, funds of knowledge, communities, families, and interests, they help bilingual students learn more (and more successfully).

Translanguaging classrooms reimagine the use of standards. Rather than start with standards themselves, we start with students' language practices. Teachers help bilingual students develop the language practices demanded by the standards using the full features of their linguistic repertoires. The following vignette shows how Justin and his co-teacher plan to expand and localize standards in their geometry unit of instruction:

Before introducing the unit to their students, Justin and his co-teacher looked at the 7th-grade Common Core math standards and found two they could use:

CCSS.MATH.CONTENT.7.G.B.4: Know the formulas for the area and circumference of a circle and use them to solve problems; give an informal derivation of the relationship between the circumference and area of a circle.

CCSS.MATH.CONTENT.7.G.B.6: Solve real-world and mathematical problems involving area, volume, and surface area of two- and three-dimensional objects composed of triangles, quadrilaterals, polygons, cubes, and right prisms.

Using these standards, among others, helped Justin and his co-teacher ensure that they were engaging students with rigorous content and helping them prepare for standardized exams. These standards also fit into their plan for helping their students create authentic, culturally relevant children's books that used local scenarios and real-world problems to demonstrate an understanding of geometry.

The translanguaging unit design is aligned with content standards. Moreover, instruction is intentionally designed to connect with and build on bilingual students' local knowledge and strengths.

Content and Language Objectives

Content and language objectives align with standards and help organize units and individual lessons. Reflecting our holistic view of language, language objectives in translanguaging classrooms are informed by the two components of the dynamic translanguaging progressions, general linguistic and language-specific performances. The translanguaging unit plan therefore distinguishes between *general linguistic performance objectives* (which encourage students to use their entire language repertoires to express complex thoughts and make inferences from multiple sources) and *language-specific performance objectives*, (which focus on meeting the objectives using standard grammar, usage, and vocabulary in a national language). While content objectives are more or less the same for all students, language objectives must be differentiated according to students' bilingual profiles and positions along the dynamic translanguaging progressions. Here are Justin's content and language objectives:

Content Objectives
- Students will be able to use formulas for measuring area, volume, and surface area for different geometric objects.
- Students will be able to accurately draw geometric shapes.
- Students will connect their mathematical understanding to real-world situations and problems.

Once they developed their *content objectives*, which aligned with Common Core State Standards (CCSS), Justin helped his co-teacher come up with *language objectives* that would help students access the content.

For example, Justin knew that to "give an informal derivation of the relationship between the circumference and the area of a circle" would require students to use content-area vocabulary, as well as abstract language structures like nominalization that are used in academic contexts. "Solving real-world and mathematical problems" would require students to break down linguistically difficult word problems and explain their solutions both mathematically and in their own words. Because their students were at different places along the dynamic translanguaging progressions, Justin made sure that there were language objectives that relied on students' general linguistic performances, as well as those that focused on language-specific performances and new features of their linguistic repertoires.

Because Justin works in an English-medium classroom he only includes language-specific performance objectives in English on his translanguaging unit plan.[1]

---

[1]Teachers who work in bilingual classrooms develop language-specific performance objectives for both languages used for instructional purposes.

Language Performance Objectives

General Linguistic

- Students will summarize solutions to real-world math problems both orally and in writing.
- Students will synthesize their understanding of geometry into stories that are linguistically appropriate for elementary school students.
- Students will use nominalization in their summaries and stories.

Language-Specific (English)

- Students will explain their choices of measurement using appropriate content-area vocabulary in English.
- Students will use nominalization in their summaries and stories in English.

Justin differentiates the language objectives for his students based on their performances in English and the other languages in their linguistic repertoires along the dynamic translanguaging progressions.

For example, one of his Chinese students, *Yi-Sheng*, has recently arrived from Taiwan, speaks little English, and needs practice with the Latin script that English uses. Justin evaluates Yi-Sheng's performance in English as *entering*. However, according to her Chinese language teacher, her performance in Mandarin is *expanding,* meaning that her general linguistic performance is at least *expanding*. Another student in class, *Pablo*, came from Argentina two months ago. Pablo had taken private English lessons in Argentina and his performance in English is *transitioning*. Furthermore, his academic performance in Spanish in the Spanish language arts class is *commanding*. Pablo can leverage his understanding of how texts work in Spanish to read and write texts in English.

Fatoumata's case is different. She is from Guinea in Africa and speaks Pular (Fula) and French, which she learned because it was used as a medium of instruction in school. However, her school attendance was sporadic because she was from a rural area. Justin considers Fatoumata's oral English to be at about the same stage as Pablo's (*transitioning*). However, her written English is at the *entering* stage. With the help of a French-speaking paraprofessional, Justin determines that Fatoumata's French is *emerging*. When Fatoumata reads, she comprehends little and has a lot of trouble expressing herself in writing. Unfortunately, Justin cannot assess Fatoumata's performance in Pular, but he always sees her engaged in conversation with students who say they speak Pular. Because Pular is not used as a medium of instruction, the other students from Guinea have told Justin that they cannot write it. So Justin's best guess is that Fatoumata's performances in Pular would be *emerging* in academic contexts. Fatoumata cannot leverage her understanding of Pular or French texts in the same way that Pablo can draw on his Spanish to comprehend English texts. Based on his students' language performances relative to the translanguaging progressions, Justin differentiated the language objectives to meet his students where they were and help propel their language performances forward.

Regarding the *general-linguistic performance objectives,* Justin noted the following:

- Fatoumata was to summarize the solution and generate stories only orally, using Pular and French. He also provided her with some sentence starters in written English so that using Google Translate, and with the help of other French-speaking peers, she could write responses.
- Yi-Sheng was to summarize the solution and generate the story in Mandarin but she would summarize her work orally in English, with the help of her Chinese-speaking peers.

- Pablo would prewrite both tasks in Spanish but then produce them in English, while supported by iPad resources and his Spanish-speaking peers in the class.

Regarding the *language-specific performance objectives,* Justin distributed a vocabulary sheet with the content-area words in English that the students would need to summarize and write their stories.

- Pablo was to use the vocabulary sheet only for guidance.
- Yi-Sheng and Fatoumata were to write ten of the words down in their notebooks.

Because nominalization is a specific structure that students would need, Justin used the internet to look up the different ways English, Spanish, Chinese, and French constructed nominalizations. He showed the students that

- English usually adds "one" or "people" (e.g., Rich people are lucky.)
- Spanish and French usually add an article (e.g., Los ricos/Les riches)
- Chinese adds a particle. He called on Yi-Sheng to show students how to add the particle 的.

Justin then told the students to use nominalizations in their stories in English, French, Spanish, and Chinese.

- Pablo was to identify them in Spanish and write them in English.
- For Yi-Sheng and Fatoumata, he supplied a paragraph in English and asked them to look for "one" and "people" and try out how it was said in Chinese and French.

Translanguaging Objectives

While content objectives set the course for *what* students will learn and language objectives outline the *general* and *specific* language practices they will need to meet the content standards, **translanguaging objectives** are planned ways of leveraging bilingualism and ways of knowing so that students can better access both content and language practices valued in school. Justin's translanguaging objectives are as follows:

Translanguaging Objectives
- Students will recognize and track math vocabulary cognates.
- Students will work in groups to solve math problems using English and their home languages.
- Students will use English and their home languages to write children's books about geometry.
- Students will rationalize their language choices in oral presentations (e.g., why certain words or problems were given in one language or the other; why a certain character used one language and not another).
- Students will read their books to bilingual children, expanding on their ideas and asking younger students questions in both languages.

These objectives allow students to appropriate content and language in ways that they could not have done alone in English or any other language. Translanguaging objectives reframe students' existing language practices and local understanding as important to classroom learning.

Building translanguaging into the unit's final project enabled *all* students to express their understanding in complex ways. Through one translanguaging objective, "Students will use both English and their home languages to write children's books about geometry," Justin and his co-teacher expected students to meet and *exceed* the standards, as well as create something that they could not have produced using only one language. For example,

---

While creating their bilingual children's books, Yi-Sheng excitedly spoke to her partner in Mandarin. Her partner, a more experienced bilingual, added a short line of dialogue in Mandarin to their book. Justin went over to the two students and asked the student who was more comfortable with English to explain to him what the character was saying in Mandarin. He did so, and Justin learned that not only did Yi-Sheng contribute an excellent explanation of the geometric concept but also had a great sense of humor! He told both students to do their best to translate the line into English and include it in the book.

Culminating Project and Assessments

The culminating project is the authentic, action-oriented product that students create and implement throughout the course of the unit. The culminating project pushes students toward taking meaningful action, and it offers an opportunity to evaluate students' understanding of content and their development of language and literacy practices for academic purposes. An action-oriented culminating project is especially important to the translanguaging classroom because it provides students with the opportunity to use their bilingualism and ways of knowing to create something new and innovative.

The culminating project also functions as a differentiated assessment that allows students to demonstrate what they know and can do with content and language along the dynamic translanguaging progressions. Here is a description of Justin's culminating project and other assessments used in this unit plan:

Culminating Project

In groups, students will create *bilingual children's books* that explain a geometric concept using English and an additional language, as well as culturally relevant examples and connections. Students will present their books to elementary school teachers and later read them to groups of elementary school students with whom they share a home language. Students will be assessed on their understanding of math content, as well as their creativity and strategic use of both languages.

Throughout this unit of instruction, teachers assess students' content understanding, intellectual curiosity, and language practices, with attention to whether students can perform tasks independently or with assistance, using all the features of their linguistic repertoires (general linguistic performance), as well as language-specific features. Specifically, Justin and his co-teacher focus on the following areas:

- *Reading Math*: Students will engage with a variety of readings from newspapers, magazines, and websites that connect geometry to the real world. Readings will be in English and the students' home languages, when possible. Students will discuss the readings in home language groups and work together to ask questions, make connections, summarize, and answer comprehension questions.
- *Writing Math*: Students will create new geometry word problems using culturally relevant situations and translanguaging. Students will be assessed on their creativity, use of language, and understanding of math content. Students will also be assessed on *why* they made the linguistic and content choices they made via short process papers.

The translanguaging unit plan also includes a *student translanguaging self-assessment,* where students provide feedback and self-assessment by responding to questions about their own learning, language development, and content understanding.

The following vignette demonstrates Justin's students' active engagement in the authentic culminating project:

Students worked in shared home language groups to create bilingual children's books that used culturally relevant examples to teach children about geometry. Students took pictures of objects in their homes and neighborhoods and created stories that taught younger students about the mathematical properties of the shapes using recognizable language and cultural objects. Students' contributions to the culminating project varied depending on their comfort with English and their literacy in their home languages. For example, *Danilo's* literacy performances were very experienced in Tagalog, but his language-specific performances in English were just emerging. His strong general linguistic performance allowed him to be an active participant in the collaborative writing process, and he planned to read the parts of the book written in Tagalog when his group presented to the elementary school students.

Before reading the books to the elementary students, Justin and his co-teacher brought elementary school teachers to listen to the students' presentations of their books. Students shared their stories, using both English and their home languages. Fatoumata read her story in French and Yi-Sheng read her story in Mandarin. These students explained the choices they had made regarding both language and math content, and discussed how they planned to present the books to younger students. The elementary school teachers gave constructive feedback to the students and to Justin, and Justin's co-teacher assessed students on both their understanding of the math content and on their strategic language choices. Students took the feedback they received, refined their projects, and later, in groups, read their bilingual math books in several elementary school classrooms.

Texts

The texts that students read, watch, listen to, and engage with are very important to the success of an instructional unit. In the translanguaging unit design, texts refer to the multilingual and multimodal resources that supplement content and language learning. Choosing texts also involves looking for relevance to students' daily lives so that meaning can be made more easily. Texts that are diverse in language, point of view, and modality provide students in English-medium and bilingual classrooms with multiple ways to understand and connect with new content and language.

For example, in classrooms like Carla's that work to develop students' bilingualism and biliteracy, this means choosing texts in both languages and allowing students to use their full linguistic repertoires to understand them. In English-medium classrooms like Justin's and Stephanie's, choosing texts includes differentiating for students according to their language-specific performances in English and considering how to leverage their general linguistic performances to strengthen what they can do in English.

Justin and his co-teacher worked hard to supplement the required Common Core–aligned textbook with diverse texts. Their unit plan included texts (e.g., math books; readings about geometry from websites, newspapers, and magazines) and children's books in the students' home languages and English. As they worked through the unit plan, teachers and students realized that there simply weren't enough books about geometry in other languages:

Justin and his co-teacher utilized the required textbook, which they had in English and Spanish, short readings from the internet in a variety of languages, and video clips in English that students discussed in groups using their home languages. In addition to reading about math content, students also read math-focused children's books but quickly realized that there were not enough bilingual books about geometry—especially not in languages like Mandarin and Tagalog. This realization pushed them toward the unit's culminating project.

Justin and his co-teacher's work expanding and localizing the standards in this geometry unit of instruction allows students to meet and exceed the standards.

Translanguaging Instructional Design Cycle

Justin and his co-teacher used the **translanguaging instructional design cycle** to structure and sequence the elements of their instruction. This section describes the five stages of the translanguaging instructional design cycle: *explorar, evaluar, imaginar, presentar,* and *implementar.* Teachers can use this model to plan instruction that scaffolds and integrates student learning and enables them to demonstrate that learning in differentiated, authentic ways. Though many curricula are created in this cyclical, integrated fashion, most are not planned specifically with bilingual students in mind. The translanguaging instructional design cycle, which teachers can use in English-medium and bilingual programs, is meant to leverage the translanguaging corriente by bringing students' complex bilingual language practices to the surface.

Explorar

When we encourage students to explore a new topic or theme, we are inspiring them to follow their natural interests or questions. This process helps them understand new content and uncover new ideas on their own terms. As students explore and build their fields of knowledge (the way Justin's students did as they explored various examples of new geometric concepts, solved different problems, and researched children's literature on the internet in both English and their home languages), they become invested in their learning and they connect new content and language to their own lives and local bilingual contexts.

Gaining a multifaceted, complex, *bilingual* understanding of a topic enables students to reimagine, transform—and in fact *redesign*—that topic in ways that improve their lives and those of their communities. In many ways, the explorar stage can be compared to the building background stage in many traditional instructional units. What makes the explorar stage different than simply building background is that students are specifically expanding their understanding of a topic from a variety of viewpoints in both their home and new languages.

Evaluar

Just as the process of explorar is ongoing, so is the process of evaluar—assessing what we learn. As students learn more about a topic, they should be encouraged to put forth opinions, raise questions, and think critically about what they're exploring, using their entire linguistic repertoires. Thus, this stage is very much connected to a translanguaging stance. Rather than asking students to passively consume information, teachers taking a translanguaging stance use this stage of the design cycle to push students to be active, critical, and creative thinkers. For example, they set up opportunities for them to ask questions:

- Whose voices do we hear in our research on the topic?
- Are the bilingual groups represented by students in class under- or over-represented in the discourse?
- Are the examples we see representative of our experiences? Of bilingual practices?
- Are there opportunities to add our local knowledge, including our bilingual voices, to the conversation?

Because of their unique position on borders and margins and their experiences in two linguistic and cultural worlds, Justin's bilingual students saw that there were not many books about geometry for children, let alone in different languages. It is this kind of criticality that opens the doors to the next stage—imagining new ways of viewing a topic or using different language practices for understanding it.

Imaginar

Equipped with the strong understanding developed in the first two stages, students use what they have learned to support and stimulate new thinking and new ways of using language to learn. This third stage can involve group and individual brainstorming, planning, drafting, hypothesis testing, and, as always, researching further, using the full features of their linguistic repertoires. It is in this stage that students shift their focus from what already exists in the field in English and other languages to imagine what *could* exist, or what is possible. For example, Justin and the math teacher engaged their students in imagining how translanguaging in math texts could change math comprehension, as well as transform the conversations and levels of access that students have in math classrooms.

Presentar

In the presentar stage, students engage in peer editing, conferences, rewriting, and, finally, presenting their work—always mindful of the language practices that they are selecting and the reasons for those choices. This opens up space for all students to participate and share their work, think about the ways they use language, and remain engaged in completing their task. This stage offers opportunities for students to receive authentic feedback before putting their work into action, and to be assessed on their authentic performances. Students can present their work to teachers and peers, members of the school community, their families, or other relevant constituents with language practices that meet the different communication needs of the interlocutors. Students' general linguistic and language-specific performances in different communicative activities can be assessed, documented, and monitored relative to the dynamic translanguaging progressions. As we saw in Justin's translanguaging unit plan, students made presentations to local elementary school teachers before sharing their books with the children. They then used their reimagined bilingual math books with the children.

Implementar

The implementar stage pushes students to demonstrate their content and language learning as they show what they know and can do using the full features of their linguistic repertoires. This stage also encourages bilingual students to use language for authentic purposes to take meaningful action. Instead of decontextualized language learning, students learn new ways of using language

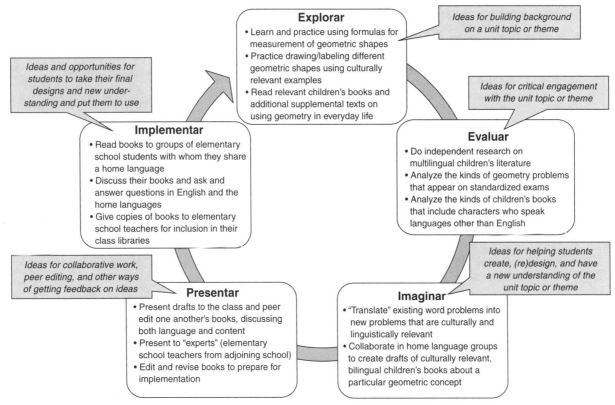

Figure 5.1   Justin's translanguaging design cycle.

to carry out a task and communicate with different people who have various language resources and practices. As students put their learning to work, they leverage their bilingualism to find academic success, contribute meaningfully to their communities, and grow as active, engaged citizens. This was indeed the case for the students involved in the math lesson that Justin supported.

Figure 5.1 shows the translanguaging design cycle template filled out for Justin's class. We include a blank template in Appendix A.5.2.

It is important to remember that each stage of the design cycle has its own linguistic demands. For example, the explorar stage, which requires students to ask questions, build background, and understand multiple facets of a topic, makes demands on students' *general linguistic performances*, as they learn and make meaning using their full linguistic repertoires. The presentar and implementar stages, which demand some kind of display, presentation, and authentic use of students' work, require more *language-specific performances,* as they make intentional, metalinguistic choices about the task, genre, audience, and context. Taking a translanguaging stance and implementing a translanguaging design require teachers to evaluate the linguistic demands of *all* instructional tasks in the classroom, and to determine what kind of scaffolding and support students need based on their understanding of students' bilingual profiles and performances relative to the dynamic translanguaging progressions.

Translanguaging Pedagogical Strategies

Teachers use *translanguaging pedagogical strategies* every day to make content and language more comprehensible to bilingual students, and to make space for students at different points on the dynamic translanguaging progressions to use all of their language resources for learning. Teachers use these flexible teaching strategies to integrate students' existing knowledge and language practices and those that are expected of them in school. Our discussion of translanguaging pedagogical strategies is organized around the four purposes of translanguaging. Recall that these purposes work *juntos* to mobilize and accelerate bilingual students' opportunities to learn and advance social justice.

Purpose 1: Supporting Students as They Engage with and Comprehend Complex Content and Texts

At all stages of the design cycle, we use translanguaging pedagogical strategies to help students make meaning of complex content and texts. For example, in the *explorar* stage of Justin's geometry unit, students worked in shared home language groups to discuss ideas and negotiate new math content through their home languages and English. They also built background on the topic of geometry through internet research, reading, and writing in both languages. Translanguaging pedagogical strategies help students to engage with, and make meaning of, complex content and texts by providing more points of entry and more opportunities for students to be active participants in their own learning. The following pedagogical strategies can be used at *any* stage of the design cycle because students are constantly engaging with complex content and texts:

- Teach students to use the internet to build background on a topic or concept in both their home and new languages.
- Assign bilingual reading and writing partners who the share same home language for mutual support and discussion.
- Encourage students to annotate texts they are reading with translations of vocabulary and other important textual information, including interesting structures and phrases.
- Encourage the use of dictionaries, glossaries, and iPads with translation apps to make meaning
- Provide multilingual books/translations of books and materials whenever possible.
- Encourage students to "read the room" to find phrases, sentence starters, vocabulary, and transition words in multiple languages that are important for their writing.
- Create a multilingual listening center composed of fiction and nonfiction texts, narratives of community members, and books recorded by students or their families (a favorite book or students' own writing).
- Allow students to explain things to each other using all their language resources.

Purpose 2: Providing Opportunities for Students to Develop Linguistic Practices for Academic Contexts

Especially in the *imaginar, presentar,* and *implementar* stages of the design cycle, all students must be taught the kind of language practices that are associated with academic contexts. This means taking what students' are *already* doing with language and expanding their repertoires to include new features and practices. For example, during the *imaginar* stage, one of Justin's Tagolog speakers was struggling to write down her ideas in *either* English or Tagalog. Justin knew that this student had creative ideas that she wanted to contribute to her group, so he used his phone to record her talking through her ideas in both languages. After she had explained her ideas orally, Justin sat her with a more experienced bilingual in her group and the two students transcribed her ideas, many of which were included in the final draft of their children's book. Rather than render this student voiceless, Justin met her where she was and helped her see connections between her own oral language and the written forms expected of her in school. Following are several more pedagogical strategies that can be used to develop students' linguistic practices for academic contexts:

- Allow students to audio record ideas using all their language resources, before writing.
- Have students prewrite using all their language resources; then select one language/voice in which to publish it.
- Provide students with opportunities to write translations to portions of a text.
- Assign language partners in class who share home languages, and differentiate language objectives (general linguistic and language-specific) based on their performances on the dynamic translanguaging progressions.
- Group students so they can use the same home language resources in collaborative work.
- Allow pairs to "turn and talk" using all their language resources.
- Allow students to raise questions, answer them, and participate in class discussion using the full features of their linguistic repertoires.
- Have students compare and contrast specific **language features** across languages to help them develop greater metalinguistic awareness.

Purpose 3: Making Space for Students' Bilingualism and Ways of Knowing

At each stage of the design cycle, but particularly in the evaluar stage, students can use their bilingualism and ways of knowing to think critically about content. To do this, we must provide opportunities for students to engage the full features of their linguistic repertoires, rather than ask them to "think in English only." For example, one of the children's books that Justin and his coteacher provided for students was *Grandfather Tang's Story*, which used tangrams, Chinese puzzles made up of different shapes. One group of Mandarin speakers immediately grabbed the book and read through it together, having side conversations in both English and Mandarin about both the story and its math-related content. Though the book was written in English, it had cultural relevance to the students, which not only helped them make connections to the content but also provided them with an opportunity to share their own stories with one another and in their own children's book. Here are some additional pedagogical strategies that make space for students' bilingualism and ways of knowing:

- Provide books/stories where authors use translanguaging and that have culturally relevant meaning.
- Encourage students to do research using multilingual reading material, especially on the internet.
- Have students write stories with bilingual characters or in situations where other bilingual language practices have to be used.
- Encourage students to write performance pieces, for example, plays that include translanguaging for voices of bilingual characters.
- Have students use translanguaging in writing for bilingual audiences, including their families and communities, besides writing for monolingual audiences.
- Engage students in language inquiry tasks, comparing and contrasting different features of spoken language and coming up with word plays.

Purpose 4: Supporting Students' Socioemotional Development and Bilingual Identities

One of the most important purposes of translanguaging is that it helps us support students socioemotionally and honors their bilingual identities. Teachers enact this purpose at *every* stage of the translanguaging design cycle, and we see it clearly in the evaluar and implementar stages. As bilingual students learned about geometry content, Justin and his co-teacher provided them with examples of children's books that related similar ideas in "kid friendly" ways. While these were important models for students, they soon realized how few books were available in languages other than English. Their teachers agreed, and explained that, for this reason, students' books *had* to include both English and their home languages—they were the ones who could fill the gaps in the literature. Students were excited about the opportunity and, when it came time to read their books to the elementary school students, they were proud of the contributions they had made. By enabling students to use their bilingualism in ways that are meaningful to them, teachers support them socioemotionally and foster their bilingual identities. The following are translanguaging pedagogical strategies that address this important purpose:

- Discuss what would have happened in a story if the characters were bilingual.
- Invite family and community members into the classroom to enrich instruction.
- Provide students with texts that highlight two or more sides of a complex issue, especially those issues that relate directly to their lives.
- Extend research projects and other culminating designs out of the classroom and into the community, where students can use their bilingualism for authentic purposes.
- Engage students in bilingual writing assignments that have a social justice focus, such as letter writing, blogging, grant writing, and editorial or newspaper article writing.
- Choose topics and texts in multiple languages that give voice to groups that are commonly silenced or left out of the traditional curriculum.
- Assess general linguistic performance, as well as language-specific performance, while encouraging students to leverage their entire language repertoire.[2]

TRANSLANGUAGING SHIFTS IN INSTRUCTION

Translanguaging shifts refer to those unplanned moment-by-moment decisions that teachers make in response to the flow of the translanguaging corriente in their classrooms. The flexible shifts are an integral part of creating the translanguaging classroom—they enable teachers to engage with the flow of the translanguaging corriente whose pulls and shifts we cannot always predict. These shifts respond to content and language needs and interests that are not built directly into the translanguaging unit plan, but which students need to be successful in the classroom. They emerge directly out of our stance and our design. Our stance enables us to see and hear the translanguaging corriente, and our design makes space for the kind of performance-based learning that illustrates what bilingual students know and can do on different tasks. Going with the flow, rather than fighting and pulling away from it, is key to the success of bilingual students and translanguaging classrooms.

Flexible translanguaging shifts are important because they open opportunities in our instructional design. When teachers go with the flow of the translanguaging corriente, they meet bilingual learners where they are in terms of their general linguistic and language-specific performances, and they leverage the corriente to accelerate student learning.

Flexibility is a key element of the translanguaging classroom. Not only must educators be flexible in terms of language use; they must also be flexible with students' understanding of new content. This means that the way *we*

---

[2]See Celic and Seltzer (2012), García and Kleyn (2017), and García and Li Wei (2014) for more translanguaging strategies.

think they will learn something isn't necessarily the way they *actually* learn it. Each group of students brings a unique set of experiences, personalities, biases, and challenges. As teachers, we must open ourselves and our classrooms to students' own interpretations and perceptions of content and language. Translanguaging shifts allow for this *flexibility* in language practices, conversations, activities, and plans because the teacher is responding to an unanticipated aspect of the translanguaging corriente. Some shifts that we have seen teachers make in translanguaging classrooms include the following:

- Helping individual students understand difficult new vocabulary or phrases by providing translation, rephrasing, and using synonyms or cognates
- Helping students make sense of new content by using culturally meaningful metaphors and/or stories
- In moments of difficulty or misunderstanding, encouraging students to talk to one another about a new concept or vocabulary word using their own language practices
- Looking up words and phrases using online translation tools or having students do so on their own
- Encouraging students to relate new content to their own worlds through stories and other text/world connections

Here we see how Justin uses translanguaging shifts to support emergent bilinguals during a science class:

Justin was going over students' homework for their science class. As he discussed the topic, heredity, he got the sense that his students, especially Fatoumata and Yi-Sheng who had recently arrived, did not understand what he was explaining. There were blank looks, some off-task behavior, and very little participation. Rather than plow forward, he stopped and asked students to talk to one another in Spanish, Mandarin, French, Vietnamese, Tagalog, or any of their languages about whether they looked like people in their families or not. Though he did not speak most of these languages, Justin could tell from the shift in energy in the room and the excited conversations that students were engaged in the discussion. After they had spoken to one another, Justin asked them to share some of their ideas in English. Danilo, with the help of his Tagalog-speaking classmates, said that he had dark skin but that his sister was fair and even had freckles. A student translated for Fatoumata that though both her parents had brown eyes, she had green eyes but no one knew why. Some students shifted the conversation to the many names for different skin colors in Spanish. Jumping off from these comments, Justin connected the idea of looking like (or not looking like) a family member to the work students had done that day with Punnett squares. Suddenly students started to make connections to concepts like dominant and recessive alleles, phenotype, and genotype that they had not tapped into before.

As we can see, rather than limit the conversation, Justin's shifts—using students' connections to strengthen their understanding of and engagement with the difficult new content—enabled him to go with the flow of the translanguaging corriente and meet his students' needs. Without paying close attention to his students, as well as applying flexibility and willingness to tap into the corriente, Justin's lesson might have ended in frustration instead of excitement and learning.

CONCLUSION

Translanguaging in instruction means that you *purposefully and strategically* design your classroom space, your unit and lesson plans, and your pedagogical strategies with the translanguaging corriente and students' general linguistic and language-specific performances at the center. Translanguaging also means responding to that corriente and to students' needs, interests, and ways of knowing through a series of unplanned, responsive shifts. Though teachers' translanguaging in different instructional contexts varies, we always find intentionality, purposefulness, and mindful flexibility in translanguaging classrooms.

QUESTIONS AND ACTIVITIES

1. Are English and students' other languages present in the ecology of your classroom? Does the ecology encourage students to use their full linguistic repertoires when learning? If not, what changes could you make?

2. Does the way you plan instruction make room for students' use of their home languages and cultural understanding? If not, what changes could you make?

3. Think about a recent unplanned decision you made while teaching. How did you came to make that decision. Can you pinpoint parts of your stance that informed that shift?

TAKING ACTION

1. Review Justin's translanguaging unit planning template in Box 5.1 and his translanguaging design cycle in Figure 5.1. Using the blank templates provided in Appendices A.5.1 and A.5.2, plan a translanguaging unit of instruction for your class. Explain how your unit plan leverages the translanguaging corriente and is informed by your students' general linguistic and language-specific performances along the dynamic translanguaging progressions. Share your thinking with a planning partner, coach, or administrator.

2. Implement the unit plan you developed. Videotape or take pictures of your unit in action and share it with your colleagues. How does your unit plan reflect your translanguaging stance? What stands out? What works well? What questions do you have?

CHAPTER 6

Translanguaging Design in Assessment

LEARNING OBJECTIVES

- Identify principles of translanguaging in assessment
- Describe the key components of the translanguaging design for assessment
- Explain how and why Carla engages in translanguaging shifts in assessment
- Design a translanguaging assessment to use with your translanguaging unit plan
- Describe some of the shifts that may be necessary to go with the flow of the translangauging corriente when implementing your design for assessment

Since the No Child Left Behind Act of 2001, assessment and accountability has focused largely on students' performance on high-stakes standardized tests in English. Likewise, college and career-readiness standards rely on academic benchmarks in English to measure students' knowledge and skills relative to those standards. It is important to take these summative assessments in English into account because they are used in most states to make decisions about student performance and teacher effectiveness. However, to better understand bilingual students and create more equitable learning opportunities, teachers in **translanguaging classrooms** assess what students know and can do on classroom tasks using the full features of their linguistic repertoires.

Translanguaging in assessment is part of the translanguaging pedagogy, and is intimately tied to translanguaging in instruction. The translanguaging design for assessment covers how teachers strategically plan evaluations of bilingual students' performances to obtain a holistic understanding of what students can do relative to the content, language, and **translanguaging objectives** of the translanguaging design for instruction. The **translanguaging shifts** in assessment reflect the moment-to-moment adjustments that teachers make in their assessment practices to go with the flow of the translanguaging corriente.

The translanguaging design for assessment relies on authentic, performance-based instruments that allow teachers to monitor students' general linguistic and language-specific performances along the **dynamic translanguaging progressions**. Recall that **general linguistic performance** refers to speakers' use of oral and written language to express complex thoughts (e.g., to explain, persuade, argue, compare and contrast, find text-based evidence, give directions, or recount events) drawing on the full features of their linguistic repertoires. **Language-specific performance** refers to speakers' exclusive use of features from a named language (e.g., Spanish, Mandarin, English) to perform classroom tasks.

Using a translanguaging design for assessment allows us to better evaluate students' content and language learning by ensuring that general linguistic and language-specific performances are never conflated. By distinguishing between these types of performances, a translanguaging design for assessment encourages bilingual children to display their entire **language repertoires** when their general linguistic performances are being assessed. Otheguy, García, and Reid (2015) discuss the differences between school assessment of bilinguals and monolinguals:

> In schools in general, but especially during testing, bilingual students, to their great disadvantage, are kept from using their entire language repertoires, are compelled to suppress a big part of their idiolect, are not allowed to translanguage. In contrast, monolingual students, to their great advantage, are forced to suppress only a small fraction of their idiolect (the part that is interpersonally inappropriate), are regularly allowed to translanguage. Both types of student are asked to be part of a teaching and testing game that each ends up playing under different rules. It is small wonder that the monolingual side usually comes out on top. (pp. 300–301)

A translanguaging design for assessment allows for a more accurate reading of bilingual children's performance by assessing students' general linguistic performance, not only their use of features of standard languages. Of course, being able to perform language-specific tasks is important, and so the translanguaging design for assessment also evaluates the bilingual child's use of English, Spanish, or any other language for academic purposes. However, this specific measure is never considered in isolation or as an accurate picture of what the child can do. Holistic assessment is always used.

This chapter provides a step-by-step demonstration of how teachers can design a holistic assessment plan that yields authentic evidence of students' performances relative to the school's content and language demands over time, with attention to how teachers can use this evidence to differentiate instruction and accelerate student learning. First we introduce principles and dimensions that guide translanguaging in assessment. Then we highlight one translanguaging unit of instruction that *Carla* developed for her 4th-grade **dual-language bilingual education (DLBE)** class to see translanguaging assessment in action. We see how Carla uses bilingual student profiles, the dynamic translanguaging progressions, the student's self-assessment tool, the families' and peer-groups' assessment tools, and her own assessment tool to understand and document what her students know and can do with content and language on the concrete tasks included in her unit of instruction. We also include examples from *Stephanie's* and *Justin's* English-medium classrooms to illustrate how they use the teacher's assessment tool, given that they do not speak their students' home languages. At the end of the chapter, we turn to the translanguaging shifts in assessment. As you read, we encourage you to think about how you can collect evidence of your students' dynamic performances on different tasks, at different times, from different perspectives.

PRINCIPLES FOR TRANSLANGUAGING IN ASSESSMENT

Teachers need to continuously monitor what students are learning throughout the unit and to give feedback for formative purposes (Popham, 2008). There are four principles of translanguaging for assessment, all stemming from the teachers' translanguaging **juntos** stance.

1. Assessment needs to consider many angles: Assessment for bilingual students needs to include many voices—families as well as teachers—and, of course, the bilingual students themselves and their peers who generate the translanguaging corriente.

A translanguaging design for assessment always attempts to integrate the home and the school juntos. Thus, assessment in translanguaging classrooms always considers how students' families, the students themselves, their peers, and their teachers evaluate what students can do with content and language on school-based tasks.

2. Bilingual students' performances in assessment must include opportunities to use all their interpersonal and intrapersonal resources, as well as external material resources, to show what they know and can do.

A translanguaging design for assessment provides students with opportunities to use all the resources they have at their disposal to make sense of, and mediate, their own learning. As Moll (2013) has explained, this ensures that the students are working in the **bilingual zone of proximal development**, thus maximizing their learning. Sometimes these resources are the people around the students (their peers and teachers) who can mediate the task. Other times the resources are the material tools of learning—glossaries, dictionaries, iPads, texts in other languages, images, videos, and so forth. Students can then be evaluated as performing independently or with moderate assistance (Bodrova & Leong, 2007). Furthermore, a student must always be given opportunities to use his or her inner voice—the intrapersonal voice that takes into account the entire language repertoire—to solve problems and show what he or she knows.

3. Assessment of what bilingual students know and are able to do must be based on authentic, performance-based tasks.

Content must also be evaluated as students perform genuine tasks. The culminating project of the translanguaging unit plan is an authentic, action-oriented product that students create and implement throughout the course of the unit. Teachers can use students' performance on the culminating project, and on the activities leading up to it, as the basis for authentic performance-based assessment relative to the content and language demands of the instructional unit.

4. Assessment of bilingual students' language use must distinguish between general linguistic and language-specific performances.

A translanguaging design for assessment always differentiates how students use language to show what they know and can do using the full features of their linguistic repertoires from their ability to do so using only language-specific features. This distinction corrects a serious flaw in contemporary assessment of linguistically diverse students. According to the American Educational Research Association, American Psychological Association, and National Council on Measurement in Education (2014), every assessment is an assessment of language. Restricting **emergent bilinguals'** opportunities to demonstrate content understanding to what they can do with a language that is just emerging is denying these students equal access to educational opportunity. However, when teachers make space for bilingual students to draw on their entire linguistic repertoires, these students can fully demonstrate their content learning without being limited to one specific language or another.

How to integrate the four principles of translanguaging for assessment—the different voices in assessment, the use of other people and other resources, the authenticity of the tasks, and the distinction between general linguistic and language-specific performances—is the topic of the rest of this chapter.

TRANSLANGUAGING DESIGN FOR ASSESSMENT

To illustrate translanguaging assessment in practice, we turn to Carla's 4th-grade DLBE classroom. Because students are at the center of the translanguaging pedagogy, we begin this section by discussing how teachers can use students' bilingual profiles, complemented by their placement along the dynamic translanguaging progressions relative to state standards, as a starting point for assessment. Then we introduce Carla's translanguaging unit for instruction and highlight the integrated approach to learning, teaching, and assessment that characterizes the translanguaging classroom.

Using Bilingual Students' Profiles

Carla begins her translanguaging instructional and assessment planning with her students' strengths and needs in mind. First she draws on information from the bilingual student profiles that we discussed in Chapter 3 to inform her assessment practices. The following information comes from individual bilingual student profiles for Erica, Jennifer, Moisés, and Ricardo that Carla compiled at the beginning of the year.

> *Erica* began the DLBE program in 1st grade. Her parents are Puerto Rican but came to the mainland as children so they spoke mostly English at home, although Spanish was also spoken. As a young child Erica grew up speaking English at home, although she understood Spanish and spoke it some. Because Erica was not officially designated as an English language learner (ELL) when she entered school, she was simply seen as an English speaker, and the Spanish she brought with her to school went unnoticed. After attending an English-medium kindergarten, her parents asked that she be put in the DLBE program so that she would develop her bilingualism and biliteracy. In the DLBE program Erica was, and is still, considered an English-dominant student.[1]
>
> Erica is now in 4th grade and her reading is at grade level in English (40 on the Developmental Reading Assessment [DRA]2), and almost up to par in Spanish (30 on the Evaluación del desarrollo de la lectura [EDL]2). Erica prefers to speak with her friends in class and during recess in English. In class, Carla notices that Erica is hesitant to speak in Spanish. Carla has also noticed that since she allowed Erica to use both languages in class she has further developed her comfort with using Spanish. At home, Erica's parents speak Spanish to her when they help Erica with her homework.
>
> *Jennifer* was born in the United States and began elementary school in the DLBE program. Jennifer's mother was also born in the United States to parents who emigrated from different regions of Mexico. Like Erica, Jennifer is officially designated as an English speaker, and traditional bilingual programs refer to her as English dominant. (We refer to Jennifer as an emergent bilingual who is learning Spanish and developing English at school.) Jennifer is a year ahead in English reading (50 on the DRA2) and on grade level in Spanish reading (EDL2), according to the district assessment. At home Jennifer speaks English to her mother and siblings, but Spanish to her grandmother, who lives with them, and who has always been Jennifer's main caretaker while her mother worked. Her teacher has recognized Jennifer's translanguaging practices with classmates and in lessons. For example, in mathematics (taught in Spanish) Carla realizes that Jennifer can explain the Pythagorean theorem better when using words and phrases that some may identify as English and Spanish, but to Jennifer are simply *her* words.

---

[1]Some educators in the world-language education or **bilingual education** fields might have identified Erica as a heritage Spanish speaker when she entered 1st grade. However, we describe Erica as an emergent bilingual who is strengthening her Spanish as she continues to develop English for academic purposes at school. We reject the term English dominant because we want to emphasize the bilingualism that Erica brings to school and its potential for full emergence as she becomes bilingual and biliterate.

Moisés is a student who emigrated from Mexico to the United States two years ago, and is thus considered a newcomer who was officially designated as an ELL when he entered school. Moisés learned to read and write in Spanish in Mexico, where he went to school until 2nd grade. (We describe Moisés as an emergent bilingual who is learning English as he continues to develop Spanish.) He scores as a level 3, *developing,* on WIDA's Assessing Comprehension and Communication in English State-to-State (ACCESS) for ELLs test. Moisés is at grade level in reading in Spanish (40 on the EDL2) and his English reading score is one grade level behind (30 on the DRA2). Moisés continues to develop both English and Spanish in Carla's DLBE classroom, although he still prefers Spanish at times. For example, when Moisés is beginning a reading or writing task in any content area in English, he verifies the task at hand with his friend *Diego*, who is comfortable using both languages. At home, Moisés communicates with his parents mostly in Spanish because they do not speak much English; with his siblings, however, he most often uses both languages to interact and play.

Ricardo was born in Tlaxiaco, Oaxaca and came to the United States at the start of 4th grade. Like Moisés he is considered a newcomer and is officially designated as an ELL. (We describe Ricardo as an emergent bilingual who is learning English, developing Spanish, and drawing on Mixteco at school.) Ricardo's schooling in Oaxaca was in a local bilingual school that taught in Spanish and in Mixteco, his other home language. On the ACCESS for ELLs test, Moisés scores as level 3, *developing.* He scores one year below grade level in reading on the Spanish EDL2 test (30) and two years below grade level in reading in English on the DRA2 (20).

Carla knows that Ricardo communicates in Mixteco and Spanish with his family, but uses some English with his younger siblings. Carla therefore encourages him to use all his language resources (Spanish, English, and Mixteco) orally and in writing. For example, Ricardo chooses to write in his daily dialogue journal in Spanish and some Mixteco. Although Carla does not speak Mixteco, she meets with him once a week so that he can explain the content of his writing to her. Many times her written comments in the journals use English and Spanish, a way of ensuring that Ricardo understands what she writes.

As we can see, Erica, Jennifer, Moisés and Ricardo's sociolinguistic histories and practices are complex and still emerging in Spanish and English, the official languages used for instructional purposes in Carla's 4th-grade DLBE classroom. These bilingual student profiles provide important information for Carla as she designs her translanguaging assessment.

Building on Students' Dynamic Translanguaging Progressions

Teachers in translanguaging classrooms need to go beyond the information they gather on students' bilingual portfolios to assess students' language practices relative to the standards of their content teaching. Recall from Chapter 3 that Carla records her students' performances along the dynamic translanguaging progressions relative to the 4th grade Reading Literature standard, which asks students to refer to details and examples in a text when explaining what the text says explicitly and when drawing inferences from it. Here we focus on Ricardo, the student whose reading scores on the DRA2 and EDL2 are a bit behind the scores of Erica, Jennifer, and Moisés. As shown in Table 6.1,[2]

---

[2]Notice that Carla uses the same template here for Ricardo that she used to assess Erica's performance in Chapter 3 (see Table 3.2).

TABLE 6.1 **Performances along the Dynamic Translanguaging Progressions**

STUDENT: *Ricardo*

Reading: Literature, Grade 4

Common Core Anchor Standard	Main Academic Demand
Read closely to determine what the text says explicitly and to make logical inferences from it; cite specific textual evidence when writing or speaking to support conclusions drawn from the text.	Draw inferences using evidence from the text
Common Core Grade Standard	**Grade Level Academic Demand**
Refer to details and examples in a text when explaining what the text says explicitly and when drawing inferences from the text.	Refer to text detail to explain and draw inferences

	Oracy	Literacy
Commanding	Refers to ample details and examples in a text that explain what the text says and can draw substantial inferences from the details and examples	Refers to ample details and examples in a text that explain what the text says and can draw substantial inferences from the details and examples
Expanding	Refers to many details and examples in a text that explain what the text says and can draw appropriate inferences from the details and examples **General linguistic** **Spanish oracy**	Refers to many details and examples in a text that explain what the text says and can draw appropriate inferences from the details and examples **General linguistic**
Developing	Refers to multiple details and examples in a text that explain what the text says and can draw relevant inferences from the details and examples **English oracy**	Refers to multiple details and examples in a text that explain what the text says and can draw relevant inferences from the details and examples **Spanish literacy**
Emerging	Refers to several details and examples in a text that explain what the text says and can draw vague inferences from the details and examples	Refers to several details and examples in a text that explain what the text says and can draw vague inferences from the details and examples **English literacy**
Entering	Refers to very minimum details and examples in a text that explain what the text says. Details and examples cited may not be appropriate	Refers to very minimum details and examples in a text that explain what the text says. Details and examples cited may not be appropriate

Translanguaging: Bilinguals from all levels can, and will be able, to refer to details and examples in a text and draw inferences from details and examples by previewing, viewing, and reviewing the texts in multiple languages, discussing orally/signing and/or exploring in writing and responding orally using their *entire language repertoires* with freedom to select all linguistic features, *or with language-specific features*

Carla's assessment of Ricardo's type of performance on each of the progressions is indicated in **bold.**

Ricardo's general linguistic performance relative to this reading standard is *expanding* in oracy and literacy. When he uses only Spanish to perform this type of task, Ricardo's oracy performances are *expanding* and his literacy performances are *developing*. Furthermore, Ricardo's language-specific performances in English relative to this standard are *emerging* in literacy and *developing* in oracy. Carla knows that she can draw on Ricardo's strong general linguistic performance, as well as his stronger performances in Spanish, to accelerate his reading in English relative to this standard.

Let's look more closely at how Carla rated Ricardo's general linguistic and language-specific performances in literacy relative to this reading standard. Ricardo's educational history gives us insight as to why his general linguistic performances in literacy *(expanding)* are more experienced than his Spanish performances in literacy *(developing)*. Ricardo started to learn to read in Mexico in ways that are different from the ways he is learning to read in U.S. schools. Thus, his reading performances relative to the reading standards in Spanish only are conditioned by his reading experiences in school in Mexico. For example, Ricardo was never asked to find text-based evidence when he read at his Mexican school. Ricardo is now developing new reading practices through his experiences at his U.S. school, including referring to details and examples, as the reading standard demands. When Ricardo is told that he can use his complete repertoire of meaning-making resources, including his new understanding of what it means to read, his general linguistic performance is more experienced than his Spanish literacy performance.

Integrating Instruction and Assessment

Equipped with information about her students' bilingualism—obtained from the bilingual student profile and complemented by the dynamic translanguaging progressions relative to state standards in reading—Carla is prepared to plan her translanguaging design for assessment. To illustrate her translanguaging assessment in practice, we introduce a translanguaging unit plan that Carla developed for her 4th-grade DLBE classroom. This unit, *Cuentos de la tierra y del barrio,* is represented in Box 6.1. It shows Carla's essential questions, content standards (in English Language Arts [ELA]: Literacy and Social Studies/History for New Mexico Common Core State Standards [NMCCSS]), content and language objectives, translanguaging objectives, and texts used that shape her design and provide important context for our discussion of Carla's culminating project and translanguaging assessment practices.

Carla's culminating project asks students to individually write an argumentative essay about local farming practices that includes text-based evidence, local sources, and human resources to support their positions. Students will first present their argument orally to their peers and then to the school community during an open house. Carla will use the culminating project for assessment purposes. She will also assess her students formatively throughout the stages of explorar, evaluar, imaginar, presenter, and implementar that make up the **translanguaging design cycle** (Fig 6.1).

Teacher's Assessment Tool

Teachers need to gather information to assess what students know and can do with content and language relative to standards, objectives, and the culminating project of a translanguaging instructional unit. To do this, teachers need to observe students as they perform different instructional tasks leading up to and including the culminating project. (We are reminded that the word assessment comes from the Latin assidere, which means to sit beside.)

A translanguaging design for assessment has teachers observe two aspects of student performance based on these two questions:

1. Is the student performing *using all the features of his or her language repertoire* and/or *using language-specific features*?
2. Is the student performing *independently,* with *moderate assistance* from other people or other resources, or is the performance *emergent*?

Up to this point, we have focused only on the first question as we demonstrated how teachers can place students along the dynamic translanguaging progressions on different tasks, at different times, and from different perspectives. Here we add the second important dimension to the translanguaging design for assessment—whether the performance is undertaken independently, with assistance, or not at all.

We developed the Teacher's Assessment Tool for Translanguaging Classrooms to help teachers look more closely at students' general linguistic and language-specific performances within the context of their translanguaging units of instruction; we include a blank form in Appendix A.6.1. This tool is organized around the academic demands of the Common Core State Standards

BOX 6.1 CARLA'S TRANSLANGUAGING UNIT PLAN: CUENTOS DE LA TIERRA Y DEL BARRIO		
Big Questions	• How are students, families, and the local community tied to their land, and by extension to their traditions? • How do communities interact with one another and their environments? • How does local farming differ from global farming? • Why is it important to sustain local farming practices? • How can students cultivate their local jardín del barrio?	
Content Standards	• NMCCSS.ELA-Literacy.W.4.1: Write opinion pieces on topics or texts, supporting point of view with reasons and information. • NMCCSS.ELA-Literacy.W.4.3: Gather relevant information from multiple sources, including oral knowledge. • NMCCSS.ELA-Literacy.RL.4.1: Refer to details and examples in a text when explaining what the text says explicitly and when drawing inferences from it. • New Mexico Standards in Social Studies/History (4th grade): Research historical events and people from a variety of perspectives.	

Content and Language Objective(s)	*Content Objectives*
	Students will be able to
	• Gather information from community leaders about their neighborhoods' agricultural, social and historical landscape
	• Summarize oral and written text-based evidence to support their position about why it is important to sustain local farming practices
	• Compose an argumentative essay to support their opinion piece
		General Linguistic Objectives
		Students will be able to
		• Review information supporting a point of view
		• Give specific details about point of view using a line of reasoning
		• Know the language differences between a logical conclusion and an emotional point of view
		
		Language-Specific Objectives
		Students will be able to
		• Use the following structures to argue a point:
		  ○ *In English*—The advantages outweigh the disadvantages because ___; From my point of view ___; The benefits are obvious, for example, ___.
		  ○ *In Spanish*—Hay más ventajas que desventajas porque ___ ; Mi punto de vista es que ____; Los beneficios son obvios, un ejemplo es que, ___.
		• Use the following signal words to argue a point:
		  ○ In English—defend, support, claim, believe, perceive
		  ○ In Spanish—defender, apoyar, reclamar, estar convencido de, percibir
		• Use the first- and third-person singular pronouns and verb endings (morphology)
		  ○ The third person singular "s" in English and the obligatory use of the personal pronoun vs. the change of ending in verbs in Spanish and the variable use of the pronoun (not obligatory)
		    ▪ In English—I defend vs. s/he defends
		    ▪ In Spanish—(Yo) defiendo vs. (él/ella) defiende

Translanguaging Objective(s)	Students will be able to • Gather information by interviewing community leaders/parents and using other local/global resources (technology) in English, Spanish, and bilingually • Complete a language analysis of bilingual texts during the Cuéntame algo activity to better understand the meaning of the bilingual texto/contexto • Collaborate in a small group to generate a list of ideas to answer a question: How do you think we can darle vida o más vida a nuestro jardín del barrio? • Select a language to write and read essay to peers • Integrate translanguaging (where appropriate) by choosing certain phrases, expressions, or words to better convey point of view	

Box continued on following page

BOX 6.1   CARLA'S TRANSLANGUAGING UNIT PLAN (Continued)

Translanguaging Assessments	*Culminating Design*	*Other Translanguaging Assessment**
	Individually, students write an argumentative essay about local farming practices with text-based evidence and local sources and human resources to support their positions. Students first present their essays to their peers and then to the school community during the annual open house.	**Teacher's Assessment:** This instructive tool provides guidance about what the student can or will do on listening, speaking, reading, and writing task to demonstrate content knowledge using general linguistic and language-specific performances. In addition, it provides teachers with an opportunity to note whether students can perform a task independently or with assistance from other people or resources. **Student Self-Assessment:** This reflective tool gives students an opportunity to express how and what they have learned throughout the project, which will better inform the teacher about his or her instruction. **Peer Assessment:** This tool offers a reflective space to explain the role of the group and the performance within it. **Family Assessment: La conexión:** This tool gives the student an opportunity to share what he or she has learned with a family member. Also, it provides a space for a family member to share their opinions, expertise, knowledge, experiences, and thoughts about the topic being learned at school.
Texts	*In Spanish* • Rudolfo Anaya's *The santero's miracle* • Literature about gardening written by the local community leader • Readings about local/ global farming practices from websites and magazines • Videos about local and global farming practices	*In English* • 5th-grade social studies textbook • 5th-grade science textbook • Readings about local/global farming practices from websites and magazines • Videos about local and global farming practices

*See Appendices A.6.1–A.6.4, respectively, for blank templates.

(CCSS) Language Arts Standards for reading, writing, listening, speaking and language. This tool also provides space for teachers to observe students' performances for evidence of their understanding, creativity, and curiosity relative to the essential ideas of the unit, both when they are using the full features of their linguistic repertoires and when they are exclusively using features of one specific language or another. Teachers of different subject areas can adapt this template to address the standards of their disciplines, with attention to specific content and language demands of a particular curricular unit of instruction.

The Teacher's Assessment Tool can be used in several different ways. First, teachers can use it to document how a student uses language to perform a specific task and with what assistance. Second, this tool can help teachers organize their holistic assessment of student performance within and across tasks relative to the standards addressed in any given unit. Teachers can see at a glance which tasks students can perform independently (IP), which they can perform with moderate assistance (PMA), and at which tasks they are still novices (NP). Third, teachers can use this template to reflect on their instruction by evaluating the types and range of performances that they are requiring of students. Teachers can use the evidence they collect with the Teacher's Assessment Tool to guide instruction and improve their translanguaging practice.

Next we see how Carla uses the Teacher's Assessment Tool to assess Ricardo's reading performance within the context of her unit of instruction and

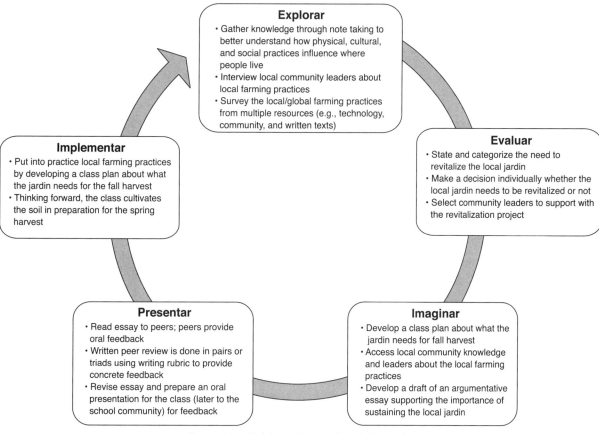

Explorar
- Gather knowledge through note taking to better understand how physical, cultural, and social practices influence where people live
- Interview local community leaders about local farming practices
- Survey the local/global farming practices from multiple resources (e.g., technology, community, and written texts)

Implementar
- Put into practice local farming practices by developing a class plan about what the jardin needs for the fall harvest
- Thinking forward, the class cultivates the soil in preparation for the spring harvest

Evaluar
- State and categorize the need to revitalize the local jardin
- Make a decision individually whether the local jardin needs to be revitalized or not
- Select community leaders to support with the revitalization project

Presentar
- Read essay to peers; peers provide oral feedback
- Written peer review is done in pairs or triads using writing rubric to provide concrete feedback
- Revise essay and prepare an oral presentation for the class (later to the school community) for feedback

Imaginar
- Develop a class plan about what the jardin needs for fall harvest
- Access local community knowledge and leaders about the local farming practices
- Develop a draft of an argumentative essay supporting the importance of sustaining the local jardin

Figure 6.1   Carla's translanguaging design cycle.

viewed through the dynamic translanguaging progressions lens. Table 6.2 shows how Carla completed the reading component for Ricardo.

Carla begins by identifying the type of reading task that Ricardo will perform, for example, *focus on providing text evidence of key ideas* or *make inferences*. Next, Carla identifies the types of general linguistic or language-specific performance she observes. In this case, Carla observes when Ricardo performs only in English, only in Spanish, or draws on the full features of his linguistic repertoire, including Mixteco. Next to each task, and according to each type of language use, Carla records the type of assistance Ricardo requires: IP, PMA, or NP. At the bottom of the form, Carla makes notes of the evidence that she collects to support her assessment. In this case, Carla identifies the patterns she observes along four dimensions (1) type of task, (2) type of language performance, (3) type of assistance, and (4) position along the dynamic translanguaging progressions (*entering, emerging, developing, expanding,* and *commanding*).

We can see that Ricardo's performance in English on many of the reading tasks, even with assistance, is still considered NP. However, when using Spanish, Ricardo can make inferences and do research independently (IP)—the two tasks that are not directly related to text analysis. In the evidence section, Carla evaluates Ricardo's Spanish language performances on these types of tasks (making inferences and doing research independently) as *expanding*. Recall that Ricardo's school in Mexico had provided him with little experience finding text-based evidence and analyzing the text's craft. As a result, Ricardo's performance on text-based tasks in Spanish, even with assistance, is still NP. However, when Ricardo is permitted to use his entire language repertoire, his performance is greatly enhanced on the text-based tasks. When we look at Ricardo's general linguistic performance, we see that he reaches the *expanding*

TABLE 6.2 **Carla's Assessment of Ricardo's Work**

Unit title: Cuentos de la tierra y el barrio

	General Linguistic Performance	Language-*Specific* Performance (English)	Language-*Specific* Performance (Spanish)
Reading			
Can the student			
• Focus on providing text-based evidence of key ideas	PMA	NP	NP
• Make inferences	IP	NP	IP
• Identify main ideas and relationships in complex texts	PMA	PMA	PMA
• Recognize the text's craft and structure (chronology, comparison, cause/effect)	PMA	NP	NP
• Associate knowledge and ideas from multiple sources and texts	PMA	PMA	PMA
• Conduct research to build knowledge	IP	NP	IP
Evidence	With assistance (technology, texts, peers, teacher) Ricardo can • Provide many details, evidence, and examples in a text *(expanding)* • Identify main ideas and relationships *(expanding)* • Recognize text structure *(expanding)* • Associate from multiple sources/texts *(expanding)* Independently, Ricardo can • Make inferences *(expanding)* • Conduct research *(expanding)*	With assistance (technology, texts, peers, teacher) Ricardo can • Identify some relationships *(developing)* • Associate from multiple sources/texts *(developing)* Without assistance, Ricardo can only • Refer to few details, evidence, and examples from a text *(emerging)* • Locate some language associated with inferences *(entering)* • Start outlining his ideas in English *(emerging)* • Recognize the text's craft *(emerging)*	With assistance (technology, texts, peers, teacher) Ricardo can • Identify some relationships *(developing)* • Associate from multiple sources/texts *(developing)* Independently, Ricardo can • Make inferences *(expanding)* • Conduct research *(expanding)* Without assistance, Ricardo can only • Provide few details, evidence, and examples from a text *(emerging)* • Compare and contrast language associated with inferences *(emerging)* • Write an essay in Mixteco and translate into Spanish *(emerging)*

IP, independent performance; NP, novice performance, even with assistance; PMA, performance with moderate assistance.

stage on all types of reading tasks evaluated in this unit, although sometimes he requires assistance from other people or material. The Teacher's Assessment Tool allows Carla to understand clearly that developing Ricardo's reading performances in English is going to require much more than simply learning a new language. It is going to require that Carla provide opportunities for him to practice using his home languages—Spanish and Mixteco—to find text-based evidence and analyze the text's craft.

The evidence that Carla collects using the Teacher's Assessment Tool paints a much more complex portrait of Ricardo's reading performance than what we see in traditional monolingual or bilingual programs. Carla uses this document as the jumping-off point for Ricardo's language arts portfolio, and she includes samples of student work to demonstrate what Ricardo can do using the full features of his linguistic repertoire alongside what he can do with Spanish and English. Carla makes instructional and assessment decisions for Ricardo based on his performance on different types of tasks over time.

The Importance of Distinguishing between General Linguistic and Language-Specific Performances

This section compares Carla's assessment of Ricardo's reading performances to Justin's assessment of *Pablo's* reading performances, in each case using the Teacher's Assessment Tool. The comparison makes it clear why teachers need to distinguish general linguistic performance from language-specific performance. Recall that Pablo has recently arrived in Los Angeles from Argentina and that he is a student in the math class that Justin supports as an English as a second language teacher. Before coming to the United States, Pablo had taken private after-school English lessons and was enrolled in a private school in Buenos Aires. Pablo has been in the United States approximately the same period of time as Ricardo. He can do all the tasks of the reading assessment inventory in Spanish only, using the full features of his language repertoire independently. Pablo's general language performance, as well as his performance in Spanish, is *commanding* on the dynamic translanguaging progressions. Because of his strong general language performance, Pablo is able to complete the English reading tasks with moderate assistance.

Teachers can use their assessments of students' general linguistic and language-specific performances on different tasks at different times to make focused instructional decisions. Let's look at a few examples in Carla's, Justin's, and Stephanie's translanguaging classrooms to highlight this point in their very different classroom contexts.

- **Moisés** is a newcomer from Mexico in Carla's DLBE classroom, and his performances in English are *developing* on the dynamic translanguaging progressions. Moisés often needs assistance from the teacher, his peers, or other visual and interactive tools to complete a task when the product is in English only, but he manages independently when he he can use his entire language repertoire to show what he can do.
- *Yi-Sheng* is a newcomer from Taiwan in Justin's class, and she needs assistance all the time when she has to perform reading tasks in English. However, Yi-Sheng performs the same types of reading tasks beautifully and independently when she uses Mandarin.
- *Luis* is a recent arrival from El Salvador in Stephanie's class, and he speaks only Spanish. As a result of his limited schooling in El Salvador, Luis' reading and writing performances in Spanish are *transitioning* on the dynamic translanguaging progressions. Luis therefore needs assistance when performing literacy-based tasks in Spanish.
- *Fatoumata* is a student in Justin's class who needs assistance whether performing using all her language resources or in one language or another. Despite her oral fluency in Pular, Fatoumata does not have any experience using this language for academic purposes. Although she speaks fluent French, in the schools she attended in Guinea she had never been asked to find text-based evidence or to write an argumentative essay.

The Teacher's Assessment Tool directs teachers' attention to what students can do with language on different types of academic tasks, with assistance and independently, which in turn helps them identify specific supports and scaffolds that bilingual students need to demonstrate their learning at the outer edges of their **zones of proximal development**. Teachers need to provide students with external resources to support them in performing tasks so that they can carry them out independently. Teachers also need to be able to differentiate how those scaffolds and supports relate to students' performances with their entire language repertoires or to performances in one language or another.

ASSESSING FROM MANY ANGLES

Teachers in translanguaging classrooms emphasize the importance of dynamic, holistic assessment from many angles. The different constituents of the translanguaging design for assessment are shown in Figure 6.2. They include the student, peer group, family, and teacher. This section illustrates these angles in action and concludes with the teacher's inclusive class assessment. As you read, we encourage you to consider how you can use the dynamic translanguaging progressions[3] lens to assess your bilingual students' performances throughout a translanguaging unit of instruction.

Student's Self-Assessment

Student learning is at the center of the translanguaging pedagogy, and students must be involved in assessing their own learning. Our Student Self-Assessment Tool asks students what essential questions they can answer, what new vocabulary or language structures they can use, whether and how they've used translanguaging to learn, what standards they've addressed, how they've collaborated with peers, their teacher's and families' roles in their learning, and what outside resources they've used. Students are also asked to evaluate their content and language performances, whether they think the culminating project was an appropriate way of assessing their learning, and what new questions they have. We provide a blank Student Self-Assessment Tool in Appendix A.6.2. Because all of Carla's students use Spanish and English, the questions on the student self-assessment are in both languages. Teachers whose students speak other languages can translate the questions as necessary.

Students can complete the questions on this self-assessment in writing or, if necessary, the teacher can ask students the questions orally and write down their answers. Or students can do so for each other or use a recorder. For example, Ricardo completes the self-assessment task orally largely in Spanish, with some Mixteco, and a few words and phrases in English. When Carla hears Mixteco on the self-assessment recorder, she invites Ricardo to discuss what he means in Spanish.

The situation is different in Stephanie's class because she does not speak or read her students' home language, Spanish. She asks her Spanish-speaking colleagues to translate to English any parts of the responses that are written or spoken in Spanish. Other students who know their classmates' home languages can also help with translation. For example, in Stephanie's class, **Teresita**, who is a strong reader and writer in both English and Spanish, works with **Luis**, recently arrived from El Salvador and just emerging in Spanish literacy, to complete his self-assessment orally, while she writes his answers in English. Stephanie uses the information derived from the self-assessment to determine what new content and language each individual student now understands and can use.

---

[3]We know that it is unrealistic for every teacher to assess every student from each of these different perspectives during each unit and then to integrate all this information. Furthermore, some perspectives may be more important than others at different times throughout the instructional unit. We recommend that teachers, especially novice teachers, try out one assessment at a time, with different students. An important advantage of having different constituents involved in assessment is that the teacher does not have to do all the work in isolation, but can share responsibility for assessment with the students themselves, peers, and families.

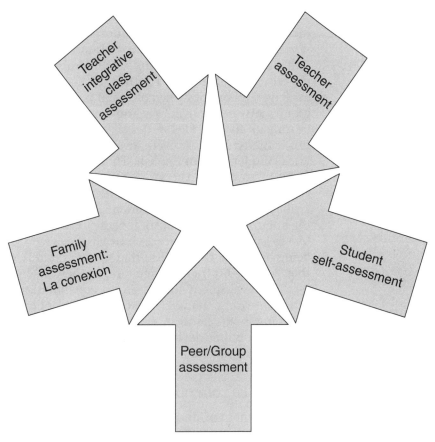

Figure 6.2   Assessment from many angles. (Courtesy of Jamie Schissel.)

Bilingual students can use this tool to express what translanguaging means for their learning, with attention to how they draw on people and external resources for support, communicate their needs for future instruction, and reflect on the design of the assessments, including the culminating project. Bilingual students are asked to articulate new questions that have emerged for them, which could lead to the development of a new unit or topic for students to explorar. This information feeds directly into the teacher's instructional design, enabling the teacher to set a different instructional course and to understand how individual bilingual students use translanguaging, as well as how they use people-resources (e.g., peers, family, and teacher) and external-resources (e.g., printed and media texts) to support their learning.

Peer Group Assessment

A collaborative instructional design must correspond to a collaborative assessment design. This means that peers are also asked to evaluate the group's work. A blank Peer Group Assessment Tool is in Appendix A.6.3, and the questions are written in Spanish and English. It is important to emphasize that this assessment is *not* of individuals by peers; instead, it is an assessment of the group's learning and the group's ways of working. This form could be filled out by one group member in consultation with the others after extensive discussion, or individual group members can take turns filling out different questions. As with individual students' self-assessments, the group is asked to assess its learning of essential ideas and questions; of content, language, and translanguaging objectives; of its use of other resources, and of the culminating project.

For one of the activities, a group consisting of Erica, Moisés, Jennifer, and Ricardo searched the web for information on local farming in Albuquerque. Jennifer and Erica searched the web in English, while Ricardo and Moisés did so in Spanish. When they came together they read from each other's notes, and the ensuing dialogue used both English and Spanish as they quoted text-based evidence. When they filled out their peer group assessment, Jennifer wrote the group's answer to no. 2: "We know now many things, but especially that it will be difficult to eat chiles verdes because there are not enough farmers." And for no. 3 she wrote, "We were awesome! Ricardo read in Spanish, and Moisés, Erica, and Jennifer in English. There is more stuff in English." Carla was especially interested in the group's response to no. 7, which Ricardo recorded: "Excellent! We discussed excellent! Y ahora sabemos más. Y abajo con una, y arriba con dos." By having students take responsibility for assessing their learning and their ability to work together, Carla is motivating them to take initiative to learn and to reflect on how language works. They not only take pride in being bilingual, they realize that "una" certainly doesn't mean "más," and so they actually lift their bilingualism as they are propelled to greater learning.

This assessment fosters group collaboration and consciousness of each other's learning, while giving the teacher opportunities to assess whether the grouping is successful. A review of this group assessment by the teacher will inform grouping decisions the teacher makes for subsequent instructional units, activities, and assessments.

Family Assessment: La conexión

The assessment of students' bilingualism and learning by families is often very different from that of school, as we saw in Chapter 3 when Noemí's parents rated her as a more experienced bilingual than did her teacher, Stephanie. When family members assess their children's learning, they shine light on the **translanguaging corriente** that connects students' homes and communities with the school, and they contribute to a more holistic view of the bilingual child. We provide a Family Assessment Tool in Appendix A.6.4 that families can use to share their perspectives on students' content and language learning. The questions are in Spanish and English.

The Family Assessment Tool, however, is not the only a way to ask family members what their children have learned and what they have learned from their children. It also taps the families' funds of knowledge and provides a vehicle for sharing their own understanding and resources with children in school. Thus, the translanguaging design for assessment recognizes families as learners *and* teachers, emphasizing the families' potential to extend their own children's understanding of content and language, as well as that of other children in the class. The family assessment is an important conexión.

As with the Peer Group Assessment Tool, the Family Assessment Tool is collaborative. It is designed so that family members work with children to complete the form. Parents can either write their own responses or share their answers with their children who then record them. In this way, parents and children are engaged in the assessment process as learners and teachers. Furthermore, when family members identify a fund of knowledge from their home or community that they would like to share, they can indicate this on the form, and teachers can invite family members to the classrooms to help students make important home–family–community–school connections.

For example, Ricardo shared the form with his mother. Ricardo read the questions in Spanish, while his mother spoke to him mostly in Mixteco with some Spanish. She also asked him to read the questions in English. Ricardo's mother was proud of her son's ability to read in English, and she repeated proudly some words: "son," "child," "song," "story," some of which Ricardo gently repeated. Ricardo filled out the form, as best he could, with his mother's words in Spanish and Mixteco. When Ricardo's father came in from work, his mother showed him the conexión and all of Ricardo's writing. She also showed him the corn plant that she had drawn on the back of the form. She spoke with excitement about the English words she learned from her son and about her pride in her son's progress in English. And then they discussed the last question. Both of them had grown corn in their tierra back in Oaxaca. They decided that they would tell Ricardo that they could visit the class to tell his classmates about their cosecha de maíz.

Teacher's Integrative Class Assessment Tool

The information provided by the different constituents of the translanguaging design for assessment (see Fig. 6.2)—the students themselves and their families, peers, and teacher—has to be integrated into instruction. We provide the Teacher's Integrative Class Assessment Tool in Appendix A.6.5. Teachers can use this template to organize the assessment data they have collected from different constituents on different tasks. Teachers may include assessments of the students' understanding of content, their language use, use of resources, and intellectual curiosity and creativity. This information then supports the teacher's translanguaging instructional design.

Teachers are the ultimate assessors of student learning. If they have paid close attention to what students say and do, teachers can surely say a lot more about their students than a score on a standardized test. But translanguaging for assessment requires that the teachers' assessment of students not be based solely on their own evaluation of student learning, but that this assessment is done in collaboration with others, especially by those who know the students best—the students themselves and their peers and families. It is then important to integrate the teacher's evaluation with the student's self-evaluation and those of the peer group and families. The equitable and fair assessment of bilingual students also requires that we evaluate students' performances according to their general linguistic and language-specific performances.

In Table 6.3 Carla has filled out the Integrative Assessment Tool for Ricardo. A few obvious patterns emerge. Ricardo is a lot more critical of his academic performances than the rest of the constituents. His parents are his biggest fans, and evaluate his performance as *commanding*. His peers are also quite proud of the group's performance. His teacher's evaluation falls between the *transitioning* one of Ricardo and the *commanding* one of his parents. Overall, however, his total integrative score of 2.63 indicates that Ricardo's performances in school are approaching *commanding* and, therefore, he is on the road to academic success.

Managing Assessments

Realistically, teachers do not have to use all of these assessment tools at all times for every child in the classroom. We offer them to help teachers get to know students and improve instruction. It is possible to try out the Peer Group Assessment in one unit and the Student's Self-Assessment in a different unit, or to send the Family Assessment home to families once a month or once a week. It might also be possible for the teacher do a full assessment of three to five students for every instructional unit. What is important is that teachers gather evidence of student performance on different tasks, from different perspectives, at different times, and then use that evidence to improve instruction and assessment of bilingual students.

TABLE 6.3   **Completed Integrative Assessment for Ricardo**

Indicate for each of the five measures whether the student's performance has been evaluated as
3 = Advanced
2 = Satisfactory
1 = Needs work
Leave blank if you do not have the data to make this determination.

1. Add up each column for a *total sum per constituent*.
2. Divide by the number of categories you can assess in the column. This gives you the *average per constituent*.
3. Add the averages per constituent and divide by 4.
4. Give the *integrative score* in the next line.

Student's name: *Ricardo*

Categories	Constituents			
	Self	Group	Family	Teacher
Content use				
Essential ideas	2		3	2
Language use				
General linguistic performance	3	3	3	3
Language-specific performance				
Spanish	3	2	3	2
Use of resources	2	3	3	3
Creativity/curiosity	2	3	2	3
Total per constituent	12	11	14	13
Average per constituent	2.4	2.75	2.8	2.6

Integrative score and comments   2.63—Ricardo's self-evaluation is harsher than that of the other constituents. He is well liked by his group who evaluate him as having *expanding* performances. But he is especially well positioned based on his parents' evaluation. The teacher's evaluation falls between the poorer self-evaluation and the positive ones given to him by parents and peers.

A 2.63 score means that Ricardo is well poised because of support from family and peers to advance to meet standards. All he needs is self-confidence to continue to perform.

TRANSLANGUAGING SHIFTS IN ASSESSMENT

Teachers in translanguaging classrooms understand that assessment is not simply a standardized test score that each child has for the year. Rather, assessment has to be flexible and responsive to students' learning needs. In addition to formally assessing students' understanding from different perspectives, teachers in translanguaging classrooms *shift* their focus as they assess different moments from students' work.

Teachers in translanguaging classrooms vary in the ways they use assessment tools. Sometimes, for example, the self-assessment is given to students after the teacher has evaluated their learning and shared the assessment with them. Sometimes teachers use different tools to assess children; they choose and adapt them for the specific learning opportunity and the characteristics of the student being assessed.

Teachers in translanguaging classrooms think about the design of their assessment, but they also assess students informally as the opportunities arise.

For example, when Carla taught the jardín lesson discussed earlier, Ricardo preferred to perform in Spanish. Carla showed Ricardo her own evaluation of his work, in which English was often left blank. Ricardo objected, and said that he was able to use English—he had just not done so for that particular task. Carla then gave Ricardo the opportunity to work in English and she assessed his performance, which showed he was able to use English, with moderate assistance, for most tasks.

Assessment in translanguaging classrooms is never just handed down. It is discussed with the learners and advice is sought for the future. Students are given a voice in their assessment through self-reflection and self-evaluation. Furthermore, students' performances are assessed on different tasks, from different perspectives, over time. Teachers' shifts in assessment are purposeful; they allow students to perform what they know and can do through different modes—drawing, speaking, writing, pointing, the use of technology, and so forth—and they encourage students to use different language practices. In these cases, collaboration means adaptation and adjustment, as teachers make moment-by-moment decisions about what counts as knowledge and how to assess it.

After designing and planning the use of assessments carefully, all teachers must go with the flow of the translanguaging corriente to ensure that students are being assessed fairly and accurately. Assessment works for the child and not the other way around. When in doubt about assessment, go with the flow of your students' needs, inquiries, and abilities.

CONCLUSION

Teachers in translanguaging classrooms design assessments carefully. They do not see themselves as the sole expert/evaluator but as one of many caring observers, ensuring that students, peers, and families also have a role in assessment.

Knowledge is collaboratively constructed and students must be given opportunities to perform certain tasks independently or with the assistance of others or other resources. For bilingual students, language is an interrelated repertoire, not simply the autonomous use of English or Spanish. Thus, assessments of bilingual students must not only assess the use of two languages independently, as schools most often require, but also include the perspective of bilingual children using their entire language repertoires. It is important for teachers to know whether a child's emergent performance on a task reflects an incomplete understanding of content, an emergent performance level in the school language, or an emergent general linguistic performance. When teachers can clearly assess the specific challenges that their students face (content, language A or B, general linguistic performance), they are in a strong position to support and scaffold students' learning and to transform their capacities.

An important lesson that we draw from this chapter is that even though we often think of assessments as fixed and rigid, they too are shaped by the translanguaging corriente. In fact, it is the flexibility afforded by translanguaging that allows teachers to assess what students know and can do using different language practices.

Translanguaging in assessment requires a strong juntos stance, careful design, and well-orchestrated shifts. There cannot be a simple linear arrangement where teaching comes first and assessment last. Instruction and assessment need to work juntos as interlocking gears to strengthen students' performances. The translanguaging corriente mobilizes students' bilingual resources, and the teacher uses flexible assessment instruments to accelerate student learning.

QUESTIONS AND ACTIVITIES

1. Think about the four principles of a translanguaging assessment design. Which are easier for you to include in your own assessment design? Why? Which are harder? Why?

2. Describe the difference between general linguistic and language-specific performances in assessment. Is this a useful distinction? Is it a difficult distinction to make?

3. Can you think of a time when it is *not* a good idea to allow students to use their entire linguistic repertoire to respond to assessment? Explain your answer.

TAKING ACTION

1. Now that you have read about assessment, see if you can add to the boxes on assessment and general and language-specific performances in the Translanguaging Unit Plan that you produced using Appendix A.5.1.

2. Select three students. After a lesson, have each of them fill out the Self-Assessment (see Appendix A.6.2), have the group fill out the Peer Group Assessment (see Appendix A.6.3), send home the Family Assessment: La conexión (see Appendix A.6.4), and fill out your own assessment (see Appendix A.6.1). What did you learn from these various assessments? How would you adapt or change your instruction based on this new information?

CHAPTER 7

Translanguaging Pedagogy in Action

LEARNING OBJECTIVES

- Identify the key components of a translanguaging pedagogy
- Explain how the three translanguaging strands—*stance*, *design*, and *shifts*—work together in the daily life of a classroom
- Describe the teacher's juntos stance toward students, languages, and content
- Explain how teachers leverage the translanguaging corriente during instruction and assessment
- Give examples of moment-to-moment shifts that teachers make in response to the translanguaging corriente
- Explain how translanguaging strategies work within the translanguaging classroom
- Use a reflective tool for adopting a translanguaging pedagogy in your classroom

When we explain each of the components (stance, design, and shifts) of the translanguaging pedagogy separately, it is possible to lose sight of the integral role of the **translanguaging corriente** in the daily life of the classroom. This chapter illustrates the integrated whole of the **translanguaging classroom** with attention to the stance, design, and shifts in instruction and assessment. This holistic portrait of the translanguaging pedagogy in action prepares us to rethink and reimagine what it means to teach, learn, and assess.

Translanguaging can "dissolve solid differences while create[ing] new realities" (García & Leiva, 2014, p. 203). The daily life of the translanguaging classroom mirrors the daily lives of bilinguals outside of the classroom. When we make the world of the classroom reflect the every day lives of bilingual people, educational opportunities for bilingual students open up. Rather than simply using students' home languages as scaffolds to English, teachers in translanguaging classrooms recognize and create opportunities for students to language, learn, express themselves, and forge relationships in unique ways. The translanguaging pedagogy shapes the classroom space, enabling us to transcend traditional rules about language, learning, and teaching—to foster new social realities in our classrooms.

A CLOSER LOOK AT CLASSROOM PRACTICE

We visit *Stephanie's* 11th-grade English-medium social studies classroom to illustrate the integrated nature of the stance, design, and shifts of the translanguaging pedagogy for instruction and assessment. Stephanie introduces students to a new genre, public service announcements (PSAs), as part of her social studies unit, *Environmentalism: Then and Now*. One assignment within this unit is for students to create their own PSAs, which they can then use to raise awareness about social issues faced by people living in their local communities.

Students First

Although Stephanie is not bilingual, and the official language of instruction in her class is English, Stephanie grouped together five of her bilingual students— Eddy, Luis, Mariana, Noemí, and Teresita—so that they can **leverage** their Spanish and English language resources to engage with complex content and texts and develop linguistic practices for academic contexts. Let's look more closely at the profiles of these students, which Stephanie has continued to flesh out based on her holistic assessment of students' performances in her class this year.

> *Eddy's* family is from the Dominican Republic, and he was born and raised in a predominantly Dominican neighborhood in New York City. His parents moved to the United States when they were very young and speak to Eddy and his siblings mostly in English. Though he understands Spanish, listens to reggaeton and bachata, and can "mess around" with his friends in Spanish, he feels more comfortable using English at school. Eddy's English literacy, especially in writing, is below grade level. Stephanie was curious about his Spanish literacy level, and she asked the Spanish language teacher about it. Stephanie found out that although Eddy was studying Spanish in the Spanish for heritage-speakers class, he had never received instruction in Spanish before this time. Stephanie tries to partner or group Eddy with newly arrived Spanish-speaking students for two reasons—he can lend his excellent oral English skills to support students who are beginning to learn English and he can learn from their Spanish-speaking strengths.

> *Luis* arrived from El Salvador in the 10th grade and he is officially designated as an English language learner (ELL). The family was from a rural area, and Luis' experiences with formal schooling are limited. Luis is now classified as a **student with incomplete or interrupted formal education (SIFE)**. When speaking with his peers and his teachers in Spanish, it is clear that he is funny, smart, creative, and tech savvy. However, Luis produces written text at a level well below his peers in both Spanish and English. Luis enjoys comic books and sports magazines, but he struggles to read academic texts in English or Spanish. Stephanie works hard to include different content entry points for Luis, such as music and video clips in Spanish, visuals, and realia. Stephanie also pushes Luis to share his ideas in Spanish while he learns more English.

> *Mariana's* family moved to the United States from Puebla, Mexico, before she was born. Raised in the United States all her life, Mariana feels as comfortable speaking English as she does speaking Spanish. She is a strong translator and constantly helps her family and friends navigate tasks that require English, like going with her mother to the doctor, talking to her father's boss on the phone, and helping her younger siblings with homework. Although Mariana can perform these tasks outside of school in English, her literacy in English is not at grade level. Mariana was labeled an ELL when she first entered school and has yet to test out of this status. Now in high school, Mariana struggles with literacy, even though she has a strong grasp of content. In school she is now classified as a **long-term English language learner**, although she prefers English to Spanish for schoolwork. Mariana is in the same Spanish for heritage-speakers class as Eddy; she is quite fluent orally in Spanish, but her teacher describes her literacy skills in Spanish as weak.

> *Noemí* and her family came to the United States from Ecuador when she was in 8th grade. When Noemí first arrived, she was one of only a few

students in her class classified as ELL. Though she got help from her teachers to learn English, she was often bored by the rote, grammar-based instruction. In her **pull-out English as a second language** class, her teacher, who did not speak Spanish, did not seem to understand that Noemí was a strong reader. Now in 11th grade, Noemí uses English orally with *commanding* performances, but she still struggles with literacy, especially in writing, and she is still classified as an ELL. Noemí finds it helpful to prewrite in Spanish before writing an essay in English and to annotate an English text with questions or ideas in Spanish.

Teresita was born in Guatemala but moved to the United States when she was very young. Though she always spoke Spanish at home, she learned English from her older siblings and television programs before she entered kindergarten. Teresita is a strong reader and writer in both English and Spanish. She consistently scores well on high-stakes exams and is a voracious reader in both languages, though she prefers reading books in English. Teresita also likes to write poetry in both languages, but says that Spanish poetry comes more easily to her. Because she is highly proficient in English, some of her teachers don't even know that she can read and write in Spanish.

These five bilingual students have a wide range of expertise in oral and written Spanish and English. Stephanie uses her understanding of what her students can do with Spanish and English, individually and in collaboration, to structure activities in her classes.

Structuring Activities

We turn now to a lengthy vignette from Stephanie's *Environmentalism: Then and Now* unit to see how she uses translanguaging strategically to (1) introduce the PSA genre to her bilingual students in this English-medium class, (2) encourage students' critical engagement with this new genre, and (3) provide opportunities for students to produce this new genre. We focus on how Stephanie structures whole class and small group activities that leverage students' bilingualism, with particular attention to Eddy, Luis, Mariana, Noemí, and Teresita. At a more general level, this activity series illustrates how Stephanie's classroom practices address the four purposes of translanguaging—supporting students as they engage with complex content and texts, providing opportunities for students to develop language practices for academic purposes, drawing on students' bilingualism and ways of knowing, and supporting students' socioemotional development and bilingual identities and advancing social justice.

Stephanie started her lesson by showing a video of a model PSA in English about human trafficking in the United States; following is a screenshot:

Public service announcement (PSA): Human trafficking in the United States. (Retrieved from Department of Homeland Security, Blue Campaign. English video: https://www.dhs.gov/video/out-shadows-psa-60-seconds; Spanish video: https://www.dhs.gov/video/out-shadows-psa-spanish-60-second)

Stephanie played the PSA a second time, in Spanish, to ensure that all her Spanish-speaking **emergent bilingual** students could draw on their entire linguistic repertoires to comprehend the minute-long PSA. This second viewing also served as reinforcement for her English-speaking students, especially those who were bilingual.

After watching both the English and the Spanish versions, Stephanie encouraged the class to discuss the end of the PSA where a man trips over a woman, and says in English (in both the Spanish and the English versions): "Sorry, I didn't even see you." The woman responds: "No one ever does." Stephanie asked the students, What did the shift to English in the Spanish PSA mean? Why was this done in English? To encourage deep thinking about the use of language, Stephanie asked students to discuss these questions in their groups using Spanish or English. This way, the groups that were stronger in Spanish could benefit from its use and explore this question deeply and participate in the discussion.

Stephanie then asked her students to come up with a definition of the PSA genre and to discuss whether the PSA they watched was effective and why. She provided the groups with printed texts about PSAs—in English only for some groups and in English and Spanish for others (e.g., for our focal group that includes Eddy, Luis, Mariana, Noemí, and Teresita). Stephanie then told the groups to look up other PSAs on the web and encouraged those who spoke Spanish to find some in Spanish. During the research, students in the focal group conducted their discussion and reading of other texts in Spanish and English.

After the groups shared their thoughts in English with the entire class, Stephanie formally introduced the PSA genre by synthesizing students' definitions and ideas. She then facilitated the discussion while students brainstormed characteristics of the genre. Mariana shared that to be effective a PSA had to "be a little shocking." Stephanie agreed and rephrased, saying, "That's true—PSAs often focus on controversial topics." Luis raised his hand and asked, "Pero todos los PSAs son videos así?" A student translated his question [Are all PSAs videos like this one?] and Stephanie responded that PSAs could be on the radio, in print, or in video form. Stephanie then transitioned the discussion to the use of persuasive language and tactics in PSAs. She emphasized that different kinds of persuasive language and tactics are used for different audiences, the same as English and Spanish are used for different audiences.

Next, Stephanie gave each group a different PSA to analyze, some in English and some in Spanish. Some of the PSAs focused on environmentalism, and some focused on other high-interest, controversial social issues. Students were told to discuss the model PSAs and to think about purpose, message, audience, and persuasive language and tactics, as well as the PSA's effectiveness. To support their work, Stephanie gave each group a handout with an image that corresponded to the different PSAs. Each handout included the same five questions, which were intended to support each group's academic conversations:

1. What is the purpose of this PSA? What message is it trying to convey?
2. Who is the audience for the PSA? How do you know?
3. What persuasive language and/or tactics are used in this PSA?
4. What is the emotional effect of this PSA on this audience?
5. Is this PSA effective? Why or why not?

Each handout also included three different languaging options:

1. Discuss your PSA in English; write down your answers in English.
2. Discuss your PSA in Spanish and English; write down your answers in English.
3. Discuss your PSA in Spanish and English; write your answers in English and Spanish (e.g., write down a word/phrase in English and expand on it in Spanish).

Students could choose the languaging option that allowed them to individually and collectively leverage all of their language resources to complete this task.

Eddy, Luis, Mariana, Noemí, and Teresita were given the following PSA from a campaign to raise awareness about teen pregnancy in Chicago:

Public service announcement (PSA): Raising aware-ness about teen pregnancy. (Chicago Department of Public Health, Office of Adolescent and School Health. Retrieved from http://d236bkdxj385sg .cloudfront.net/wp-content/uploads/2015/07/ pregnant-boy-post.jpg)

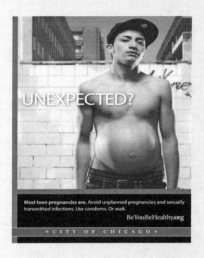

The group shared their first reactions to the image. Eddy thought the PSA was "crazy," "weird," and "unexpected." Luis did not understand the word "unex-pected," and Teresita offered "inesperado, que no se espera." When he under-stood the meaning, Luis said, "OK, ahora entiendo. Es muy unexpected que el muchacho esté embarazado!" [OK, now I get it. It's very unexpected that the guy is pregnant!] All students worked collaboratively to answer the questions, and those in our focal group moved between Spanish and English to discuss their thoughts and, eventually, write down their answers.

After the groups had shared their thinking on their PSAs, Stephanie opened up the discussion to the whole class to see if anyone had anything else to add. A stu-dent from another group asked angrily, "Why'd they have to make him Spanish, though?" Luis volunteered an answer immediately, saying "Porque siempre los Latinos cargan con la culpa." [Because Latinos are always blamed]. Teresita added that the PSA played on stereotypes about Latinos and teen pregnancy. Stephanie jumped in, sharing that this playing on stereotypes, as well as its controversial image and short, blunt text, made it a very effective PSA—even if it made them mad.

After all the groups shared their assigned PSAs, Stephanie told them that they would be creating their *own* PSAs for their group's chosen social issue. She told students that they should focus their work not only on the PSA's content, but also on its *language* and *style*. Because our focal group chose an environmental issue that specifically affected Latinos, Stephanie asked students to create their PSA using English and Spanish. This meant that students had to keep two different audiences in mind and make appropriate linguistic and stylistic choices.

When students finished drafts of their bilingual PSAs, they made short, infor-mal presentations to the class. Stephanie required every student in the group to participate in the presentation. Noemí, for example, introduced her group's PSA. Stephanie explained to Noemí that she should do her best to explain the work in English, but that she could use Spanish to expand on or clarify ideas. When Noemí spoke in Spanish, Stephanie relied on students like Mariana and Teresita to trans-late so that she could fully understand Noemí's contributions.

Each group then filled out the Peer Group Assessment (see Appendix A.6.3) for the work they did. Each student in the group also filled out a Student Self-Assessment (see Appendix A.6.2).Stephanie then asked the students to show their families the bilingual PSA that their group had produced. The families assessed what they learned, as well as what they thought the students had learned, by filling out the Family Assessment: La conexión (see Appendix A.6.4). These evalu-ations contributed to Stephanie's holistic assessment of students' performances, and helped engage students and their families in the assessment process.

After students had presented to the class, Stephanie asked her principal if they could post their PSAs around the school. The principal agreed and asked Stephanie if students would explain the project to the community during the morning announcements. Stephanie asked Mariana and Luis to work together to come up with an explanation of the PSA assignment in both Spanish and English that they would read during the announcements the following week.

This rich vignette provides an opportunity for us to look closely at how the translanguaging strands—stance, design, and shifts—are manifested in Stephanie's classroom. We highlight important principles in each of the strands to keep in mind as you create your own translanguaging classroom.

STANCE: STUDENTS, LANGUAGE, AND CONTENT JUNTOS

The **translanguaging stance** informs all our classroom work. Though each of our translanguaging stances will be a little different, there are three fundamental elements that are integral to the stance of *any* teacher working with bilingual students. As we discussed in Chapter 4, these three core beliefs are as follows:

1. Students' language practices and cultural understanding encompass those they bring from home and communities, as well as those from school. These practices and understanding co-exist, work **juntos**, and enrich each other.
2. Students' families and communities are valuable sources of knowledge and must be involved in the education process juntos.
3. The classroom is a democratic space where teachers and students juntos create knowledge, challenge traditional hierarchies, and work toward a more just society.

Stephanie's translanguaging stance is reflected in many aspects of the classroom vignette. For example, Stephanie's choice to strategically group students heterogeneously in terms of their English language performances illustrates her belief that all students have something important and meaningful to contribute to the classroom work, regardless of what they can do with oral and written English. Returning to our focal group, Noemí's more experienced literacy performances in Spanish help Eddy with his writing in Spanish, and Eddy's strong oral language performances in English provide Luis with an opportunity to grow more confident using English. Luis' comfort with technology and his ability to find things on the internet makes him the resident expert on research, even though, as you recall, he has been classified as a SIFE. Mariana and Teresita, both of whom have strong Spanish and English, love explaining ideas to the group in both languages.

Putting these five students into one group juntos builds on their different linguistic strengths. This kind of strategic grouping also fosters strong relationships and enables each student to leverage his or her entire **language repertoire**. These relationships can also help address tensions that often exist between Latino newcomer students and Latino students who have been in the United States longer and speak more English, as well as among Latino students from different national origins. Rather than segregate newcomers from experienced English speakers, Stephanie chooses to integrate them, which enriches the group's learning and contributes to their intellectual and socio-emotional growth. It is also an important way of supporting students' bilingualism and biliteracy in this English-medium classroom.

A second aspect of the lessons that illustrates Stephanie's translanguaging juntos stance is how she views the use of one language or the other. To the administration, Stephanie teaches in English. However, Stephanie believes that all her students learn more when they can use the full features of their language repertoires. Thus, she presents the PSA in two languages juntos to enable her bilingual students to learn more about topics and to become familiar with different discourses and genres. Allowing students to make different language choices to express what they know demonstrates her belief in the interrelationship of language practices. This kind of focus on genre, audience, and language also raises students' metalinguistic awareness, one of the major benefits of translanguaging.

A third aspect of the lesson that illustrates Stephanie's translanguaging juntos stance is her choice of content. A focus on PSAs allows students to put their research to work in an authentic, real-world genre and pushes them to think critically about both audience and discourse. By "hooking" students with model PSAs that are high-interest, controversial, and relatable, like the one that focused on teen pregnancy, Stephanie sets them up to create their own PSAs on topics related to the unit. Asking students questions about a text's expected audience, purpose, impact, and effectiveness moves them past simple "comprehension." These kinds of questions challenge students to "read the word and the world" (Freire & Macedo, 1987) more critically, to assess *everything* they encounter with a critical lens. These kinds of tasks ask students to use their unique ways of knowing and languaging to foster a consciousness that helps them recognize, challenge, and transform the structures that uphold the status quo.

Stephanie's juntos stance is also manifested in her use of assessment, which like instruction, is collaborative. She not only evaluates students' learning herself, she also gives the students themselves, their peer groups, and their families opportunities for assessment, which makes everyone co-learners and co-teachers. Stephanie's assessment practices evaluate whether students can perform tasks with moderate assistance or independently and also differentiate between students' understanding of language and content. By allowing students to perform tasks using English and Spanish some times and English only other times, Stephanie also differentiates between the students' **general linguistic** and **language-specific performances**. These translanguaging practices also greatly benefit her African American students who are learning some Spanish from their peers. Also, they are no longer judged solely on whether they can use standard English **language features**, but rather on the *kind* of language users they are, regardless of specific language features.

DESIGN: PURPOSEFUL AND STRATEGIC

Incorporating translanguaging into instruction and assessment design is a powerful means of enhancing bilingual students' learning opportunities, because translanguaging enables students to engage with complex content and texts and develop linguistic practices for academic contexts. Simply put, if we limit students to the use of only part of their language repertoires—especially the part that is considered their *weaker* language—we also limit their ability to learn. Teachers can use a **translanguaging design** to tap into and leverage the translanguaging corriente in ways that accelerate bilingual students' content and language learning at school.

This section, which is divided into three parts, looks more closely at the vignette from Stephanie's classroom to examine her translanguaging design. First we introduce Stephanie's translanguaging instructional unit design, *Environmentalism: Then and Now*. Then we focus on the stages of the translanguaging instructional design cycle that structure the activities in her unit plan. Finally, we use Stephanie's classroom to illustrate the myriad opportunities for translanguaging assessments present in everyday instruction. These assessments, some small and informal, others more formal, give Stephanie authentic information about what her students know and can do with content and language and enable her to learn from their languaging and build on their strengths so that all students can meet or exceed the unit goals and objectives.

Translanguaging Unit Design

We start by looking at the vignette through the lens of Stephanie's translanguaging instructional unit design, which is shown in Box 7.1. This unit design is the flexible structure that Stephanie uses to enact her translanguaging stance and pedagogy in the classroom. Stephanie's stance is reflected in the four essential questions that connect social studies content to students' everyday lives, relate contemporary issues to the historical context, and work to address social justice issues.

Stephanie's unit design is clearly aligned with state standards and she includes content and language objectives, as required by district and school administration. Stephanie plans for translanguaging in this unit of instruction is reflected in the **translanguaging objectives**, culminating design, and assessment from many angles. This flexible design provides the structure and space that Stephanie needs to leverage students' bilingualism for learning.

Translanguaging Instructional Design Cycle

Now we look at the vignette of Stephanie's classroom practices through the lens of the translanguaging instructional design cycle, which, as we saw in Chapter 5, includes five stages: explorar, evaluar, imaginar, presentar, and implementar. These stages provide a way of envisioning an active, engaging, and responsive instructional unit. Here we use the translanguaging instructional design cycle, shown in Figure 7.1, as a framework for examining a cycle of instruction within Stephanie's *Environmentalism: Then and Now* translanguaging unit. If students are to be active learners throughout a unit, we must design instruction so that they are *constantly* engaged in exploring and evaluating what exists, imagining something new, and presenting and implementing new ideas outside the four walls of the classroom.

We now go through each stage of the translanguaging instructional design cycle and discuss how Stephanie and her students used translanguaging within each stage during this cycle of instruction. We illustrate how to use this design cycle as a tool to plan the "big picture" of the unit, as well as the smaller instructional designs that occur from week to week *within* a unit. At each stage of the cycle, we identify concrete translanguaging pedagogical strategies that Stephanie uses to help her students learn.

Explorar

The first stage of the translanguaging instructional design cycle is explorar, which encourages students to explore a new topic or theme, follow their natural interests and questions, and build their background knowledge. Multifaceted exploration occurred throughout the *Environmentalism: Then and Now* unit as a whole. Stephanie worked hard to provide her students with multiple content entry points through a variety of texts (in both Spanish and English, and representing different perspectives) and a variety of modalities (e.g., film, print, internet sources). These design choices reflect her belief that one must view a topic from multiple perspectives to understand it. They also reflect her understanding that all students, but especially emergent bilinguals, benefit from rich, thematic, interdisciplinary instruction (Freeman & Freeman, 2007). Stephanie organized each unit around a central theme, bringing in

BOX 7.1 STEPHANIE'S TRANSLANGUAGING UNIT DESIGN—ENVIRONMENTALISM: THEN AND NOW

Essential Questions	• What does it mean to live sustainably? • How does our environment influence our lives and actions? • How have people fought for what they believe in throughout history? • In what ways can we make change on the local level?
Content Standards	**New York State Social Studies Standards** 3.1.6: Students explain how technological change affects people, places, and regions. 3.2.3: Students select and design maps, graphs, tables, charts, diagrams, and other graphic representations to present geographic information. 4.1.3: Students understand the nature of scarcity and how nations of the world make choices, which involve economic and social costs and benefits. 5.3.4: Students explore how citizens influence public policy in a representative democracy. 5.4.6: Students prepare a plan of action that defines an issue or problem, suggests alternative solutions or courses of action, evaluates the consequences for each alternative solution or course of action, prioritizes the solutions based on established criteria, and proposes an action plan to address the issue or resolve the problem **Common Core Learning Standards** CCSS.ELA-LITERACY.RH.11–12.2: Determine the central ideas or information of a primary or secondary source; provide an accurate summary that makes clear the relationships among the key details and ideas. CCSS.ELA-Literacy.RH.11–12.7: Integrate and evaluate multiple sources of information presented in diverse formats and media (e.g., visually, quantitatively, as well as in words) to address a question or solve a problem. CCSS.ELA-LITERACY.RH.11–12.9: Integrate information from diverse sources, both primary and secondary, into a coherent understanding of an idea or event, noting discrepancies among sources.
Content and Language Objective(s)	*Content Objectives* • Students will trace the development of the U.S. environmental movement from the early 20th century to today • Students will make connections between the environmental movement and larger societal events and developments in recent U.S. history • Students will relate ideas, such as sustainability, to their own lives as young people in an urban environment • Students will create an action campaign that attempts to solve a local school- or community-based issue related to environmentalism and sustainability	*Language Objectives* *General linguistic* • Students will read and synthesize a variety of text sources in order to make connections and draw conclusions • Students will use appropriate and relevant text evidence to support their ideas • Students will create action plans that they will present both orally and in writing in ways that persuade an audience to support their position *Language-specific (English for English-medium class)** • Students will use content-specific vocabulary, both orally and in writing, to explain their ideas and connections to the content • Students will use a structured essay-writing format for persuasive writing that includes an introduction, two supporting body paragraphs, a counter-claim paragraph, and a conclusion • Students will present their action plans orally in English
Translanguaging Objective(s)	• Students will use oral and written Spanish and English to analyze and critique both the content and discourse of bilingual PSAs. • Students will create bilingual PSA texts across a variety of genres (announcements, posters, persuasive essays, oral presentations, and short dramatic plays) and rationalize their linguistic choices.

Box continued on following page

BOX 7.1	STEPHANIE'S TRANSLANGUAGING UNIT DESIGN (Continued)	
Assessments	*Culminating Design* Students will create bilingual action plans and presentations for improving the environmental sustainability of the school or local community in a way that would reach and be understood by diverse, bilingual audiences.	*Other Assessments†* **Teacher's assessment tool:** Teachers assess the student's content understanding and linguistic performances, with attention to what the student can do with or without assistance, using all the features of their repertoire (general linguistic performance) or language-specific features. **Student's self-assessment tool:** Throughout the unit, students provide feedback and self-assessment via questions about their own learning, language development, and content understanding in English and their home languages, orally and in writing. Self-assessments in the home languages will be assessed by the teacher using technological resources (e.g., translation apps) and human resources (bilingual colleagues; bilingual students). **Peer-group assessment tool:** Members reflect on their work as a group via questions about their content learning, languaging performances, and further questions the group has about the unit theme. **Family assessment tool: La conexión:** Students and their families assess what the students learned about the unit topic at school and what families learned from students about the topic. Families also identify relevant funds of knowledge that they might share with the class.
Texts	*In the Home Language(s)* • 11th-grade U.S. history textbook (Spanish version) • Documentary film with Spanish subtitles • Readings in Spanish on César Chávez and the Farm Worker's Association • Supplementary readings on the same content-area topics in Spanish (found via teacher's research and students' online research)	*In English* • 11th-grade U.S. history textbook • Various content-area readings from newspapers, magazines, blogs, and websites • Documentary film • Readings on César Chávez and the Farm Worker's Association • Podcasts and music • Content-related fiction/creative nonfiction

PSA, public service announcement.

*Differentiated according to students' English oracy and literacy performances.

†See Appendices A.6.1–A.6.4, respectively, for blank template tools.

social studies events and ideas from a variety of time periods. This helped her students to see the connections across historical periods through today, as well as to better understand the breadth of a topic.

In the unit of instruction depicted in the vignette, students explored a new genre, the PSA, in a variety of ways. They were given models or "mentor texts" of PSAs in both video and print form. They collaboratively defined the genre, working from the models to formulate ideas about audience and purpose, as well as linguistic and stylistic characteristics. As they explored, Stephanie and her students engaged in translanguaging in a number of ways, including the following:

- Stephanie showed the PSA in English and Spanish. Both short videos had subtitles so that students were able to read the text as they watched.
- Students shared questions and comments in English and Spanish; Stephanie took notes for the class in English.
- In groups, students analyzed print PSAs in Spanish and English.

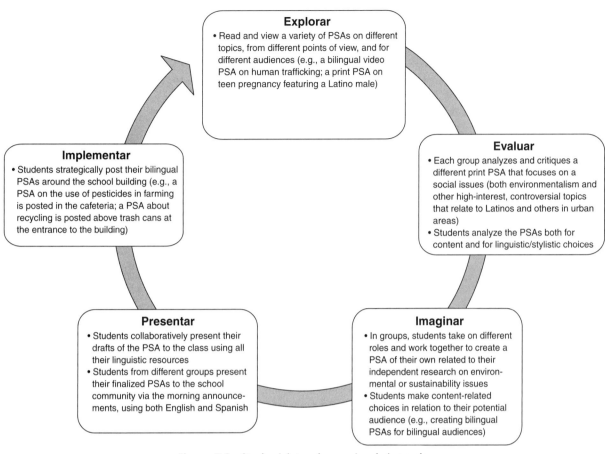

Figure 7.1   Stephanie's translanguaging design cycle.

- To answer the five questions about the model PSAs, students discussed, debated, and analyzed in Spanish and English, and were given three options, including translanguaging options, to arrive at their answers in English.

Evaluar

As students explore, they also evaluate what they are learning. This second stage in the instructional design cycle is important because it helps students strengthen their ability to read texts critically. In Stephanie's classroom, students focused on comprehending the content of the PSAs and on the tactics and discourse used within them to play off a potential audience's fears and deep-seated prejudices. This evaluation of the content deepened learning and helped students think critically. Though students were evaluating PSAs in this lesson, they could just as easily have evaluated a content-specific reading. This kind of critical evaluation of texts both expands and localizes the traditional curriculum, making it more complex and more specific to bilingual students' lives. The translanguaging strategies that Stephanie and her students used to evaluar include the following:

- In groups, students used Spanish and English to express their thoughts and analyze the PSAs. The emergent bilinguals performed better in English on the handout because they were able to first use Spanish to engage with complex content and texts.
- Stephanie drew students' attention to specific linguistic and stylistic choices made within the PSAs. This raised students' metalinguistic awareness and helped them pick out these choices in other texts.

- Stephanie chose model PSAs that portrayed situations or social issues that Latino bilingual students might relate to (i.e., directly related to Latinos or directly related to young people in urban contexts). This allowed students to bring their local knowledge to the analysis of the texts and think critically.

Imaginar

The third stage of the translanguaging instructional design cycle is imaginar, which supports and informs new ideas and new ways of using language to learn. Students are encouraged to use what they have learned in the explorar and evaluar stages to imaginar something new. During the *Environmentalism: Then and Now* unit, students in Stephanie's class were asked to imagine a PSA related to the groups' independent research on environmental or sustainability issues. Our focal group members worked together to build on what they had learned from the PSA on teen pregnancy and in other activities in this unit. In the group, students were able to draw on their strengths to carry out different tasks and translanguage in different ways. Here are some of the ways that Noemí, Eddy, Teresita, Luis, and Mariana contributed within the imaginar stage:

- Noemí contributed ideas orally in Spanish to the group's bilingual PSA. She also took the lead in writing the Spanish text, choosing the evidence from the group's research that was most persuasive.
- Eddy contributed ideas orally, mostly in English but also in Spanish. He lent his creativity to the task of writing a short but powerful "hook" that would catch a reader's attention. He drafted versions of this hook in English and worked with the group to edit it for the final draft.
- Teresita used her strong bilingualism to synthesize group members' comments in English and Spanish. She worked closely with Luis to translate his ideas from Spanish into English. She also translated a quote from a newspaper article from English to Spanish.
- Luis contributed many content-related ideas orally in Spanish. Though he did not have strong writing skills in English or Spanish, he had creative ideas for the visual format of the PSA. He sketched out plans, explained his vision, and worked with the whole group to brainstorm the look of the PSA.
- Mariana worked on both the English and Spanish texts for the PSA. She helped Teresita translate pieces of their research from English to Spanish. Together they imagined how to construct a PSA that would be understood by both Spanish-speaking and English-speaking audiences.

Presentar

The fourth stage of the translanguaging instructional design cycle is presentar, which involves students in peer editing, conferencing, rewriting, and presenting their work, with attention to the choices they make about using language. Stephanie's translanguaging design helped students pool their linguistic resources and present their work orally in English in several ways. First, she had groups present *collaboratively*, rather than individually. This was beneficial for two reasons. First, it lessened the anxiety that some students felt about presenting. For those students newer to English, like Noemí and Luis, sharing responsibility with three other people enabled them to participate in the presentation with much less worry. Second, it gave *all* students an opportunity to practice their oral language for an authentic purpose. Following are some of the steps that Stephanie and her students took to make these presentations successful.

- Stephanie provided specific sentence frames for students that supported their presentations. Students whose performances in English were emerging, like Luis, first expressed themselves in Spanish and then used the English sentence frames and added short, English responses, with the help of other group members.
- During presentations, Noemí and Luis read their prepared English responses, but clarified and expanded on their thinking in Spanish.
- Teresita, Mariana, and Eddy presented in English and built on Noemí's and Luis' Spanish comments by summarizing them in English.

We want to stress the importance of making any presentation an opportunity for *all* students to practice English and the other language orally for a variety of audiences (monolingual audiences, bilingual audiences made up of monolingual speakers of one language or another, and bilingual-speaking audiences). This participation improves their confidence as public speakers and gives them practice in adapting language to the needs of listeners.

Stephanie carefully guided her students' performances throughout the unit so that each task would provide a foundation for the public presentation. First, students made an informal, in-class presentation for their bilingual peers using the full features of their linguistic repertoires. Second, they made a more public presentation, using English and Spanish, during the school's morning announcements. Third, they prepared a formal presentation in English for the larger school community. Finally, they made a presentation to the local community outside of school that leveraged translanguaging practices to engage the very diverse community. These different types of task-based performances provide bilingual students with opportunities to make the "same" presentation to diverse audiences, drawing on their language resources to reach a larger and more diverse audience than a monolingual English or Spanish presentation would allow. These presentations, or performances, provide opportunities for authentic assessment throughout the unit.

Implementar

The implementar stage moves students' work from the classroom to the larger community. This action-based step does not have to be monumental—it merely means that students' work should be applied in authentic ways. In this instructional unit, Stephanie and her students used a number of translanguaging strategies to implementar, for example, displaying their bilingual PSAs around the school building. Because students' PSAs were both bilingual *and* geared toward the local audience of the school (fellow students, teachers, administrators), their placement around the building contributed to the **multilingual ecology** of the school and raised awareness about important issues that affected community members. In addition, when Mariana and Luis used the school's morning announcements to explain the genre of the PSA and the purpose of their work in both Spanish and English, they used their bilingualism to communicate with their school community about important issues of sustainability and environmentalism. Rather than mere social studies students, Mariana, Luis, and their classmates became *activists*, informing their community at the local level. We saw the following translanguaging strategies in Stephanie's instructional design at the implementar stage:

- Students posted their bilingual PSAs around the school building, strategically placing certain PSAs in particular locations (e.g., a PSA on the use of pesticides in farming and the dangers to the environment and to health was posted in the cafeteria; a PSA about recycling was posted above trash cans at the entrance to the building).

- Mariana and Luis prepared a bilingual statement explaining the PSA genre and the class' work with the genre. They gave examples of PSAs that were posted around the school and previewed the larger culminating design that their class would present.

Like Stephanie, teachers in translanguaging classrooms can use the translanguaging instructional design cycle to plan and deliver their week-to-week instruction within a specific unit of instruction *and* to plan and deliver their entire unit.

Translanguaging Pedagogical Strategies

Teachers choose different translanguaging strategies during different stages of this cycle to help students use *all* of their languages and ways of knowing to learn.

Translanguaging to Explorar

- Build background knowledge by engaging students in meaningful collaborative dialogue that includes translanguaging and the use of all students' language resources.
- Show short video clips with subtitles in English and students' home languages.
- Post content-related pictures around the classroom and do a gallery walk and discussion in any language.
- Have student groups brainstorm their prior knowledge on a topic in any language.
- Provide an engaging discussion question in one language and ask students to discuss it in any language.
- Provide content-related readings and have students make connections to text and analyze the text in any language.
- Create a multilingual listening center composed of fiction and nonfiction texts, narratives of community members, podcasts, interviews, and music that are relevant to the topic being explored.
- Use graphic organizers to help students track their learning on a topic (e.g., KWL charts, semantic maps, word walls) and provide opportunities to do so in all languages.
- Invite community leaders to talk about local issues or topics using their own language practices.

Translanguaging to Evaluar

- Have students compare different texts on one topic. Focus students' comparison on what perspectives are included and excluded, what linguistic and stylistic choices are being made, and what readers take away from each text.
- Whenever possible, provide students with multilingual versions of reading texts to use as needed or to use for textual contrastive analysis.
- Have students do outside research on a topic. Provide relevant, bilingual websites or have students find their own. Have students present on how new research supports, refutes, or adds to what is covered in a textbook or set of readings.
- Provide students with "counter-stories" or alternative points of view on a topic. This can be done in English and the students' home languages through readings; guest speakers; and/or multimedia such as podcasts, video clips, film, and so forth.
- Come up with a set of questions that can help students think critically about a text of any kind. Make the use of these questions a routine when encountering a text or the overall topic.

Translanguaging to Imaginar

- Plan activities that can be differentiated for students according to what they can do with content and language. Make sure that there are ways for all students to participate meaningfully in any activity.
- Have students work in groups or partnerships to brainstorm, plan, draft, and revise an assignment, project, piece of writing, and so forth. No matter the language in which the final product is presented, students can use all of the languages in their linguistic repertoires to create that product.
- Provide students with models of what you want them to create for their performances. This could be a mentor text, a teacher-created resource, a sample poster, or anything that provides an example of what students should be working toward.
- Have students write stories with bilingual characters or situations where other language practices have to be used.
- Encourage students to write performance pieces, for example, plays or readers' theater, that include translanguaging to give voice to bilingual characters.
- Have peers review the translanguaging used in written texts to verify meaning.

Translanguaging to Presentar

- Provide time for students to engage in peer editing, revision, and rewriting using all their language practices, and then redesign based on feedback from you and their peers.
- Have students present collaboratively, with different students taking on different roles. These roles should be appropriately differentiated according to their oracy, literacy, and content knowledge.
- Make linguistic and stylistic choices part of students' presentation grade, which can enhance students' metalinguistic awareness.
- Provide students with a presentation outline, format, or set of appropriate sentence starters in English and their home languages.
- Have students create PowerPoint presentations for their multilingual families, using translanguaging for meaning-making and images and multimodal texts for support.
- Encourage students to do their best to present in one language (English), but allow them to expand on, clarify, or further explain their ideas in the other language (Spanish).

Translanguaging to Implementar

- Attach some kind of action to students' learning. For example, lessons can be expanded by asking students to
  - Interview family members about an instructional topic using appropriate language practices and report findings back to the class
  - Share their writing on different public websites, blogs, Facebook pages, or other social media sites, being mindful of choice of language practices for different audiences
  - Write emails or use social media to communicate with both teacher and peers about their learning, using appropriate language practices
- Expand students' learning to the school community by
  - Posting student work with translanguaged texts around the school
  - Encouraging students to submit translanguaged work to a school newspaper, magazine, or website
  - Creating opportunities for students to discuss their translanguaged work in other classrooms or with teachers and administrators

- Compiling translanguaged student work into bound books that can be accessible in a school library or resource center
- Expand students' learning to the larger community by
  - Partnering with local organizations whose work is relevant to the classroom topic/project/subject area and using relevant language practices
  - Planning bilingual events that feature student work and are open to students' families and other community members
  - Helping students submit their work to local newspapers, websites, radio stations, TV stations, and funding organizations, using appropriate language resources

These strategies promote the connections among teachers, students, families and communities, as well as across language and cultural practices, that translanguaging classrooms require.

ASSESSING FROM MANY ANGLES

Like Carla's assessment practices discussed in Chapter 6, Stephanie's pedagogy includes others' voices in *assessing from many angles*. Stephanie's authentic assessment of student learning is never done in isolation. Stephanie relies on students themselves, on the group, and on families as part of her inclusive class assessment of what the students are learning. Because her instruction leverages authentic collaborative performances in groups, she can also assess whether students are performing independently, with moderate assistance from other people or resources, or at a novice stage.

As we saw in the opening vignette, Stephanie's informal assessment practices differentiate between language and content understanding by ensuring that specific language features do not become a barrier to assessing what students know about content. Moreover, when assessing language performances, Stephanie makes sure to differentiate between students' ways of using language to express complex thoughts, make inferences, associate ideas, explain, persuade, and so forth—general linguistic performance—and the use of specific, school-sanctioned English language features. Although Spanish is not an official language of instruction in Stephanie's class, her design for formal and informal assessment reflects the power of translanguaging for learning in this English-medium classroom.

When teaching or assessing within a translanguaging unit, a teacher taps into his or her stance, enacts the design, and uses the third strand—shifts—to weave the strong rope that pulls students' learning forward along the translanguaging progressions.

SHIFTS: GOING WITH THE FLOW OF THE TRANSLANGUAGING CORRIENTE

Throughout the translanguaging instructional design cycle, Stephanie served as facilitator for the class' inquiries and learning. Rather than present a scripted, teacher-centered lesson, Stephanie provided students with information (the model PSAs and questions that made students think about those PSAs) and let them run with it. For example, when a student in the class voiced his anger about the Latino youth portrayed in the teen pregnancy PSA, Stephanie built on that anger to help the class understand the purpose of the genre. Rather than deflect the question or avoid a difficult conversation, Stephanie opened the question up to the presenting group and facilitated an important discussion of how ideology is transmitted through discourse. This unplanned shift, and others like it, contributed to the sense that Stephanie and her students were a part of a small, tight-knit community of thinkers who were, as Stephanie puts it, "moving and shaking our society." This kind of shift is also clearly connected to Stephanie's stance, in that she believes that the *classroom is a democratic space where teachers and students juntos create knowledge, challenge traditional hierarchies, and work toward a more just society.*

A second shift is Stephanie's linguistic flexibility that is also tied, of course, to her stance. Because Stephanie is not a Spanish speaker, she could not always understand her students' contributions to classroom discussions around content. However, Stephanie knew how important it was for students to draw on *all* their languages at *all* times to make meaning and share their ideas. For this reason, Stephanie often encouraged students to use Spanish to express their content knowledge and relied on other students in the class for help understanding their comments. For example, when Noemí presented her group's PSA, she sometimes elaborated on her ideas in Spanish. Rather than impose a rigid language policy that forced Noemí to speak English only, Stephanie sat back and let her express herself on her own terms, bilingually. This shift, the embracing of flexibility in response to students' linguistic needs, contributed to the sense that all voices were welcome and valuable in the shared classroom space.

Like Stephanie, teachers in translanguaging classrooms must adapt their instruction to the flow of the translanguaging corriente. To do so requires that teachers think of their classrooms as a tight community of thinkers who are exploring content on their own terms. As co-learners, teachers in translanguaging classrooms also rely on students and other resources, such as technology, to ensure that all students learn.

ENACTING A TRANSLANGUAGING PEDAGOGY IN YOUR CLASSROOM

We have provided this integrated view of Stephanie's translanguaging pedagogy in action as a model to help you develop your own translanguaging pedagogy. To support your work, a blank protocol that aids teacher reflection and planning for translanguaging is included in Appendix A.7.1. Teachers can use this protocol to document how they use (or do not use) translanguaging, and to generate concrete ideas for new ways to use it. This tool encourages you to consider the various aspects of your pedagogy—your own stance, design, and shifts—and think critically about whether those aspects make space for the translanguaging corriente to flow. Specifically, when examining your own stance, to what degree do you

- Think of students' languages and cultural practices as equally valuable and interrelated?
- Value and include students' families and communities in their education?
- Challenge traditional hierarchies, such as teacher/student, English/additional language, native/non-native speaker, ELL/English fluent learner, and work toward a more just classroom and society?

When examining your own design, to what degree do you

- Design the physical space of the classroom for collaboration and create a multilingual and multimodal ecology?
- Design instruction (e.g., in unit planning, activities, instructional strategies) so that all learning promotes translanguaging?
- Design assessments that differentiate between general linguistic and language-specific performances?
- Design assessments that evaluate whether students perform tasks independently, with moderate assistance, or at novice levels?

Finally, when examining the moment-to-moment interaction in your classroom, to what degree do you use shifts to allow for flexibility and changes to your design that are responsive to students' needs, interests, and language practices?

These are not easy questions, and we encourage you to explore them within a professional learning community of teachers who are also thinking deeply about their own practices. Asking questions about our own pedagogy helps us grow as educators, which can only benefit the bilingual students in our classrooms.

CONCLUSION

In this chapter, we walked you through a unit of instruction in Stephanie's translanguaging classroom, and we demonstrated how her translanguaging pedagogy—her stance, design, and shifts—is integral to the success of her classroom. We also explored how she uses specific translanguaging pedagogical strategies across the five stages of the translanguaging instructional design cycle. We closely linked this translanguaging instructional design with the translanguaging assessment design. Stephanie's integrated translanguaging pedagogy helped students draw on their linguistic strengths, connect new learning to their own local knowledge, and use their unique positions as Latino bilinguals to analyze a new genre with a critical eye.

We also drew from Stephanie's instruction to identify the general principles that teachers in translanguaging classrooms should hold within each of three strands:

1. *Stance:* bringing juntos students, languages, and content
2. *Design:* purposefully and strategically including translanguaging in unit planning, stages of instruction, classroom activities, and student performance assessments
3. *Shifts:* responding to students' needs and interests

Lastly, we provided you with a protocol for reflection and planning that you can use to think deeply about your own instruction. You can then use these reflections and observations to make positive changes that strengthen how you work with the translanguaging corriente in your specific context.

QUESTIONS AND ACTIVITIES

1. How do you envision translanguaging practices occurring in your classroom? What opportunities exist? What challenges? How might you build on these opportunities and work to address these challenges?

2. What kinds of texts, genres, or resources do you think lend themselves to translanguaging practices? How might you incorporate these into a unit or lesson?

TAKING ACTION

1. Design a lesson using translanguaging. Work off of the lesson planning structure you already use and make space for translanguaging in each aspect of your instruction.

2. On your own or with a group of colleagues, fill out Appendix A.7.1, Reflecting and Planning for a Translanguaging Pedagogy. Work through each strand of the translanguaging pedagogy (stance, design, and shifts) and discuss where you are now and how to make room for the translanguaging corriente in your classroom.

PART III

REIMAGINING TEACHING AND LEARNING THROUGH TRANSLANGUAGING

CHAPTER 8

Standards in the Translanguaging Classroom

LEARNING OBJECTIVES

- Distinguish how teachers in traditional monolingual and bilingual classrooms use standards from how teachers in translanguaging classrooms use them

- Describe how a translanguaging perspective on standards helps teachers address the first purpose of translanguaging—to support students as they engage with complex content and texts.

- Explain how teachers can use their translanguaging stance, design, and shifts to help students meet or exceed the expectations of state content and language standards

- Design lessons that expand and localize the standards by drawing on and extending familiar language and cultural practices

Good teachers use standards to help them focus and organize their instruction. A set of standards can help you think big and highlight those practices that will help your students engage with literacy and content in deep, authentic ways. These days, however, it is easy to feel like standards are using *us* more than we are using *them*. It is important for all teachers, especially those teaching emergent bilingual students, to "take back" standards, to reclaim them as part of the toolkit of good instruction. Here we reimagine how standards can be used in a **translanguaging classroom** and we come to see them as a way to meet students where they are *and* build paths toward new understanding.

In this chapter, we return to *Stephanie's Environmentalism: Then and Now* unit design that we introduced in Chapter 7. We focus on how Stephanie uses content standards to set goals and create a strong, engaging, culturally sustaining translanguaging unit of instruction.

Let's look more closely at Stephanie's classroom practices to see how she uses these standards and her translanguaging stance, design, and shifts to address the first purpose of translanguaging—to support students as they engage with and comprehend complex content and texts. As you read about Stephanie's planning process using standards, we encourage you to think further about how *you* would use standards in the development of your translanguaging unit.

STANCE: JUNTOS TO "TALK THE TALK" AND "WALK THE WALK"

When standards affect everything from testing to graduation to teacher ratings, we naturally come to view them as the benchmarks of academic success. Though helping students meet standards is important, it is essential to remember that that these standards, and especially the standardized tests used to evaluate student performance relative to these standards, are not infallible, particularly with regard to **emergent bilinguals**. If we think of scores on standardized tests as the *only* measure of success, we may see our students through a deficit lens—lacking something, missing something, behind, or below. In other words, this standardized test lens emphasizes what students *don't have* rather than what they know and can do. This is especially the case for emergent bilinguals, whose developing English—often described in terms of a lack of English language proficiency—can become the defining characteristic of their academic identities in a standards-driven world.

Taking a **translanguaging stance** means trading this deficit lens for one that highlights students' strengths and ways of knowing. It means viewing students' **dynamic bilingualism** as an advantage, rather than as a problem to be solved. It also means using that dynamic bilingualism to ensure that students learn. And it means starting by designing challenging and relevant instructional units while being mindful of standards, rather than starting with the standards themselves in isolation of content and purpose. In sum, it means making the standards work for students, rather than the other way around.

In the following vignette, we see how Stephanie's use of standards arose from her understanding of what her students knew, what they were passionate about, and what she thought would be important to their growth as thinkers and active, informed citizens. Stephanie's stance toward the standards also reflects her passion and personal goal of living a life of which she can be proud.

In every unit she taught, Stephanie noticed her 11th-grade students found ways to make connections between the content they were learning and current events; stories they had been told by their families; historical events from the United States and their home countries; and pop culture like music, movies, and TV (both English language channels and Spanish ones like Univisión and Telemundo). Seeing how excited they were when they brought up these connections, Stephanie knew she had to build on her students' knowledge, no matter what content she introduced in English. Recently, Stephanie was moved by a documentary she saw about a controversial aspect of the environmental movement and knew that her students would jump at the chance to discuss a part of history that is not usually afforded much time in social studies classrooms. Stephanie also knew that the New York State Social Studies Standards (NYS SSS) addressed the study of geography and civics, so a unit on sustainability and environmentalism would help her students meet these content-area standards. When looking through the textbook, however, Stephanie found the section on environmentalism to be lacking. There was a short discussion of the history of the environmental movement, but Stephanie couldn't find a trace of the kind of passion and urgency she had seen in the documentary. Thus, Stephanie went about designing a unit, *Environmentalism: Then and Now* that addressed both the Common Core State Standards (CCSS) for literacy in social studies and the New York State content-area standards through the study of the past and present of the environmental movement. The unit included an action-based culminating project and, of course, a translanguaging pedagogical framework.

When asked about the inception of this unit, Stephanie recounted:

I knew that the history of the environmental movement was often left out of social studies curricula, so I thought I'd design a unit that taught us about the history and pushed us to put ourselves into the movement *today*—"walking the walk" through culminating projects that could actually do something for the community.

This idea of "walking the walk" meant that Stephanie wanted her students to do *more* than just "talk the talk," that is, more than just meet the standards by learning about and discussing the environmental movement. Stephanie believed that deep student learning would occur from *taking action*. By encouraging her students to look at new content with a critical eye, designing a project that required local action, and using local ways of languaging, she hoped her students would be emboldened and inspired to think about real change. In this way, Stephanie used translanguaging to support her students' bilingual identities and work toward social justice.

Though Stephanie did not start with the standards themselves, they were an integral part of her planning. She knew that having both CCSS and state social studies standards in her unit was necessary for herself and her students. Stephanie enacted her belief that designing a critical and creative unit on a timely and important issue would engage her students and allow them to meet the standards' requirements, but prevent the standards from taking over the unit. She also believed that her emphasis on students' use of Spanish and English in interrelationship and the inclusion of community and families would play a similar role. Without access to both Spanish and English, many of Stephanie's students would be unable to engage with complex content and texts to meet the rigorous standards set forth by both New York State and the Common Core. Thus, Stephanie uses translanguaging to ensure deep understanding of content. In addition to accessing the content, students' use of all their language practices allows them to go *beyond* the standards, opening up opportunities to hear different voices and stories, compare different perspectives, and take action that benefits the local, bilingual community. Furthermore, when bilingual students (and bidialectal African American students in her class) can use the full features of their linguistic repertoires (i.e., their **general linguistic performance**), they are able to offer more experienced academic performances in English (and Spanish for her bilingual students) than if they are allowed only to use features from, in this case, "standard English."

When teachers adopt a translanguaging stance, their instruction can become *more* rigorous than when they rely exclusively on state-mandated standards. Furthermore, teachers can use translanguaging in their standards-aligned classrooms to open up a democratic co-learning space. Learning in translanguaging classrooms can become deeper and more authentic, enabling bilingual students to (1) meet and exceed state-sanctioned standards and complete school-defined tasks ("talk the talk") and (2) take action as informed, critical, and empowered members of their communities and families ("walk the walk").

DESIGN: EXPAND AND LOCALIZE THE STANDARDS

When thinking about the role of standards in the **translanguaging design**, it is important to reiterate that we use standards; standards do not use us. When designing instruction and assessment, we have to take this point a step further and embrace what may seem like a paradox: to use standards well, we must both expand *and* localize them. We must enlarge the scope of the standards, moving past monolingual, monocultural, decontextualized understanding to, as Stephanie put it, "bring home" or *make local* that understanding. This means carefully selecting standards and aligning them to an instructional unit that draws on students' language practices, funds of knowledge, communities, families, and concerns to help them understand and meet those standards *on their own terms and with their own language practices*.

Designing a Translanguaging Unit Starting from the Local

Stephanie begins designing every unit by drawing on her knowledge of her students. As she began gathering resources for her *Environmentalism: Then and Now* unit, Stephanie realized that a general study of the environmental movement would not be enough to engage and stimulate her students. In her words, she needed to find a lens that would "bring the issues home" for her students.

After talking with her fellow teachers, running ideas by some of her students, and doing additional research, Stephanie decided that in addition to learning the history of the movement, the unit would focus on current environmental issues that disproportionately affected Latinos, such as air and water pollution and pesticide poisoning, as well as those that affected the students' local community in New York City. Because she knew that her students would already have connections to these kinds of topics, Stephanie saw this focus as a connection between what students already knew and what they would learn. She also saw this unit as an opportunity to help her students expand their passion for social justice and learn about how change could be made on the community level.

With this new emphasis on the "local," Stephanie turned her attention to the content understanding she wanted her students to grasp and the language and literacy she knew they would need to best express their understanding of these important topics.

Using the Standards to Meet Students' Needs

Stephanie's planning around standards arose organically from the understanding she wanted students to gain from the unit. Once Stephanie had decided on her focus and found a few anchor texts in English, she looked for supplementary texts in Spanish and asked her bilingual colleagues, as well as some of her experienced bilingual students, to check them out for her. She also looked for relevant passages on the topic in the social studies textbook and reviewed the CCSS for literacy in social studies.

As Stephanie read through the list, she saw that many of the standards already applied to what she wanted her students to do in the unit. For example, one of the unit goals was for students to synthesize information from multiple sources—the documentary, textbook, public service announcements (PSAs), supplemental readings, music, and so forth—to get a holistic view of the topic. Stephanie could see this goal clearly in CCSS.ELA-Literacy.RH.11–12.7, which reads, *Integrate and evaluate multiple sources of information in diverse formats and media (e.g., visually, quantitatively, as well as in words) to address a question or solve a problem.* After Stephanie found other CCSS that lent themselves to the unit (e.g., CCSS.ELA-Literacy.RH.11–12.2, CCSS.ELA-Literacy.RH.11–12.9), she moved on to the NYS SSS. Stephanie thought about the resources she already had—and the understanding she wanted the class to grasp—and, again, found standards that met her students' needs. For example, Stephanie knew she wanted her students to use their understanding of environmentalism and sustainability to locate a problem in the school or community and come up with possible solutions.

With her students' local needs clearly in mind, Stephanie selected the following NYS SSS to include in her *Environmentalism: Then and Now* unit.

> 3.1.6: Students explain how technological change affects people, places, and regions.
>
> 3.2.3: Students select and design maps, graphs, tables, charts, diagrams, and other graphic representations to present geographic information.
>
> 4.1.3: Students understand the nature of scarcity and how nations of the world make choices, which involve economic and social costs and benefits.
>
> 5.3.4: Students explore how citizens influence public policy in a representative democracy.
>
> 5.4.6: Students prepare a plan of action that defines an issue or problem, suggests alternative solutions or courses of action, evaluates the consequences for each alternative solution or course of action, prioritizes the solutions based on established criteria, and proposes an action plan to address the issue or resolve the problem

Figure 8.1 shows how Stephanie expands and localizes content-area standards by choosing activities that connect this content standard to students' lives, in this case with a focus on one of the NYS SSS.

Stephanie also expanded and localized the standards through her choice of texts, an important element in her unit design. Stephanie used the required English-language social studies textbook in the *Environmentalism: Then and Now* unit. However, she, knew that to localize the content (as well as help build students' literacy in English), she would need to supplement with multimodal texts—videos, film, music, tables, graphs, maps, blogs, websites, and so forth—in English and Spanish. To this end, Stephanie chose high-interest texts from different genres and with different levels of complexity, as we show in Figure 8.2.

Seeing Content Standards through a Language Lens

Although many of us have experience creating language objectives that are language-specific (e.g., in English or Spanish), most language objectives we see in classrooms do not focus on language *practices*, the ways that students use oral and written language for academic purposes. All teachers need to identify the language practices necessary for all students to meet every standard successfully. This isn't always easy. As Gibbons (2009) writes, "the fish doesn't recognize the water in which it swims" (p. 46), meaning that many of us can't point out the specific language practices that we use to communicate and make meaning on a daily basis. However, as we saw in Chapter 3, teachers of bilingual students—especially emergent bilinguals—can look closely at the content and literacy standards to highlight the kinds of language practices that students at different positions along the **dynamic translanguaging progressions** will need to engage with and comprehend the complex content and texts included in an instructional unit.

New York State Social Studies Standard: 3.2.3
Students select and design maps, graphs, tables, charts, diagrams, and other graphic representations to present geographic information.

Expand and Localize

- Analyze U.S. maps for areas of air pollution and compare to demographic factors, such as language, race (including Latinos and non-Latinos), and socioeconomic levels.
- Survey school and local communities and make graphs and charts that represent percentages of people who suffer from pollution-related diseases like asthma and compare those to percentages in other areas (surrounding areas and across the United States).
- Survey Latinos and non-Latinos in the school and local communities, using both Spanish and English, and represent the percentages of asthma sufferers in each group.
- Use data (those collected by students and those found through research) to support plans of action for increased sustainability in school/local communities.

Figure 8.1   Connecting content standards to students' lives.

Standards-based English-language social studies textbook

Expand and Localize

- Newspaper articles from local Spanish and English publications
- Public service announcements in Spanish and English
- Bilingual readings on César Chávez and the Farm Worker's Association
- Excerpts from documentary films such as *An Inconvenient Truth* and *Food, Inc.*
- Bilingual music and poetry with messages about the environment, community action, and social change
- Thematically relevant podcasts
- Blogs, websites, social media, and other internet resources about local environmental/sustainability projects and campaigns

Figure 8.2   Supplementing a standards-aligned textbook with multimodal bilingual texts.

Here we see how Stephanie views the content standards included in the *Environmentalism: Then and Now* unit through a language lens:

Prepared with ideas for content understanding, Stephanie began to think deeply about the language practices her students would need to meet the standards. She also thought about her students, who used English and Spanish differently, and whose performances she had evaluated at different places on the dynamic translanguaging progressions. For example, even though **Eddy** was confident using English in class, he struggled with writing. **Noemí** was one of the strongest writers in class in Spanish, but her English literacy performances were still developing. Other students had different strengths and needed practice with different kinds of language. With her specific students in mind, Stephanie looked again at the social studies and Common Core standards she had chosen, the texts and resources she planned to use, and the project students would complete at the end of the unit and brainstormed what kinds of language practices all students would need to be successful.

Let's look more closely at the NYS SSS and the CCSS that Stephanie has included in her translanguaging unit plan. We see that all students will need to use oral and written (including graphic) language to *explain, explore, integrate,* and *evaluate* information, as well as *select* and *design* graphic representations. We see that the language demands of NYS SSS 5.4.6 are particularly complex. As noted earlier, to meet this content standard, students will need to use language to prepare a plan of action that

- Defines an issue or problem
- Suggests alternative solutions or courses of action
- Evaluates the consequences for each solution or course of action
- Prioritizes the solutions based on established criteria
- Proposes an action plan to address the issue or resolve the problem

Stephanie knows that the complex language performances this standard demands require language practices that may be particularly challenging for her emergent bilinguals. Stephanie also knows that it is unrealistic for her to expect that some of her students, for example, Eddy, Noemí, Mariana, Luis, and Teresita, will be able to perform these language functions with the same levels of expertise.

Stephanie determined how she would need to differentiate instruction and assessment for students in the different activities in the unit, considering their general linguistic performances and their language-specific performances in English and Spanish. Realistically, Stephanie couldn't create individual language objectives for each student. Therefore, she loosely grouped her students into the five different placements along the dynamic translanguaging progressions: *entering, emerging, developing,*[1] *expanding,* and *commanding.* She used these groupings to think about the expectations, scaffolds, and assessments she would use throughout the unit to help her meet students where they were and enable them to access content, share their ideas, and strengthen their oracy and literacy performances in English.

As we discussed in Chapter 3, teachers can use the Can-Do descriptors or model performance indicators articulated by their state-mandated English

---

[1]Recall that we use the term *developing* on the dynamic translanguaging progressions rather than the term *transitioning,* used by the New York progressions in new and home languages, to emphasize that students never transition from one language to another; they always develop both languages side by side.

language development (ELD) systems (e.g., WIDA, ELPA 21, New York New and Home Language Arts Progressions [NLAP and HLAP]) to get a preliminary idea of what students at different stages of development should be able to do with English (and other languages) relative to the content-area standards used in their state. Stephanie loosely draws on the New York State system, because the progressions provide model performance indicators in the new and home languages, and because she teaches in New York.[2] Teachers must also remember how the dynamic translanguaging progressions complement and extend these state-mandated ELD systems, for example, in their distinction between general linguistic and language-specific performances.

Creating Translanguaging Objectives

While New York's NLAP and HLAP can help teachers think about what students can do in each of their specific languages relative to content standards, they may still be interpreted as focusing on the new and home languages as separate and separable entities. However, teachers in translanguaging classrooms understand that bilingual students have one holistic **language repertoire** that includes general linguistic and language-specific performances, and that they can **leverage** students' general linguistic performances for learning. Therefore, in addition to creating language objectives that target specific languages like Spanish and English, these teachers also create **translanguaging objectives**:

Stephanie looked for opportunities for her students to use all their language practices, not only to help them communicate and express their thinking, but also to look at the topic from multiple points of view, write for different audiences, and compare environmentalism and sustainability across different cultures. Thus, she chose texts, planned lessons and activities, and planned the details of the culminating design so that students could use all of their languages to dig deeper into the content and access it on a variety of levels. To keep students' language practices front and center in the unit, Stephanie challenged herself to create *translanguaging objectives* for the unit. This meant thinking of ways that students' existing language practices could be used to meet content standards and learn school-sanctioned language practices in English. For example, Stephanie decided that students would be required to create *bilingual* culminating projects, action plans, and presentations for improving the environmental sustainability of the school or local community that would reach and be understood by a diverse, multilingual audience.

In addition to identifying the kind of language practices necessary for students to comprehend content in English, Stephanie knows how important it is for them to use all their language practices to engage deeply with that content. Stephanie believes that, more so than monolingual students, bilingual students can understand a concept from more than one linguistic and cultural perspective. In effect, bilingual students have the ability to see multiple sides of an issue because of the multiple worlds they inhabit. Stephanie knew that this deeper understanding of the content would not only help students better meet the standards, but would also engage them with the learning in a more meaningful way.

---

[2]Remember that the New York progressions only correspond to language arts, and Stephanie needs to determine what her students can do with language relative to the social studies standards. No system is perfect, but all can provide useful guidance.

Stephanie's use of translanguaging objectives *expands* on the use of language objectives, which focus mainly on English, and only occasionally on another language like Spanish. Translanguaging objectives leverage students' general linguistic performance, asking them to use all their language practices to do *more* with the standard than they could through the use of only one language. Translanguaging objectives also provide opportunities for all students to engage meaningfully with the content, no matter their experience with English.

There is an integral relationship between content standards and translanguaging objectives in the translanguaging classroom. Content standards are the "what" of instruction and translanguaging objectives are the "how," that is, how to leverage students' general linguistic performance for learning within this unit of instruction. For example, as shown in Table 8.1, one of the content standards targeted in the *Environmentalism: Then and Now* unit of instruction is CCSS ELA-Literacy.RH.11–12.7. As noted earlier, it asks students to *integrate and evaluate multiple sources of information presented in diverse formats and media (e.g., visually, quantitatively, as well as in words) to address a question or solve a problem.* Stephanie then generated the following translanguaging objectives that focus on how bilingual students would draw on their general linguistic performances to meet this standard:

- Students will use their oral and written Spanish and English to analyze and critique both the content and the discourse of bilingual PSAs.
- Students will create bilingual texts across a variety of genres (PSAs, posters, persuasive essays, oral presentations and short dramatic plays) and rationalize their linguistic choices.

As we saw in Chapter 7, Stephanie found several PSAs, in both print and video form, in Spanish and English.

Because students would eventually create their own bilingual PSAs, Stephanie asked students to synthesize different kinds of information into a relatively small space (a 1-page print PSA), and to use language persuasively to move an audience to think about an issue in a new light. Because students' audiences (the school and local community) were bilingual, Stephanie required students to look at PSAs in both languages to analyze persuasive tactics for these different audiences. Using textual evidence (i.e., the PSAs in both languages), Stephanie asked her students to demonstrate whether and how the PSAs directed at Spanish-speaking Latinos differ from those directed at English-speaking Latinos. Then, using the concrete differences they identified in the texts, Stephanie asked her students to explain why one audience might be moved by one tactic rather than another. Through the use of both

TABLE 8.1   **Relationship between Content Standards and Translanguaging Objectives**

Content Standards: *The What* ⟺	Translanguaging Objectives: *The How*
CCLS ELA-Literacy.RH.11–12.7 • Integrate and evaluate multiple sources of information presented in diverse formats and media (e.g., visually, quantitatively, as well as in words) to address a question or solve a problem.	• Students will use their oral and written Spanish and English to analyze and critique both the content and the discourse of bilingual PSAs. • Students will create bilingual texts across a variety of genres (PSAs, posters, persuasive essays, oral presentations, and short dramatic plays) and rationalize their linguistic choices.

PSAs, public service announcements.

languages—with a critical focus on discourse—Stephanie was able to expand on this standard, deepening what it meant to *evaluate* sources of information and see information in *diverse formats*. Students were prepared to create bilingual PSAs using the most persuasive features for different audiences.

SHIFTS: SEIZING THE MOMENT

To this point we have seen how the translanguaging design for instruction and assessment allows teachers to purposefully and strategically leverage students' bilingualism to meet or exceed standards. This section turns to the moment-by-moment **translanguaging shifts** that teachers in translanguaging classrooms make to respond to the dynamic flow of bilingual students' language practices throughout the course of unit implementation. For example, teachers may shift course when they

- Get informal feedback on unit planning and implementation through conversations with colleagues *and* students
- Make spontaneous choices about language use in classroom activities, such as when to ask for translations of ideas and how to facilitate whole class brainstorming and participation
- Relinquish the role of "expert" and enlist the help of bilingual students
- Seize the moment to make a specific language or content turn
- Reference students' questions and connections throughout planning and instruction

The shift we want to focus on here is Stephanie's way of using language in the classroom. Remember that Stephanie is one of the few people in her classroom who is not bilingual—a fact she thinks about often. When Stephanie plans activities to help students meet standards and engage with complex content and texts, she knows that she needs to step back and allow students to use language in ways that benefit them the most. Other teachers and administrators constantly question Stephanie about her stance on language in the classroom. When asked about this, Stephanie said,

When I first started teaching, I was really nervous that I couldn't understand everything my students said. I kept thinking, "How can I teach them if I can't understand them?" Now though, I just let them go if they're on a roll—if I can tell they're really into a discussion or a debate, I just sit back and listen. Later, if I feel like it's something I can build on, I'll ask a student like Teresita or Eddy to fill me in on what I missed.

Stephanie sees her flexibility as integral to her strong relationships with students; to students' rapport with one another; to the high levels of engagement and participation she sees; and, of course, to students' ability to tackle rigorous, complex content and demonstrate their understanding in ways that align with standards. By stepping back and allowing students to use language in their own way, Stephanie is *seizing a translanguaging moment* and not only honoring the authentic language practices of her students, but making space for them to grapple with ideas and make sense of new information in a deeper way than they could if they were forced to use only one language.

Aligning instruction to standards is important. However, teachers in translanguaging classrooms also know that they must make shifts in their instruction so that they can work with, and not against, the **translanguaging corriente**. Teachers can use translanguaging shifts spontaneously to make sure that bilingual students meet and *exceed* standards.

STANDARDS AND CURRICULA: A CAUTIONARY NOTE

One unfortunate result of the implementation of standards has been that many states have adopted commercial curricula that are prescriptive and pre-planned. Most Common Core–aligned curricula have been developed for elementary schools, so fortunately Stephanie is still free to think creatively about how to align her curriculum and instruction to the standards. However, her friend, *Sarah*, teaches 3rd grade in an elementary school in the same school district, and there the school administration has adopted a ready-made curriculum that all teachers must use in the same way. Although Sarah teaches in an English-medium classroom, there is tremendous linguistic diversity among her students, as is the case with Stephanie's class. Some of Sarah's students come from homes where only English is spoken and others from homes where languages other than English are spoken. Some speak and write English very well; others speak English fluently but read and write English at *emerging* and *entering* levels. Some of Sarah's students have been classified as English language learners and get support in English as a second language programs. Despite this diversity, Sarah is expected to follow the scripted curriculum in the same way for all her students, regardless of their individual language performances.

Sarah's colleague, *Lina*, teaches bilingual 3rd grade in the same school. Lina is also expected to use the district curriculum, but she has not found texts in Spanish that readily align to the topics of the English curriculum. And she has not found a way to teach this curriculum in two languages that makes pedagogical sense. To teach bilingually, Lina is expected to translate the English anchor texts to Spanish, but, of course, something is lost in translation and the texts in two languages are not in any way equivalent. Lina is struggling to find a balance between English and Spanish in her dual-language bilingual classroom. However, the space for Spanish is shrinking every day, while attention is focused on getting students to achieve standards in English only. Not only are these scripted curricula taxing the bilingual children more than the monolingual children, but bilingual teachers are also being burdened. When these planned curricula are adopted without taking into account either the variation in bilingual students' language performances (in terms of general linguistic and language-specific performances), or the ways that teachers can leverage students' dynamic bilingualism for learning, these curricula burn out teachers and they fail children.

This, of course, creates inequalities among students and teachers. It is imperative that bilingual learners, including emergent bilinguals, meet college and career-readiness standards. But this cannot be done without stretching and transforming the standards-aligned curricula that publishers are producing and selling. Bilingual teachers cannot be expected to carry this burden alone. It is the responsibility of publishers to also produce bilingual curricula that acknowledge the complexity of the dynamic translanguaging progressions, and that are aligned to what bilingual children know and can do, not simply to external standards. It is also the responsibility of districts to provide professional development for all teachers who work with bilingual students to learn how to leverage translanguaging for learning.

Developing standards-based translanguaging instruction like we see in Stephanie's classroom is not easy. It is perhaps faster and cheaper to buy scripted curricula than to prepare teachers who are creative and knowledgeable about translanguaging instruction. But the costs to children and to society are very high. Rather than using bilingual students' language practices to meet and exceed content and language standards, following scripted curricula without regard for the students' diversity will ensure that bilingual children be left behind, and bilingual teachers with them.

CONCLUSION

Standards shape much of what happens in classrooms. In Stephanie's translanguaging classroom, however, standards are shaped by the translanguaging corriente and are not blindly adopted. They are used, but always with a translanguaging *stance* informing their use. Stephanie not only "talks the talk," she also "walks the walk" by *designing* instruction and assessment that takes up the standards, expands and localizes them, and connects them with action-oriented, culturally and linguistically sustaining work, thus adapting them to the translanguaging corriente. Part of the adaptation involves the *shifts* Stephanie makes to seize moments of learning. These moments are unplanned but they expand students' learning and language development opportunities, enabling them to meet standards. Stephanie is always on the lookout to leverage the translanguaging corriente for learning.

For many, standards mean an emphasis on English-only instruction, with teachers blindly following scripted curriculua that is said to be aligned to those standards. But, as Stephanie shows us, this doesn't have to be the case. A translanguaging pedagogy, including a translanguaging stance, design, and shifts, can actually *expand* the power of the standards because teachers use instruction and assessment to leverage students' use of their entire language repertoires, not part of it, to meet their important goals.

QUESTIONS AND ACTIVITIES

1. Compare Stephanie's translanguaging stance, design, and shifts to your pedagogy relative to standards. What does Stephanie do differently from you? What can you learn from Stephanie (and what could *she* learn from *you*)?

2. Review the translanguaging pedagogical strategies across the stages of the translanguaging instructional design cycle that were discussed in Chapter 7. Which strategies do you think would be most helpful to support Stephanie's students in meeting the standards throughout the five stages?

3. Can translanguaging classrooms work with mandated state curricula? If yes, how?

TAKING ACTION

1. On your own or with a colleague, design a lesson or activity in which you *expand* and *localize* a particular standard through the use of translanguaging. If possible, use the translanguaging unit of instruction that you have been developing while reading this book. What differentiation strategies might you need for the bilingual students in your class at different stages of the design cycle?

2. Implement the lesson or activity. Reflect on how you used translanguaging to address the standards. In what ways did translanguaging help advance bilingual students' content and language learning, leverage their bilingualism, promote stronger socio-emotional identity, and work toward social justice?

CHAPTER 9

Content-Area Literacy in the Translanguaging Classroom

LEARNING OBJECTIVES

- Explain how teachers can use translanguaging to teach content-area literacy, specifically through their stance, design, and shifts
- Design activities that support the development of bilingual students' literacy practices for academic purposes by leveraging their dynamic bilingualism

Literacy is a very important part of schooling. It is in school that we learn how to interact with written texts in the ways that academic contexts demand. At home, we may read the newspaper, discuss the news, read and write for informal purposes (e.g., memos, lists, personal journals, letters to families), read and post to Facebook, tweet, and text. However, we seldom use the literacy practices at home that we encounter in school. For example, we are rarely asked by family members to evaluate our ideas using text-based evidence, analyze how texts are constructed, or write a persuasive document that compares and contrasts competing perspectives or approaches on an issue. Yet, these are precisely the types of literacy practices with which students are expected to engage in school.

While all students must reach equally high standards in content, language, and literacy, we know that the bilingual students in our classes are likely to differ considerably in the ways that they can use oracy and literacy for academic purposes—in English and other languages. One important differentiating factor relates to quantity and quality of prior schooling, which of course varies cross culturally. As Street (1984) has so aptly shown, literacy is not autonomous; it is situated in specific contexts. For example, bilingual students who have been educated in good bilingual schools (in the United States or in other countries) will generally be able to read and write for academic purposes in two languages, using appropriate discourse conventions in each language. Bilingual students who have been educated in monolingual schools (e.g., in English in the United States; in Spanish in Mexico) will likely display stronger literacy performances in the language used in their prior schooling. **Emergent bilinguals** who are learning how to read and write in an additional language will need explicit attention to cross-cultural differences in literacy practices in their home and new languages. And **students with incomplete/interrupted formal schooling (SIFE)** generally will need to learn to develop a foundation for literacy in any language, as well as an understanding of cultural norms of schooling.

Educating bilingual students equitably requires identifying and building on the specific content, language, literacy, and cultural strengths these students bring with them to school, and leveraging their **dynamic bilingualism** for academic purposes. This chapter focuses on *Stephanie's* English-medium 11th-grade social studies classroom in New York City, and addresses the second purpose for translanguaging—providing students with opportunities to develop language and literacy practices for academic contexts. We see how Stephanie structures activities that engage her diverse learners with complex texts and literacy practices. We return to the bilingual profiles of our five focal students in Stephanie's class, which illustrate some of the variation teachers can expect to find in their classrooms:

- *Eddy* was born and raised by Dominican parents in a Dominican neighborhood in New York City. He has excellent English oracy and can speak Spanish. Eddy is below grade level in English literacy and is beginning to develop literacy in Spanish.
- *Luis* arrived from El Salvador last year and speaks Spanish. Luis is officially designated as an English language learner (ELL), has been identified as a SIFE, and struggles to read and write academic texts in English and Spanish.
- *Mariana* is of Mexican descent, was born and raised in the United States, and is equally comfortable speaking English and Spanish. Mariana has been officially designated as an ELL since she entered elementary school, and is considered a **long-term ELL** who struggles with literacy in English and Spanish.
- *Noemí* moved to the United States from Ecuador in the 8th grade, is a strong reader in Spanish, and is still classified as an ELL. Noemí's English oracy performances are *expanding*, although she still struggles with English literacy, especially in writing.
- *Teresita* moved to the United States from Guatemala when she was very young, and her oracy and literacy performances in English and Spanish are *commanding*. She is a voracious reader in both languages, scores well on standardized tests, and loves to write poetry.

This chapter demonstrates how Stephanie's **translanguaging stance**, **design**, and **shifts** throughout the *Environmentalism: Then and Now* unit enable all of her students, particularly emergent bilinguals, to engage with and create complex texts. As you read, we encourage you to think about how you can **leverage** your students' bilingualism to promote content-area literacy in your classes.

STANCE: CONTENT AND LITERACY JUNTOS

A defining feature of all **translanguaging classrooms** is the teacher's **juntos** stance, which informs everything from how the teacher views students and their language and cultural practices to the way he or she plans instruction. Here we see how Stephanie's juntos stance is reflected in how she brings content and literacy together in her curriculum and instruction.

Throughout her unit on the history of the environmental movement, Stephanie constantly made connections between the social studies content and students' lives, interests, and concerns. One of the most important connections she made was putting Latinos at the center of the curriculum. In addition to focusing on environmental issues that disproportionately affect Latinos, Stephanie incorporated readings about Latino historical figures that were given little treatment in the standards-aligned textbook. For example, though her social studies textbook provided a short autobiography of César Chávez and briefly outlined his role in fighting for workers' rights, Stephanie felt it was too cursory for such an important voice in the struggle, or as her students referred to it, la lucha. Stephanie decided to devote a unit of instruction to learning about Chávez's life and contributions to both the environmental movement and the struggle for human rights.

Stephanie's stance, which included pride in her students' bilingual Latino identities, strongly informed her instructional design and the ways in which she had students engage with texts. Her choice to *expand* the learning outside the bounds of the textbook was in response to her own and her students' belief that an important figure in la lucha had not been given adequate coverage. By *expanding* the learning to focus on an important Latino figure—who some students, especially those who were not Latino, had never heard of—Stephanie also *localized* the learning. This helped students connect and engage with content and learn about a historical figure whose role in the movement was both important and controversial, and helped affirm the identities of her Latino students. Though Chávez was Mexican American, and most of Stephanie's Latino students are Dominican and others African American, *all* students expressed deep pride as they learned about his legacy. This change to the curriculum through the simultaneous expansion and localization of the content resonated with *all* students and made them more active learners. In this way, Stephanie used translanguaging to make space for students' ways of knowing, which supported their socioemotional development and bilingual identities. Her stance reflects a social justice approach to teaching content. Stephanie supplemented the traditional curriculum with voices and stories that are often underrepresented, and pushed her students to see themselves and people like them as powerful agents of change in society.

Stephanie's stance also influenced the way she approached texts. As she expanded the instruction past the textbook, she made important choices about texts that would supplement students' study of Chávez. Though her students' language and literacy performances were at different positions across the **dynamic translanguaging progressions**, Stephanie believed that each one of them could engage with complex, grade-appropriate content. Here we see how Stephanie chooses texts:

Stephanie did some research and found several websites that had readings about Chávez in both English and Spanish. For example, the entire United Farm Workers website was in both languages and had a great deal of information on Chávez's work. Because she wanted her students to get a full picture of Chávez, rather than the flat rendering she found in the textbook, Stephanie also found articles that examined Chávez's legacy from different angles. Some were glowing retellings of his role in the movement. Others highlighted criticism about Chávez and looked at the controversies around his life and work. While some of the readings she found were in Spanish, many were only in English. As such, Stephanie knew she would have to use different kinds of strategies to help her students—especially emergent bilinguals like Noemí and Luis—access the texts. She knew that her students could handle the content of such nuanced, complex readings; they just needed the language supports to do so.

Stephanie does not "water down" the content and texts that she chooses. Instead, she strategically scaffolds her instruction to support student learning. As we see in the sections that follow, through purposeful student groupings and a variety of translanguaging strategies and activities, Stephanie sets up her students to participate successfully in a rigorous academic experience, no matter what their experiences are with English.

Stephanie's view of bilingualism as a resource for creativity and criticality shines through all aspects of her thinking about content and literacy instruction. Rather than view students' languaging as a problem to solve, Stephanie plans her approach to content-area literacy instruction so that students have authentic opportunities to use their bilingualism to understand texts in deeper ways than they would have if they only had access to English. These opportunities for students to use their bilingualism and ways of knowing make space for them to show off their linguistic strengths and cultural understanding and engage with English texts in more meaningful ways.

DESIGN: ENGAGING WITH CONTENT-AREA TEXTS

To leverage the **translanguaging corriente**, Stephanie had to find ways to help *all* students—bilingual or not—engage with complex texts in English and create their own texts in English. Though her students had different experiences using English for academic purposes, Stephanie knew that the right design would meet each student where they were and enable them all to meet the language demands of the *Environmentalism: Then and Now* unit of instruction.

Using Two Languages Side by Side to Increase Comprehension

Stephanie's translanguaging unit design provides opportunities for students to engage with multilingual texts, and reflects her content and literacy juntos stance.

On the first day devoted to the Chávez study, Stephanie had students read a biography of Chávez that she found on the United Farm Workers website. The website had the short biography in both English and Spanish, so Stephanie created a handout that put the two versions side by side. After watching the trailer for a new movie about Chávez and having a short discussion about what, if anything, students knew about him, Stephanie distributed the following reading handout, which contained an annotation system for reading and the side-by-side English and Spanish versions of the biography. Rather than giving some students English and others Spanish, Stephanie gave each student both versions, telling them that they could choose to read one or the other or both. Before they read, Stephanie went over the reading handout, especially the annotation and note-taking system the class had been working with, which was a way for students to track their thinking in *any* language and improve their comprehension. Stephanie reviewed the different annotations—circling unknown vocabulary, looking up and writing the meaning of unknown words in English or Spanish, underlining main ideas, putting a star next to important/interesting moments, putting a question mark next to moments of confusion or wondering. Stephanie also emphasized that students' notes could be taken in English, Spanish, or both, regardless of the written language of the text.

Student name _____

Date _____

Directions
Read the biography of César Chávez independently. Make sure you *annotate* and *take notes* on what you read. Your annotations can include the following:

(Circling) unknown vocabulary words *or* Spanish/English cognates
Writing the *Meaning* of the word in English or Spanish
Underlining main ideas
Putting a ★star★ next to things you think are interesting or important
Putting a ? next to your questions, wondering, or moments of confusion

Your note taking can include the following:

Noting and explaining things you agree or disagree with
Writing down your questions or wondering
Making connections
Making predictions
Summarizing or writing out the main ideas

You can make notes in English, Spanish, or both, regardless of the written language of the text!

The Story of César Chávez
The Beginning

The story of César Estrada Chávez begins near Yuma, Arizona. César was born on March 31, 1927. He was named after his grandfather, Cesario. Regrettably, the story of César Estrada Chávez also ends near Yuma, Arizona. He passed away on April 23, 1993, in San Luis, a small village near Yuma, Arizona.

He learned about justice, or rather injustice, early in his life. César grew up in Arizona; the small adobe home where César was born was swindled from them by dishonest Anglos. César's father agreed to clear eighty acres of land, and in exchange he would receive the deed to forty acres of land that adjoined the home. The agreement was broken and the land sold to a man named Justus Jackson. César's dad went to a lawyer who advised him to borrow money and buy the land. Later, when César's father could not pay the interest on the loan, the lawyer bought back the land and sold it to the original owner. César learned a lesson about injustice that he would never forget. Later, he would say, "The love for justice that is in us is not only the best part of our being but it is also the most true to our nature."

La historia de César Chávez
El principio

La historia de César Estrada Chávez empieza cerca de Yuma, Arizona. César nació el 31 de marzo de 1927. Lo llamaron como su abuelo, Cesario. Lamentablemente, la historia de César Estrada Chávez también termina cerca de Yuma, Arizona. Falleció el 23 de abril de 1993, en San Luis, un pueblo pequeño cerca de Yuma, Arizona.

Aprendió sobre la justicia o más bien la injusticia temprano en su vida. César creció en Arizona; unos Anglos deshonestos les quitaron la casa pequeña de adobe en dónde nació. El padre de César aceptó limpiar ochenta acres de terreno a cambio del título de propiedad de cuarenta acres de terreno que colindaban con su casa. El acuerdo no se cumplió y los Anglos vendieron la tierra a un hombre llamado Justus Jackson. El papá de César fue a un abogado que le aconsejó pedir un préstamo y comprar el terreno. Después, cuando el padre de César no pudo pagar el interés del préstamo, el abogado volvió a comprar el terreno y se la vendió al dueño original. César aprendió una lección sobre la injusticia de la cual nunca se olvidaría. Después diría, "El amor por la justicia que está dentro de nosotros no sólo es la parte mejor de nuestro ser pero también es la parte más verdadera de nuestra naturaleza."

Notes/Notas

Reading handout. (Excerpt in English retrieved from United Farm Workers www.ufw.org. Translation adapted by authors. Photograph Copyright © Jocelyn Sherman. Used with permission.)

These design choices clearly illustrate how *any* teacher can leverage students' bilingualism to promote reading for academic purposes in English. Remember that Stephanie doesn't speak Spanish and that English is the official language of instruction in this social studies classroom. Stephanie brought in readings in English and Spanish on the same topic and set up opportunities for students to draw from their full linguistic repertoires, regardless of the text's written language. The use of side-by-side English/Spanish texts also provided *all* students with an important opportunity to develop and display **critical metalinguistic awareness**. For the students who were bilingual, putting their two languages next to one another allowed them to compare syntax, vocabulary (including Spanish/English cognates), word choice, and discourse structure. For those who were monolingual, seeing one text in two languages raised their linguistic awareness and enabled them to see how many similarities exist between languages that they may have thought of as totally separate and different. Drawing explicit attention to language helps *all* students—bilingual or not—think more deeply about language in relation to literacy practices.

Through the use of an explicit strategy for annotating their ideas, Stephanie also encouraged students to be in dialogue with their intrapersonal translanguaging voices while they read independently. As students read the English and/or Spanish texts, some annotated and took notes in English, some in Spanish, and some used both languages.

Using a Reading Jigsaw to Differentiate Content-Area Literacy Instruction

Stephanie has the same high standards, goals, and objectives for all of her students. However, not all bilingual students perform equally in oracy and literacy in English and in Spanish. Teachers therefore need to differentiate their content, language, and literacy instruction to meet students where they are individually and engage all students in learning. Here we see how Stephanie strategically groups her students and differentiates tasks in ways that help *all* students to engage with complex content and texts, develop language practices for academic contexts, and strengthen their metalinguistic awareness.

Later that week, Stephanie organized a "jigsaw" of different readings in English. First, she thought about her students' dynamic translanguaging progressions and assigned students to five different groupings according to their English language development—*entering, emerging, developing, expanding,* and *commanding.* Though the groups' assigned readings were at different levels, each dealt with the legacy that Chávez left behind and the three questions they had to answer were the same. This ensured that when students went back to more heterogeneous groups, their discussions and comparisons would be aligned.

Once students had settled into these more-or-less homogeneous groups, Stephanie explained the activity and distributed the reading activity handout.

READING ACTIVITY HANDOUT FOR GROUP WORK

Student name _____

Date _____

Directions
After you have read your assigned text independently and used our annotations and note-taking strategies
1. Share out your thoughts and questions with your group.
2. In your group, answer the following questions about your assigned text (write in English, Spanish, or both):
   1. What do you think is the most important idea from this reading?

   2. What is the message about César Chávez given by the author?

   3. Do you agree or disagree with this message? Why?

Remember: Once you join your new groups, you will be the only expert on your reading, so make sure you know what you're talking about!

Stephanie told students that they would

- Read their assigned text independently, using the annotation and note-taking procedures they had been practicing
- Discuss their annotations and notes with the group
- Answer the three questions on the handout

Stephanie also told her students that after they completed the questions on the handout, they would join a new group to report on what they had read. Stephanie reminded the students that they would be the only expert on their reading when they joined the new group, because members of the new group had read a different article.

After students read their assigned English-language texts about Chávez independently, they discussed what they had read with group members who had read the same text and prepared to report as experts on their reading. Some groups used both English and Spanish, but they used the languages in different ways that reflected the translanguaging *corriente* flowing through each group. For example, some students annotated texts and took notes in Spanish about the English texts they had read, while others annotated texts and took notes in English. Other students had annotated texts and made notes in the same language as the text, but then discussed what they had written in the other language. Group members worked together to jot down some notes for each of the three questions, in both English and Spanish, preparing to report back in English to their new groups. The bell rang just as students were finishing up their work, so Stephanie told them to review their readings and notes for homework in preparation for the second part of the jigsaw the next day.

When students arrived to class the following day, they went back in their groups to review and ensure that everyone was prepared to present their ideas. Stephanie instructed students to discuss each of the three questions they had answered. Students took notes, sometimes in English and other times in Spanish, as they listened to others sharing. Once the groups had finished discussing the three questions, they collaborated to write a summary of their reading in English (which they negotiated in both languages in many cases), and they were prepared to report as experts on their reading.

Afterwards, Stephanie sent all students to groups composed of students at different progression levels who had read different texts. Thus, in each group, there were five different points of view on the issue of Chávez's legacy, reflecting the five different texts they had read.

Stephanie purposefully uses the structure of a jigsaw activity to leverage the translanguaging corriente in her class and engage all of her students with complex content and texts in English, particularly those who are emergent bilinguals at earlier stages of English development.

First, Stephanie made strategic choices as she grouped her students and assigned texts and tasks throughout the jigsaw activity. The objective for the first part of this activity was to have all students read a text written in English about César Chávez and respond to the same three questions about the text they had read. Though Stephanie generally preferred to organize her students heterogeneously, she understood that students with *expanding* English literacy performances on this type of task needed to be challenged with higher level texts while those with *entering* or *emerging* English literacy performances on this type of task needed practice with less linguistically complex texts. Stephanie therefore organized students into homogeneous groups with peers at similar stages in English literacy along the dynamic translangauging progressions for this first activity, and she gave each group of students a text written at a different level of linguistic complexity. In this way, Stephanie supported those students who needed a less complex English text, as well as those who could take on something more linguistically challenging, so that every student would be able to engage with the same complex content in English.

We can see strong evidence of the translanguaging corriente in this activity. Though all the texts for this jigsaw were in English, Stephanie encouraged students to use all their language resources to take notes, discuss and analyze the texts, and answer the discussion questions. When students utilized all of their languages to engage with those texts, they were able to comprehend and analyze them on a much higher level. Students like Noemí and Luis, who were bright and curious but did not yet have the ability to comprehend complex texts written in English, were not left out. Instead, Stephanie's purposeful design and students' translanguaging provided them with access to both the texts and the conversations occurring around those texts.

Then Stephanie sent students to a different group, where students were at all stages of the progressions. She distributed her jigsaw activity handout (Box 9.1). In those groups, every student was able to learn about *all* of the readings. Though some groups had read complex English texts that others would not have been able to understand, they were able to access the content by listening to their group members' reports. They answered the questions using all their language resources. Each group wrote summaries of what they had learned from all five readings in English, which they then presented to the whole class.

BOX 9.1 HANDOUT FOR JIGSAW ACTIVITY	
Student name _____	
Date _____	
Jigsaw Group Work	
Reading	**My Notes** Write down what you learned about the other texts your group members read; notes can be written in English, Spanish, or both.
Reading no. 1:	
Reading no. 2:	
Reading no. 3:	
Reading no. 4:	
Reading no. 5:	
Summary paragraph (written in English) _____ _____ _____ _____ _____ _____	

Re-Presenting English Texts with Translanguaging

Though it was very important that students comprehended the content-area texts in English, Stephanie knew it was equally important for them to *create* texts that interacted with the content. Through the combination of reading and creating texts, students were able to learn about and "talk back" to the content, which made them active and engaged learners. Rather than assign a writing assignment like an essay, Stephanie designed an opportunity for students to *re-present* a text they had read with different language practices and in a different genre. She wanted students to re-present complex, linguistically challenging texts such as primary source documents, textbook chapters, and scholarly journal articles, as dramatic dialogue, poems, stories, interviews, advertisements, newspaper articles, emails, and postcards (to name only a few!). Walqui (2006) writes of text re-presentation:

> It has been argued. . .that there is a progression in the ability of language users to use different genres within academic discourses. In terms of language use, this continuum starts with asking students to say what is happening (as in drama or dialogue), then what has happened (narratives, reports), then what happens (generalisations in exposition) and, finally, what may happen (tautologic transformations, theorising). In this fashion, students can access content presented in more difficult genres by. . .transforming it into different genres, especially those that are more easily produced. (p. 213)

Stephanie's design for re-presenting academic texts in new genres and with new linguistic practices helped students extend their learning *and* draw on their bilingualism and ways of knowing.

Stephanie paired students to create imagined dialogues between César Chávez and another character from the readings they had done throughout the week. To get them started, Stephanie modeled a short dialogue she had written between César Chávez and the writer of a particularly critical article one group of students had read for the jigsaw. Stephanie showed students how she was taking what she had read and presenting it in a new way—through a dramatic dialogue. She pointed out a part of her dialogue that used a specific piece of textual evidence from the article, which she had re-presented as a line of dialogue in her scene. She told students that they could choose any character—for example, Chávez's wife, a farm worker who joined the movement, the owner of a large farm—and that their dialogues should represent an aspect of Chávez's legacy. Stephanie explained that they should include in the dialogue at least two direct quotes from the texts they had read that were relevant and appropriate to the character and scene. She also told students that depending on whom Chávez was talking to, he might use English, Spanish, or both. Thus, students' dialogues could be written in either or both languages. Students worked in pairs, co-creating their dialogues, which they later performed for the class.

By re-presenting what they learned about César Chávez in the form of a dramatic dialogue, students were able to demonstrate their knowledge and understanding in an engaging way that was accessible to all.

Performing these dialogues helped students teach one another more about Chávez and his legacy and provided Stephanie with an important assessment opportunity. Reading and watching her students' co-created dialogues helped Stephanie understand the extent to which they had comprehended the texts they read without the burden of writing a linguistically complex, decontextualized genre like an essay. Though Stephanie appreciates the importance of teaching students how to write in all genres, she believed that students' understanding of texts could be better assessed without relying solely on written essays in English.

In addition, Stephanie took Walqui's ideas a step further by making space for students' re-presentations to include translanguaging. Because Chávez was Latino and interacted with his family and many of the farm workers he organized in Spanish, their imagined dialogues were authentic opportunities for students to create bilingual, translanguaged texts. Encouraging students to use all of their languages while interacting with an English text served a number of purposes. First, it gave emergent bilinguals like Noemí and Luis the opportunity to express their knowledge in the language they knew best. It also opened up space for *all* students, including those who spoke English only, to draw from their entire **language repertoires**, making the dialogues more interesting, nuanced, and authentic. Lastly, it provided an opportunity for students to develop and demonstrate their metalinguistic awareness as Stephanie facilitated conversations around why students made the linguistic choices they made. As students explained their rationale for including certain words or phrases in one or the other language, Stephanie could assess what they knew about how to use Spanish and English for different audiences and purposes.

There are many strategies that content-area teachers can use—in any content area—to set the course of the translanguaging corriente with texts, including the following:

- Purposefully create groups or partnerships so that students can read various texts, use different language practices, and engage in activities that differ but that are on similar topics.
- Supplement the curriculum with texts that are linguistically and culturally relevant to students.
- Look for or create versions of English texts in students' home languages (and vice versa).
- Use the internet as a resource for finding bilingual texts on the same topic, perhaps reflecting different perspectives.
- Supplement the reading of texts with multilingual film clips, music and other audio, art and other visuals, and realia.
- Explicitly teach students how to annotate and take notes on a text in the language in which they are most comfortable, regardless of the text's written language (e.g., students can annotate an English text with a LOTE or vice versa).
- Encourage students to be in dialogue with their intrapersonal voice as they read and write, no matter the language of the text.
- Encourage students to work in groups and use all their language resources in collaborative dialogue to make meaning of complex texts.
- Assess students' understanding of texts by having them *re-present* those texts with different language practices and in different genres (e.g., a textbook chapter in English as a dramatic bilingual dialogue or a scholarly journal article in English as a poem in English or a LOTE)

When teachers enact a juntos stance through their translanguaging design that brings content and literacy together, and that leverages the translanguaging corriente for learning, bilingual students in English-medium classrooms can engage more meaningfully with complex texts and build their literacy practices for academic purposes.

SHIFTS: ENHANCING CONVERSATIONS AROUND TEXT

Stephanie made several shifts that helped her follow the translanguaging corriente flowing through her classroom as she focused on her bilingual students' literacy performances. On the first day of the Chávez study, Stephanie made copies of excerpts from his biography in both Spanish and English. Stephanie had intended for students to work on the English text, and only refer to the Spanish text if they needed additional help for comprehension. However, she soon realized that this approach might unintentionally stigmatize Spanish, and support the idea that students use Spanish *only* if they are incapable of using English. Stephanie's stance toward Spanish and English is that they are of equal status, and she wanted her classroom practices to reflect this stance. She had first thought of creating a handout with the two texts on separate sheets, but she then decided to put the languages side by side. Right before the lesson, Stephanie decided not to tell students which text to read, contributing to the sense that Spanish was *always* available to *all* students, no matter their performances in English.

Stephanie also made important moves that demonstrated her ability to shift in response to her students' translanguaging. Stephanie's flexibility with language enabled *all* students to participate meaningfully in the literacy activity:

After students read the short biography of Chávez independently, Stephanie told them to discuss their annotations and notes with their groups. Students jumped into conversations about the reading while Stephanie circulated around the room, listening in, contributing ideas, answering questions, and jotting down things she heard that she wanted to bring up with the whole class. After the groups had talked, Stephanie asked them to come up with one question and one comment about the reading to share with the class. She asked that they prepare to share in English, but told them they should know how to explain their ideas in Spanish as well. When it came time to share, Stephanie asked Luis to share his group's answer in English; recall that Luis is an emergent bilingual with limited formal schooling, and he struggles with literacy in any language. Referring to his notes, Luis was able to explain the group's thinking in English saying that "César Chávez's father was a victim of discrimination." After he finished, Stephanie asked Luis if there was anything he wanted to add in Spanish. Luis expanded "que eso que le pasó al papá de César continúa pasando hoy también. Le pasó a un amigo mío." [What happened to Cesar's father continues to happen today. It happened to a friend of mine.] Though Stephanie did not understand most of what Luis said in his follow up, she saw that many students were nodding in agreement. She asked Mariana to translate Luis' comments, which she praised in English.

Although Luis had successfully completed the task in English, Stephanie sensed he had more to say than what he shared in English. By asking Luis if there was anything he wanted to add in Spanish, Stephanie made space for him to expand on what he said in English in the language with which he was more comfortable.

This shift illustrates how attuned Stephanie is to her students. Rather than limit emergent bilinguals like Luis to what they can express in English, Stephanie consistently pushes students to use Spanish to expand on their comments in English. Though she does not always understand what is said, she allows the translanguaging corriente to flow, leveraging students' bilingualism for learning, and making space for increased comprehension and production of content-area texts.

There are many different kinds of shifts that teachers can use to teach content while building literacy, including the following:

- Help students make meaning from texts by providing on-the-spot translations and explanations (if you are not bilingual in students' home languages, you can use translation apps, online or print dictionaries, and/or bilingual students and staff members)
- When students seem stuck, use strategies like "turn and talk" that permit pairs of students to use all their language resources privately to clear up confusion and spark conversation about texts.
- Encourage students to add to, and expand, their understanding of texts in English with discussion or writing in their home languages whenever they need to.
- Help students make connections to texts by providing culturally relevant examples or metaphors or asking students to supply them whenever necessary.

CONCLUSION

The main lesson of this chapter is that all teachers need to see themselves as content and literacy teachers of diverse learners. Some content teachers claim that students must be proficient in the language of the text before they can learn complex grade-level content. However, this is simply not the case. Almost every classroom is multilingual, and the bilingual students in these classrooms have very different experiences and expertise with language and literacy practices for academic purposes—in English and other languages. Thus, *all* teachers have to leverage students' dynamic bilingualism to engage diverse learners with complex content and texts. This means that all content teachers must become literacy teachers; the translanguaging framework makes this possible.

The chapter identifies the stance, design, and shifts of one content teacher, Stephanie, in a translanguaging classroom. Stephanie teaches content and literacy juntos, and she draws heavily on local interests and understanding as she works to expand students' language and literacy practices for academic purposes in her English-medium 11th-grade classroom. Important characteristics of Stephanie's teaching include the strategic grouping of students, use of bilingual texts, and emphasis on different language practices and genres. Stephanie's translanguaging classroom demonstrates how teachers can engage students with content-area literacy more effectively when they do not restrict students to working exclusively with the language of the text. When teachers make space for students to draw on the full features of their linguistic repertoires, they have more opportunities to develop language and literacy for academic contexts in any language.

QUESTIONS AND ACTIVITIES

1. Review the excerpts from Stephanie's classroom practices in this chapter. What else could Stephanie have done to expand her students' literacy performances?

2. Why did Stephanie include readings of a Latino historical figure? Do you think this is useful for *all* students, Latino or not? How could you localize the content *you* are teaching?

3. Discuss the kinds of moment-to-moment shifts that teachers can use to go with the flow of the translanguaging corriente and teach content while building literacy. Do you engage in any of these shifts in your own instruction? What additional shifts have you taken to respond to your students' language practices to engage them with complex content and texts?

TAKING ACTION

1. Design a jigsaw activity or a text re-presentation activity for your classroom that uses translanguaging, ideally as part of the translanguaging unit design that you have been working on while reading this book. What resources do you need? How will you structure activities throughout the jigsaw or text re-presentation to leverage the translanguaging corriente in your class?

2. Implement the jigsaw activity in your class and then think about the following activities on your own or with a group of colleagues:

   • How did the ways that you grouped students, differentiated texts, and structured tasks support students' efforts to engage with complex content and texts?

   • What translanguaging strategies did your students use in the different activities?

   • What shifts did you make to go with the flow of the translanguaging corriente?

CHAPTER 10

Biliteracy in the Translanguaging Classroom

LEARNING OBJECTIVES

- Describe how translanguaging works to promote biliteracy
- Analyze the differences between traditional models of biliteracy and the flexible multiple model of biliteracy used in translanguaging classrooms
- Describe how teachers can implement a flexible model of biliteracy through their translanguaging stance, design, and shifts
- Design and implement activities that use translanguaging to engage students with complex biliteracy texts in your classroom

Not all **translanguaging classrooms** have biliteracy, in the traditional sense of being able to read and write two languages, as an explicit goal and anticipated outcome. But biliteracy, as described by Hornberger (1990), is a very important part of all translanguaging classrooms—bilingual and English-medium. For Hornberger, biliteracy includes "any and all instances in which communication occurs in two or more languages *in or around writing*" (p. 213, italics added for emphasis). We have seen many examples throughout this book illustrating how *Stephanie* and *Justin* leverage students' bilingualism in and around writing in their English-medium classrooms. Here we look more closely at how *Carla* uses a flexible, dynamic model of biliteracy in her **dual-language bilingual education (DLBE)** classroom.

This chapter highlights the third purpose of translanguaging—making space for students' bilingualism and ways of knowing. We begin with a broad look at different models of biliteracy that we find in bilingual schools today, and we reimagine what biliteracy—as an explicit instructional goal and as a language practice—might look like from a translanguaging perspective. Then we return to Carla's DLBE classroom to see how she leverages the **translanguaging corriente** to promote biliteracy in her class through her stance, design, and shifts. As you read, we encourage you to consider how you could use translanguaging to strengthen biliteracy in your bilingual classroom.

DYNAMIC BILITERACY

The goal of biliteracy is slowly but surely being embraced in the United States. DLBE programs are more popular than ever, and the Seal of Biliteracy continues to be adopted in an increasing number of states. However, we don't find a clear definition of biliteracy in most policy discussions, nor do we find clear articulations of different pathways to biliteracy.

Flexible Model

García (2009) has posited four models of language and literacy use in biliteracy practices that we find in different types of **bilingual education** programs.

1. **Convergent monoliterate model.** This model uses two languages (English and a language other than English [LOTE]) to discuss an English language text. The objective, however, is simply comprehension of the English written text. In this sense, it is not truly a biliterate model.

    English and LOTE ⟶ English text/literacy

2. **Convergent biliterate model.** This model uses texts in two languages with a goal of literacy in English. Although texts written in two languages are used, minority literacy practices are simply calqued on majority literacy practices. For example, in many English–Spanish bilingual programs, initial literacy in Spanish is often taught in ways that mimic the reading strategies used to decode English, thus the emphasis on phonemic awareness (see Goldenberg, Tolar, Reese, Francis, Ray Bazán, & Mejía-Arauz, 2014).

    English and LOTE calqued on English
    ⟶ English text/literacy

3. **Separation biliterate model.** Here, one language or the other is used to interact with a text written in one language or the other, but there is strict separation based on the sociocultural and discourse literacy norms of the cultures that the texts represent. In practice, however, we rarely find the sociocultural and discourse norms of Spanish-speaking cultures reflected in bilingual classes.

    English ⟶ English text/literacy

    LOTE ⟶ LOTE text/literacy

4. **Flexible multiple model.** In this case, the two languages are used to interact with texts written in both languages and in other media, according to a bilingual flexible norm capable of both integration and separation.

All translanguaging classrooms, whether officially English-medium or bilingual, use a flexible multiple model of biliteracy. A translanguaging pedagogy in instruction and assessment encourages bilingual students to draw on the full features of their lingusitic repertoires to read texts in different languages as they think, discuss, interact with, and produce written texts, sometimes in one language.

Traditional bilingual education classrooms most often follow either the convergent biliterate model or the separation biliterate model. The convergent biliterate model is generally found in **transitional bilingual education** classrooms, where reading and writing is performed in two languages, but usually following the reading and writing norms of English. The separation biliterate model is generally found in DLBE classrooms, where the use of English and Spanish in literacy activities always occurs separately. Students read in one language and write in the same language. In contrast to the convergent and separation biliterate models, the flexible multiple model reflects the type of biliteracy that Escamilla, Hopewell, Butvilofsky, Sparrow, Soltero-González, Ruiz-Figueroa, and Escamilla describe in *Literacy Squared* (2014), where literacy contexts and topics across languages are interrelated and cross-language connections are made. We also see this model enacted in Carla's DLBE classroom as she teaches for biliteracy.

Broad Notion of Texts and Literacy

The written texts used in a translanguaging classroom have a myriad of forms. Sometimes the texts are *monolingual* and are discussed using language practices that are different from those of the text. Sometimes the texts are *bilingual*, by which we mean texts with translations with different layouts—often side by side, sometimes top and bottom, and other times at the end. Sometimes the *texts have been constructed using translanguaging*, by which we mean that the two languages are used in relationship with each other throughout the text. For example, the dialogue between characters in a story is spoken in different languages or spoken with features that are considered two languages. The features of what are traditionally thought of as belonging to two different autonomous languages are used sin fronteras to enable bilingual voices to emerge.

We want to emphasize that texts are not only in print format. Sometimes they are audio-based, in the form of oral interactions, or visual, in the form of videos or movies. Most of the time texts' multimodalities are experienced simultaneously. For example, shared reading practices enable students to see, listen to, and speak about the text at the same time. It is also possible to view a video clip, read its subtitles, and listen to the text in the language of the subtitles or the video itself. When we write, we read silently to ourselves, listen to what the text says and the way it sounds in our heads, and often use internal dialogue or make notes as we read the text. So how we interact with text requires all our meaning-making resources to make sense of texts and to create new ones. In the case of bilingual students, this means leveraging all their language and semiotic (meaning-making) resources to engage with and produce complex texts.

Translanguaging is important in developing biliteracy because a bilingual's inner voice (the *intrapersonal voice*) always contains features that are traditionally considered two languages, but to the bilingual are a single, complete **language repertoire**. That is, even with a monolingually written text, a bilingual student is always *constructing meaning bilingually* to make connections to themselves, their worlds, and to the texts of those worlds. When teachers require bilingual students to use only one language as they engage with texts inter- and intrapersonally, they limit these students' opportunities to learn.

Hornberger's (2003) **continua of biliteracy** posit a first language/second language continuum that addresses the complex relationship between the two languages. Hornberger (2005) adds "Bi/multilinguals' learning is maximized when they are allowed and enabled to draw from across all their existing language skills (in two+ languages), rather than being constrained and inhibited from doing so by monolingual instructional assumptions and practices" (p. 607). Translanguaging offers a way for students to draw on the diverse aspects of Hornberger's continua of biliteracy. A translanguaging classroom helps students use their entire language repertoires to develop a dynamic biliteracy, a way of interacting with texts that focuses on how and why texts are used. Teachers sustain and shape the many ways that translanguaging generates thinking, expression, and creativity as they encourage and enhance students' biliterate performances.

Literacy is much more than merely decoding a text, although this is important. Following Freire (1970), literacy involves reading the world, not just the words. We enact biliteracy by reading el texto to decipher the meanings and to reflect on the text itself, and by developing the critical dialogue about el contexto—social, political and economic—in which el texto exists and is produced.

Multiple Pathways

In a traditional bilingual classroom that uses traditional biliteracy instruction for emergent and experienced bilinguals, the course from home language to new language is generally represented as linear and unidirectional, moving from home to school. Even in DLBE programs where Spanish literacy is a goal, the ways of using Spanish permitted in schools move away from vernacular varieties of Spanish used in U.S. Spanish-speaking communities and toward a more "standard" Spanish. Acquiring a new language in any type of program is also generally represented as a linear, stage-like process, with students moving from *entering* to *emerging* to *developing* to *expanding* to *commanding*. Under this perspective, students at particular stages of new language development are expected to be able to do certain things with language and not others; thus, teachers often deny students access to texts that are beyond their level. Because learning is represented as more-or-less straightforward and linear, the roles of teachers and students in reading instruction are often described in terms of three stages: teacher-directed (the teacher reads *to* the students), shared responsibility (the teacher reads *with* the students), and independent-production (texts are read *by* the students). That is, the teacher first leads the actions and then turns over the actions to the students.

The movement in the translanguaging classroom is very different. Students do not have to wait to act by themselves until they reach a particular developmental stage. The **translanguaging design** for instruction and assessment allows teachers to move seamlessly among the three roles (reading *to* students, *with* students, and *by* students) because students are always actively performing tasks, even when they are new to English. Teachers use translanguaging strategies and shifts to adapt to the ecology of the classroom, the tasks at hand, and the individual student's placement along the translanguaging progressions. Teachers continually identify what students and their families know and can do with content, language, and literacy, and they help students make connections between home language and literacy practices and the language-specific practices required at school. Because students' language and literacy practices are so varied, and because the translanguaging corriente differs across contexts, teachers in translanguaging classrooms emphasize multiple pathways to (bi)literacy.

STANCE: RE-MEDIATING LITERACY JUNTOS

Since the enactment of No Child Left Behind (2001), the literacy education of **emergent bilinguals** has been increasingly remedial and prescriptive, focusing on the teaching of basic skills. That is, teachers are being asked to follow scripted curricula that more often than not have been developed to remediate learning for "students at risk." Carla's stance focuses, however, on *re-mediating* literacy. Gutiérrez, Morales, and Martínez (2009) refer to the concept of re-mediation as "a framework for the development of rich learning ecologies in which all students can expand their repertoires of practice" (p. 227). Carla understands that literacy is not an autonomous skill, that it is also mediated by social, cultural, political, and economic factors (Street, 1984). Carla's **translanguaging stance** demands that reading to learn has to be done **juntos**—using all their language practices and with the help of other people and technology—while acknowledging the influence of culture on literacy practices.

Recall that Carla teaches in a DLBE program in New Mexico that stresses the separation of Spanish and English for instructional purposes, similar to many such programs in New Mexico and throughout the United States. However, Carla has carved out a space for translanguaging where she and her students bring Spanish and English together, and draw on their bilingualism and ways of knowing. Carla calls this space Cuéntame algo. During this instructional time, Carla and her students draw on the full features of their linguistic and cultural repertoires as they make connections between home, school, and community language and literacy practices.

Carla's translanguaging stance reflects her understanding that there is no such thing as academic language per se (although there are ways of using language differently for academic purposes), or even English or Spanish per se (although there are ways of using what is known as English or Spanish in certain settings). Instead, Carla recognizes that her bilingual students develop their language and cultural practices as they move between home, school, and other key contexts in their everyday lives. Thus, when bilingual students use language for academic purposes in either English or Spanish at school, we can expect to find **language features** generally associated with home and community settings. Likewise, when bilingual students use language for specific purposes at home and in the community, we are likely to find features that are associated with academic settings. This makes sense because home and school are not two separate and separable contexts. Teachers can also strengthen these home, school, and community connections by encouraging the translanguaging corriente to flow.

Carla's teaching also reflects her stance that biliteracy practices are jointly constructed with others in communicative activities through two or more languages around writing. For example, she provides students with bilingual and multimodal texts (both fiction and nonfiction) from published sources and from the community. She integrates the language used in academic texts in one language or the other with those of bilingual community members, and she encourages her students to take a holistic view of their bilingual linguistic repertoires, using different linguistic features to strengthen their literacy performances and develop their voices.

Carla's ideological orientation is enacted by how she treats the language and literacy practices of the home and community as resources in her pedagogy, encouraging the translanguaging corriente to flow freely. In her classroom, knowledge is drawn not only from the school, but also from home, as teacher and students work *jointly* to include cuentos from home, community, and school in the translanguaging unit of instruction, *Cuentos de la tierra y del barrio*. Works of fiction are experienced not just as cuentos de hadas [fairy tales]. Rather, they are placed alongside nonfiction texts—including the oral histories of family and community members—so that fiction can be seen as a mirror of life and nonfiction can be understood as another cuento. Thus, Carla constructs biliteracy in her classroom using home, school, and community practices juntos.

On a personal level, Carla is a bilingual, bicultural educator who understands the language practices of her students at home—not solely English or Spanish, not solely oral or written. Carla knows that her students' literacy practices are varied and include texting, posting on social media, surfing the internet, and reading from iPhones and other screens, all performed using their entire language repertoires. The space provided during Cuéntame algo encourages students to value, support, and enact their biliteracy learning como la corriente. In so doing, students develop their bilingual identities as they leverage their bilingualism and ways of knowing.

DESIGN: BILITERACY ACOMPAÑAMIENTO

In traditional **English as a second language (ESL)**, whether **push-in**, **pull-out**, or **structured English immersion**, classrooms students are given texts in English and asked to make sense of them (and produce them) in English only. In traditional bilingual classrooms much biliteracy instruction is sequential, which means that students learn to read and write in one language first (usually their home language), before they are introduced to reading and writing activities in the additional language. Thus, when students are reading in a language that they are just learning (e.g., at the *entering* or *emerging* stages), they are only expected to perform low level actions—"point," "draw," "sequence the pictures"—to demonstrate their comprehension of complex content and texts. In those cases, the teacher has to come up with a way of scaffolding literacy instruction that often seems artificial.

In a translanguaging biliteracy classroom, students are expected to analyze, infer, synthesize, present evidence, and perform other higher order activities by drawing on the full features of their linguistic repertoires. At all times, even when students are reading or producing monolingual texts, they are using all their language resources, including the other language, to make meaning. Translanguaging classrooms enable bilingual students to display a wide range of **general linguistic performances** from the very beginning, including the following:

- Offering opinions on issues raised by texts, regardless of language of text
- Questioning the texts, regardless of language of text
- Discussing relationships among ideas in bilingual texts
- Evaluating different language features in the bilingual texts and explaining their meanings
- Comparing and contrasting language features and discourse structures in bilingual texts
- Extending their engagement with published texts by making connections to those produced by community members

As students draw on their bilingualism and ways of knowing to demonstrate what they can do with their general and **language-specific performances**, they also have opportunities to develop their metalinguistic awareness and deepen their cultural understanding.

Students in Carla's classroom draw on the full features of their language repertoires as they participate in meaningful dialogue, conduct research, perform important literacy tasks as translators and linguists, create their own cuentos and scripts, make multimedia presentations, and even write sophisticated argumentative texts. Recall the varied profiles of our four focal students:

- *Erica* was born in New Mexico, although her parents were born in Puerto Rico. She speaks mostly English at home. Erica can speak, read, write, and comprehend Spanish and English. Her reading and writing in Spanish and English are just about grade level, but she is much more comfortable speaking English than Spanish.
- *Jennifer* is of Mexican descent, was born in the United States, and is learning Spanish at school. At home, Jennifer speaks English to her mother and siblings and Spanish to her grandmother. Jennifer reads at grade level in Spanish and above grade level in English.
- *Moisés* emigrated from Mexico two years ago, can read and write at grade level in Spanish, and is officially designated as an English language learner (ELL). At home, Moisés communicates with his parents mostly in Spanish because they do not speak much English; however, with his siblings he most often uses both languages to interact and play.
- *Ricardo* emigrated from Mexico (where he learned through Spanish and Mixteco at school in Oaxaca) last year, is officially designated as an ELL, and scores below grade level in reading in Spanish and English. Ricardo communicates in Mixteco and Spanish with his family, but uses some English with his younger siblings.

It is important to remember that in a traditional DLBE program, Erica and Jennifer would both be considered English dominant, and Moisés and Ricardo would both be considered Spanish dominant ELLs. The bilingual profile that Carla uses allows her to find bilingual resources in every case that are masked by traditional labeling conventions.

As we saw on Carla's translanguaging unit plan, *Cuentos de la tierra y del barrio,* in Chapter 6, Carla taught fiction and nonfiction texts in multiple modalities in her literacy instruction. The unit included a large number of books in both English and Spanish about farming and soil conservation. For example, Carla chose the following texts in Spanish:

- Rudolfo Anaya's *The Santero's Miracle*
- Literature about gardening written by a local community leader
- Readings about local/global farming practices from websites and magazines
- Videos about local and global farming practices

In English, she chose the following:

- 4th-grade social studies textbook
- 4th-grade science textbook
- Readings about local/global farming practices taken from websites and magazines
- Videos about local and global farming practices

We turn now to Carla's classroom to see how she skillfully conducts **biliteracy acompañamiento** in ways that engage students deeply with texts.

Read-Aloud: Linking Language and Cultural Practices

During the Cuéntame algo translanguaging space, Carla read en voz alta *The Santero's Miracle,* a bilingual cuento written by a local New Mexican writer, Rudolfo Anaya. In the story, Don Jacobo and his grandson are finishing a wood carving of San Isidro Labrador, the santo patrón of farmers, as a heavy snowstorm hits New Mexico. San Isidro works a miracle for the grandfather by clearing the road, making it possible for an ambulance to reach his sick vecino, and for his children to get home for Christmas.

In the book, Anaya's English text has been translated into Spanish, and the English–Spanish texts are laid side by side or top and bottom. Carla reads some paragraphs in English and others in Spanish, and students participate in the collaborative dialogue that ensues without regard to the language in which she read. As they read el cuento en voz alta, they drew the action of the text on chart paper (Fig. 10.1). Although the book was written in both languages, and Carla read some text in English and some in Spanish, the dialogue was mostly in Spanish, so she decided to write the action of the text on the chart paper in Spanish.

Notice in the following vignette how a student's questions about the use of Spanish lead to a metalinguistic discussion about differences between Spanish and English, and about challenges with translation.

"Is 'm'ijo' even a word?" Jennifer asked. Ricardo responded that this was a word in Oaxaca. They then looked it up in the dictionary and couldn't find it. Moisés then said that it meant "mi ijo," but he still couldn't find "ijo" in the dictionary. Then Jennifer pointed out that "hijito" had an "h" and they wondered if this was why they couldn't find the word. They looked up "hijo" and found it. Jennifer said: "The problem is Spanish. In English we hear the "h," so we wouldn't be confused." After much disagreement with Jennifer's statement, they discussed what "hijito" meant. Ricardo said that his family often called him "Ricardito," and then Jennifer chimed in, "I call my grandmother, abuelita." They asked Carla why some Spanish words use "ito/ita" and together they decided it meant "little." Carla told them this was called a "diminutive."

Figure 10.1 Action in cuento for read-aloud. (From Johnson, 2013.)

Carla then gave them a sentence from the cuento: "Don Jacobo se bajó de la cama, se vistió y fue a la ventana para ver el pueblo entero" and asked them to add the suffix "ito/ita" whenever possible, and discuss what it did to the meaning of the sentence. She then asked them: "What is necessary to create the same sentence in English?" The class came up with an English translation with which they were totally unsatisfied. For example, Jennifer said, "Little village is not the same as a pueblito. You love a pueblito, and that's why you add 'ito'. It has nothing to do with size!" Carla then talked about the complexities of translation. She pointed out that this particular book had a translator. The class discussed the well-respected (and well-paid) profession of translator. Erica said that she was always translating for her family and didn't get paid! Although they all laughed, they agreed that they did much translating in their families, and that this was a valuable skill.

Carla then engaged students in a metalinguistic discussion of how bilingual authors make choices about language having to do with what they want to express. They also discussed the importance of biliteracy. Referring back to the cuento, Carla reminded them that Don Jacobo and his grandson worked all day on the wood carving of San Isidro and spent a lot of time selecting and mixing the colors to get the right shade. She then told them: "It says in the story: 'All day they worked at painting the carving.' Authors have to do the same thing with their words." And Erica exclaimed: "Yes, but as bilinguals we can paint with more colors. We have to use all our colors!"

As we can see in this vignette, reading, writing, listening, and speaking are experienced *juntos*, as are all the linguistic features of the children's two languages. Carla's use of translanguaging with her bilingual students in the discussion following the read-aloud provides many opportunities for meta-linguistic analysis. The strict separation of the two languages that we see in traditional DLBE programs would have made this kind of opportunity unavailable.

In the following excerpt from the same class discussion, we see how students' questioning of the text leads to an exploration of cultural practices, again made possible by translanguaging.

During the reading of the story Erica heard the word *santero*; she jumped up! She told the class that in Puerto Rico, where her family came from, a *santero* was not someone who carved images of *santos*, but someone who practiced a religion that she was unfamiliar with and who dressed in white. Moisés got very excited and said: "Mentira. Mi mamá es católica, y ella siempre le reza a sus santos, y no se viste de blanco." [That's a lie. My mother is Catholic, and she always prays to her saints, and she doesn't dress in white.] Carla decided that she needed to respond to Moisés in Spanish, and that this would be a good topic to pursue for research—the meanings of *santeros* and *santos*. In Spanish, she gave the class an assignment. They were to go home and interview their family members about their understanding of the words *santos* and *santero*, take notes on what the families said, and be ready to do an oral report to the class.

Carla is always looking for ways to build student engagement with texts, especially when students question the text or each other. Carla goes with the flow of the translanguaging *corriente* and adds a new activity to the unit— the family interview—to help students understand differences in the terms *santos* and *santeros*, and gain a deeper understanding of associated cultural practices.

As we see in this next excerpt, the read-aloud can also engage students with each other and with the text when they discover shared background experiences and knowledge:

When Carla got to the part in the story where the grandfather repeated a well-known prayer to San Isidro, she made sure to read the rhyme in Spanish. Immediately Moisés said: "No es lo que digo" [It's not what I say], and he added: "San Isidro Labrador, quita el agua y pon el sol" [Saint Isidro the Farmer, take away the rain and make it sunny.] And Erica exclaimed, "That's also what we say in my family when we want the rain to stop!" They then had a discussion about the role of the rain and the sun in farming.

In this case, Moisés questions the text because the prayer that he knows is not what is written in the text. His engagement with the text functions to bring Moisés and Erica closer together, because their families (one Mexican that uses largely Spanish at home and the other Puerto Rican that uses largely English at home) say the same prayer for sun.

After the discussion, which focused primarily on the meaning of the text, Carla invited her students to reflect on how the author chose to use translanguaging in his text. Anaya's text in English was peppered with words that some would call "Spanish," but that for many bilinguals are just part of their lexicon. Carla pointed this out to her students, and together they made a list of those words. In groups of four they then discussed why these words and not others were written in Spanish. The groups reported back to the class, and with Carla's help they came up with these categories:

- Informal greetings and interactions: "Buenos días," "Vamos," "Gracias," "Entre" "¿Qué pasa?"
- Terms of relationship and endearment: "abuelo/a," "hijito," "compadre" "m'ijo" "mujer," "amor"
- Food: "tortillas," "posole," "biscochitos"
- Other cultural practices: "santero," "santo"

Carla and her students discussed ways that authors use language to involve particular audiences in the texts they create, in this case using Spanish to invoke authentic cultural practices in U.S. Latino homes.

Assessing Learning: Writing a Research Report

Carla pays attention not only to instruction, but also to the close assessment of how her students engage with texts and use language (general linguistic and language-specific performances) to describe, explain, question, report, and so forth. Carla uses the Teacher's Assessment Tool (see Appendix A.6.1) to place students along the **dynamic translanguaging progressions**, which she complements with other assessments, to yield a more holistic portrait of what students can do with content, literacy, and language on different tasks throughout the translanguaging unit of instruction. For example, one of Carla's culminating projects asks students to individually write a research report about local farming practices using text-based evidence, local sources, and human resources to support their positions. Students present their arguments to their peers and then to the school community during the annual open house.

First, Carla told her students to go home and share what they had learned about the story with their families, using the Family Assessment: La conexión (see Appendix A.6.4). Carla specifically had students ask their families about stories on farming and legends of San Isidro.

Carla then put students into groups of four and asked each group to write a research report putting together the findings from their families on cultural practices about farming and San Isidro. She also asked them to conduct internet research using websites in English and Spanish. Carla instructed some groups to write in Spanish and others to write in English. But she also told them to quote directly from the texts they had gathered from friends, family, and the internet in whatever language they had read or heard them. Carla reminded them that Rudolfo Anaya had chosen some words to render in Spanish, and that they could do the same. She explained to them that they would then use their research reports to make a public oral presentation to the school community.

The culminating research report for this part of the unit reflects Carla's juntos stance. For Carla and her students, reading *The Santero's Miracle* was a translanguaging literacy event where they strategically used Spanish and English juntos, orally and in writing. Carla's translanguaging design also enabled the bilingual students to make use of all their language and cultural resources juntos, while bringing home and school experiences juntos. These translanguaging practices encouraged students to engage with complex content and texts while deepening their experiences reading and writing monolingual and bilingual texts. Students demonstrated their performances through different tasks leading up to and including the research report that each group wrote.

Close Reading: Using the Full Features
of Students' Linguistic Repertoires

Later in the unit, Carla formed heterogenous groups of four students at different stages in Spanish and English along the dynamic translanguaging progressions. Each group read a different story about farming and soil conservation. Some groups read in English and others in Spanish, although each group had access to resources in both languages, including peers who could translate and iPads and bilingual dictionaries. Carla grouped both Moisés and Ricardo, students whose English literacy performances were still developing, with two more experienced bilinguals so that they would have access to peers who would facilitate their reading of the English text. In this case, Carla wanted to make sure that Moisés and Ricardo grappled with a complex text in English, and she supported their work by providing additional Spanish texts on the same topic. Carla included both Jennifer and Erica in the group that was reading in Spanish, because they were both more comfortable reading in English, and Carla knew that they needed the extra challenge of reading in Spanish. Jennifer and Erica were supported by peers with more literacy experience in Spanish and other resources. Students worked in their groups to do a close reading of their assigned text:

Although groups of students were reading a text in either English or Spanish, they were using all their language resources to make meaning. That is, they were actively using translanguaging as they discussed and strategically raised questions about the text being read and provided answers. They also took notes with all their language resources for a later discussion.

Carla, working with individual groups, some in English, some in Spanish, through this close reading activity, reminded them to use the general questions that were visible in a large classroom poster. These questions, in both English and Spanish, included the following:

- What picture or drawing could help me understand this text?
  [¿Qué fotografía o dibujo me puede ayudar a entender este texto?]
- Visualiza. ¿Qué sientes, hueles, o oyes? Explica.
  [Visualize. What do you feel, smell, and hear? Explain.]
- What does the text remind you of? In your life or experiences? In other texts that you've read?
  [¿De qué te recuerda el texto? ¿En tu vida? ¿En otro texto que hayas leído?]
- What is the text about?
  [¿De qué se trata el texto?]

Carla also encouraged students to seek her support, as well as that of each other, as they read and took notes about the topic. As she walked the room, she supported the students by paraphrasing ideas in Spanish or English, as appropriate, and reminded them to use their iPads and dictionaries.

Besides the close reading of bilingual published texts that told cuentos about farming and soil conservation, Carla and her students drew on cuentos from community and family members about the history of farming practices in New Mexico. Carla wanted her students to understand that la tierra y los barrios go through changes. For homework the students were told to ask family or community members for cuentos de la tierra in New Mexico (or Mexico or other countries) and to take notes on the cuentos told by different people in various ways and with different language practices. Carla wanted to ensure that her students understood that reading meant engaging not only with published written fiction and nonfiction texts that they read at school but also with oral stories from their homes and the larger community.

Assessing Learning: Writing an Argumentative Essay

Prepared with the deep knowledge that came from examining texts closely, both established ones written by published authors and those produced by community members, the students were ready for the culminating project of the unit's lessons—the writing of an argumentative essay.

In their groups, students shared cuentos and brainstormed about the position they would take in their collectively written argumentative essay on whether farming and the soil in el jardín del barrio was better or worse than in the time of their parents and grandparents. They were told to identify text-based evidence to support their positions as they debated the topic and came to agreement about which position they would support in their essays.

Carla referred the class to the bilingual bulletin board where she had placed two examples of argumentative essays, one in English and the other Spanish, which had been written by students from her previous 4th-grade class. She read each example, giving students opportunities to ask clarifying questions and make recommendations as to how to extend the arguments made.

The students were then asked to choose one language in which to write, rendering the final argumentative text *in only one language*. To make this determination Carla asked the groups: "Which audience are you writing for? To whom are you making the argument?" And then continued, telling them, "The answer to these questions will help you determine the language and language practices that you would want to include in your essay." Once the groups had selected the language of publication of their argumentative essay, Carla reminded them that it was possible to use the other language to make the writing more authentic, in the same way that Rudolfo Anaya had done.

Individual students then prewrote in the language of their choice. For example, as expected, Moisés and Ricardo prewrote in Spanish, but Erica and Jennifer did so in English. In their groups they read each other's prewriting and made observations on how to extend arguments and use evidence. They then started to write their group's argumentative essay in the language they had selected for their chosen audience.

Writing in Carla's classroom is always accompanied by collective thinking, speaking, listening, and reading. That is why so much time is spent leveraging the students' collective language and literacy practices to discuss and find text-based evidence in readings. Carla's biliteracy acompañamiento approach allows her to continuously assess what students know, inviting their self-reflection and that of the peer group, and also inviting family members to contribute.

Strategies for Deep Engagement with Texts

The teacher's translanguaging unit plan and the **translanguaging design cycle** provide structures to support students' efforts to generate questions and think deeply about texts, interact meaningfully with texts, and design and perform texts for specific purposes. These types of literacy practices are key to academic success.

Carla provides students with opportunities to learn and use these kinds of strategies throughout the unit design cycle. For example, Carla uses bilingual read-alouds and multimodal texts and encourages her students to engage in discussion of the texts that they read, using their own voices and language practices, not just those of the chosen text. Carla also observes and documents the concrete strategies that her students use to engage with texts:

- Moisés made sense of the text by doing a close read and jotting notes and questions in the margins in English and Spanish. To better understand the main ideas and concepts, he asked his peers for help and used iPads for translations.
- Erica read the Spanish text that was assigned to her group, but wrote notes and questions in English.
- Jennifer collaborated closely with Moisés by reviewing the main ideas and concepts that he had written in Spanish. She asked clarifying questions in both English and Spanish to make sure she understood what he wrote.
- Ricardo translated key terms from English to Spanish in the text he was reading. He frequently asked questions of his peers, asked Carla for help, and looked for other resources on the iPad.

These are just a few of the ways that teachers can use the translanguaging design to enact biliteracy acompañamiento in the bilingual classroom. This approach to teaching for biliteracy accomplishes much that is impossible when the two languages are kept strictly separate. Carla's translanguaging design for biliteracy instruction and assessment meets students where they are; links home and school language and cultural practices; identifies and builds on students' general linguistic and language-specific performances; strengthens students' metalinguistic awareness and cultural understanding; and propels their content, language, and literacy learning forward.

SHIFTS: MOVING "UNMOVABLE" TEXTS

Carla makes moment-by-moment shifts in her instruction and assessment as she strategically adapts her language practices to those of her students. This doesn't mean that Carla used one or the other language randomly. Rather, Carla planned the language of the texts that they read and wrote. But she frequently went outside of the design that she had planned to follow the translanguaging corriente more freely. For example, when Moisés reacted in Spanish to Erica's meaning of santos, Carla immediately understood that she needed to discuss this matter, and follow it up, in Spanish, although this was not part of her design.

Teachers in translanguaging classrooms challenge the notion that written texts are often considered "unmovable," written in one or the other language in static ways. Translanguaging enables teachers to strategically shift the course of instruction and assessment to put the readers (and not simply the authors of the texts) in charge of the text. Furthermore, translanguaging allows readers to "hear" the written text in their heads a través de/through their own language practices. Only by creating an intimate relationship with the text can readers generate deep meaning and create new texts. Teachers have to engage in these moment-by-moment shifts because they cannot possibly anticipate all of their students' responses to texts.

CONCLUSION

Translanguaging enables bilingual students to become better readers and writers in two languages, precisely because all their language resources are put in the service of constructing the text in their own voices to appropriate it, even when the text is monolingual. Unlike traditional bilingual classrooms, translanguaging classrooms take up a flexible multiple model of biliteracy. When students own the language of the text itself—even if only "in their heads"—they can become good readers and writers, especially in two languages.

At times, translanguaging classrooms also promote the use of language features that are considered two languages when constructing texts. By representing the language practices of bilinguals in the same text, the translanguaging classroom legitimizes students' **dynamic bilingualism**. Translanguaging is not just a scaffold for one language or the other. Reading and writing translanguaged texts show the potential of a bilingual repertoire for both academic and home functions. It also enables a student to write using his or her own voice, one that is bilingual and expresses multiple, dynamic ways of knowing el texto y el contexto.

QUESTIONS AND ACTIVITIES

1. Consider the four models of biliteracy posited by García (2009) and reviewed in this chapter. What models have you observed or worked with?

2. Identify the types of texts that use translanguaging and consider how you can use them in your classes.

3. Do you see translanguaging as simply a scaffold to literacy in an additional language or as a resource for becoming better readers and writers in an additional language or in two languages? Explain the reasons for your answer.

TAKING ACTION

1. Review the four biliteracy models discussed in this chapter. Which biliteracy model is enacted in your context? What steps would you need to take to move toward a flexible, multiple model?

2. Design a lesson, ideally within the context of the unit plan you are developing while reading this book, and implement that lesson. If possible, videotape your lesson and look closely at the video, thinking about the following questions:

   • How does your lesson reflect a flexible, multiple model of biliteracy?

   • How do you use translanguaging strategies to promote dynamic biliteracy among your students?

   • How do your students take up these opportunities?

CHAPTER 11

Socioemotional Well-Being and Social Justice

LEARNING OBJECTIVES

- Describe how translanguaging supports bilingual students' socio-emotional well-being through valorización
- Explain how translanguaging classrooms can advance social justice
- Identify how you can use translanguaging to foster your students' socioemotional well-being and critical consciousness

The **translanguaging corriente** is the key to **translanguaging classrooms**. To feel the translanguaging corriente, all you have to do is take a step back from your daily routine and listen and look. Listen hard to what your students say to you and their peers, inside the classroom, hallways, and cafeteria and on the playground. If you listen hard enough, you might be able to perceive their intrapersonal voices (what they're saying in their heads, in imaginary dialogues with themselves and their friends). Listen also to the conversations that take place when their families and peers are present; try to hear what is being said and how it is said, as well as what is not being said and why. Listening in this way allows you to hear your students' voices anew, and puts you in touch with the flow of the translanguaging corriente, even if it is not obviously at the surface of your classroom.

Look at your students through a translanguaging lens. Focus so that you see, as Carini (2000) always says, the whole child. Observe closely so that you can describe fully what the student is doing with language. When, with whom, and where is the student languaging in certain ways? Let the students' own language practices bloom by giving them control of the tasks at hand or putting them in situations where they're interacting freely with others. After listening deeply to the students in your class and seeing them in their entirety, you become aware of their languaging. And if your students are bilingual, you will come into contact with the translanguaging corriente. Let the translanguaging corriente flow through your classroom. What happens? What is the translanguaging corriente able to do for your teaching and your students' learning?

Once you feel the translanguaging corriente you are unable to ignore it, and you learn to use the translanguaging pedagogy purposefully and strategically:

1. Supporting students as they engage with complex content and texts
2. Providing opportunities for students to develop linguistic practices for academic context
3. Making space for students' bilingualism and ways of knowing
4. Supporting students' socioemotional development and bilingual identities

Your teaching will then acquire a higher purpose—advancing social justice—ensuring that bilingual students, especially those who come from language minority groups, are instructed and assessed in fair and equitable ways.

This concluding chapter highlights two fundamental reasons for education—upholding and supporting the socioemotional strength of students and advancing social justice for the improvement of society as a whole. Placing these two goals alongside each other emphasizes that it is impossible to uphold and support the socioemotional strength of each individual student without also considering the sociopolitical and economic context in which bilingual students are being educated.

STANCE: CON RESPETO, CON CARIÑO, COMO FAMILIA, Y CON ACOMPAÑAMIENTO

The development of students' socioemotional well-being is an important part of teaching, for one cannot learn without feeling secure in one's own identity and performances. A translanguaging classroom provides extended opportunities for bilingual students to be valued participants who draw on rich linguistic and cultural resources for learning. Thus, a translanguaging classroom enables students to create identities for themselves that are also academic.

Teachers in translanguaging classrooms believe that, as *Carla* put it, "la enseñanza y el aprendizaje comienzan valorizando a nuestros estudiantes." [Teaching and learning begin with valuing our students.] This valorización derives from teachers' understanding about what their students can do, and from how translanguaging both uncovers and strengthens those assets. Here we identify four elements of the translanguaging classroom for socioemotional support—con respeto, con cariño, como familia, y con acompañamiento:

1. *Con respeto* refers to the respect that needs to be shown for the struggles and ways of life of bilingual communities. This was the title of Valdés' (1996) study of ten Mexican American families, mothers, in particular, in a U.S.–Mexico border town. Translanguaging is a tool to teach con respeto because the students' language and cultural practices are valued, leveraged, and strengthened.

2. *Con cariño* means the authentic caring between teachers and students that is the core of the successful education of bilingual Latino students.[1] However, con cariño goes beyond care; it builds on the love that brings **juntos** teachers, students, school, and community and English and other languages. Con cariño is at the core of the translanguaging classroom, where the languages of bilingual students are no longer conceived as separate but as working juntos. The translanguaging classroom recognizes not just a harmonious cariño, but an "armed love" to "fight, to denounce, and to announce" (Freire, 2008, p. 209). The language practices of bilinguals work con cariño to fight against their representation as autonomous languages in which bilingual practices are considered "illegitimate."

3. *Como familia* refers to how translanguaging classrooms are like familias, always acting together to promote the well-being of the whole, but sometimes also struggling with each individual member. It also refers to language practices that, like families, sometimes act juntos, and sometimes as separate individuals. Furthermore, como familia refers to how pláticas/conversations in classrooms cannot just be about content or language,

---

[1]See especially Valenzuela, 1999; see also Bartlett and García, 2011; Bartolomé, 2008; García, Woodley, Flores, and Chu, 2013; and Johnson, 2013.

but also need to be about sharing inner truths and connecting deeply (Flores-Dueñas, 1999; Johnson, 2013).

4. *Con acompañamiento* (Sepúlveda, 2011) means that teachers in translanguaging classrooms accompany youth as they share stories and experiences. Further, the act of teaching con acompañamiento includes "not only 'being' with another, or feeling with another, but also 'doing' with another" (Goizueta, 2001, p. 206). Teachers in translanguaging classrooms set up instruction so that they and their students are always languaging and learning juntos. The students' voices are never just in English or Spanish; they are experienced con acompañamiento.

The **translanguaging stance**—understanding that the **language features** of your students' bilingual repertoires always function juntos—is the first step toward setting up a translanguaging classroom. This stance extends to understanding that language, literacy, and content are learned juntos, that students' home and school experiences go juntos, and that critical consciousness is developed junto with meaningful learning.

Valorización of Students' Experiences

Supporting students' socioemotional positions con respeto, con cariño, como familia, y con acompañamiento means valuing their language and cultural practices as strengths in learning. In this vignette from Carla's translanguaging unit, *Cuentos de la tierra y del barrio*, Carla displays her stance of valorización of bilingualism and bilingual students through her assessment practices.

During the lesson of el jardín, Carla and Sonia wanted to "valorar el conocimiento y apresamiento que tenían los estudiantes hacia el jardín de su vecindad" [validate the knowledge and appreciation that the students had of their community garden]. Throughout the translanguaging unit design cycle, Carla immersed her students in authentic activities, discussed their performances with them, gave them further opportunities to show what they knew, and supported them in new ways of demonstrating their learning. She put her own collaborative assessment of students' performances alongside that of students in their self-assessment, and of the peer groups in which they worked. And finally she had students show their families what they had learned and enabled family members to give feedback.

Carla knew that her students' socioemotional states were important to their learning throughout the stages of the translanguaging instructional design cycle, especially during assessment. She understood that she could not just design assessments that evaluated student work and identified their weaknesses. Rather, she designed dynamic and flexible assessments that informed her understanding of what her students knew and could do, which contributed to the students' socioemotional well-being. Carla put her students first, and her primary purpose in assessing was not for herself as a teacher or for the school or state, although each of these constituencies is important. Her primary purpose in assessing was to allow her students to learn. She knew students had to feel secure in their bilingual identities and they had to feel positive about their lives inside and outside school.

Carla's assessment is intimately tied to her instruction. For example, she selected stories and contexts with which students could identify. She honored students' bilingual voices and practices. All instruction and assessment stemmed from Carla's stance that her students' socioemotional well-being was central to their learning, and that a translanguaging classroom offered them the spaces to fortify their bilingual identities.

A valorización stance requires you to first ask yourself as an educator: "How do I view my students' home language and cultural practices? Do I see the students' bilingualism as a problem or a resource?" Teachers in translanguaging classrooms need to answer these questions con respeto for who their students are and what they bring with them to the classroom community.

DESIGN: VALORIZACIÓN DEL TEXTO Y CONTEXTO

Designing a translanguaging classroom to support bilingual students' socioemotional standing involves attention to the classroom space and the instructional and assessment design. Having a valorización design can improve bilingual students' educational experiences by sustaining and strengthening socioemotional qualities developed at home and throughout the community. We return to Carla's and *Stephanie's* classrooms for examples.

Carla treated her students con respeto, con cariño, como familia, y con acompañamiento, and made the world around them and the words on the page more comprehensible by putting forward opportunities to learn from meaningful and relevant multilingual and multimodal texts. Her translanguaging unit plan validated and supported the students' biliterately lived experiences by having them read, write, and discuss bilingual Latino/a textos and contextos. This affirmed the students' socioemotional strengths as Latino bilingual students.

Carla designed her (bi)literacy lessons by first selecting stories that facilitated the use of textos bilingües written by well known Latino/a authors—Sara Poot Herrera's *Lluvia de plata,* Sandra Cisneros' *Three Wise Guys: Un cuento de Navidad,* and Rudolfo Anaya's *The Santero's Miracle.* One of the activities that Carla used during her literacy time was Cuéntame algo, which began with her reading en voz alta a bilingual text to her students. Carla also invited guest speakers, such as family members and community leaders, to platicar about their cultural practices, thus extending to a much broader contexto. The Cuéntame algo activity culminated with the students using translanguaging to develop and write their own cuentos from the barrio, which were then performed by the students with community participation.

Carla opened up a space that offered the students opportunities to translanguage to communicate their ideas about relevant textos and contextos with her. This meant that students felt socioemotionally supported at all times.

Carla designed her literacy activities knowing that each text needed to be read within a larger context. Carla knew that reading *Lluvia de plata* would generate a discussion with her students because many were from Chihuahua, Mexico. Through the Cuéntame algo literacy activity, the students communicated using their bilingual voices and identities, which affirmed their socioemotional well-being. By promoting the use of translanguaging to communicate their thoughts, imaginings, and curiosity, Carla was helping students develop strong identities as Latino bilinguals, not simply as speakers of **English as a second language (ESL)** or speakers of Spanish as a **heritage language** who were not up to the standards of a so-called "native speaker" of one or the other language. Rather than identifying with labels that seem truncated, deficit-oriented, or dated (e.g., second, heritage), Carla's students are developing a sense of who they are as bilingual Americans. They are starting to view bilingual languaging as authentic and fuller than monolingual performances in one or the other language. Carla's design recognizes and draws out the students' **dynamic bilingualism** as a resource to be nurtured.

Stephanie's teaching with valorización was always present in her trans-languaging classroom, even though she did not speak Spanish. Stephanie acompaña her students con cariño y respeto as they provide socioemotional support for each other in learning. As we have seen, she involves all of her students in creating a public service announcement (PSA) for the school community, regardless of their levels of oral and written English.

Stephanie required every student in the group to participate in the presentation of their collaboratively created PSAs. To scaffold this work, she provided sentence frames to each group to help them prepare. Stephanie explained to *Noemí* that she should do her best to explain the group's choice in English, but that she could use Spanish to expand on or clarify ideas.

After students had presented to the class, Stephanie made copies of students' PSAs and asked her principal if students could post them around the school. The principal agreed and even asked Stephanie if two students would explain the project to the community during the school's morning announcements. Stephanie asked *Mariana* and *Luis* to work together to come up with an explanation of the PSA assignment in both Spanish and English that they would read during the announcements the following week.

In Stephanie's instructional design, acompañamiento was always present as she designed lessons with appropriate scaffolding and mediation from other people and material resources. She grouped students for support. She provided students, especially **emergent bilinguals** like Noemí, with sentence starters and frames and translations as needed. She urged her bilingual students to use the full features of their linguistic repertoires to express their ideas. At the end of the preceding vignette, the students show what it means to acompañarse— with Mariana and Luis accompanying each other as they collaborated in sharing with the school community their PSAs in both English and Spanish. Students in Stephanie's class were never left to feel insecure about their identities, their understanding, or their language use. They were always acompañados.

There are many ways to set the course of the translanguaging corriente to build and strengthen bilingual students' socioemotional well-being within your instructional and assessment design:

- Group students con acompañamiento, as they would be in a familia, con cariño, y respeto, to encourage and foster their different strengths and insights.
- Open up a dialogue space that engages teacher and students in discussion about their insights and experiences inside and outside the classroom with all their language resources.
- Encourage the bilingual voices of community and families in the lessons, using multilingual and multimodal texts, and inviting family members to become the classroom's familia.
- Place students at the center of learning and teaching by encouraging them to draw on their bilingual language practices at school.
- Have students share with the entire school community their bilingual understanding, as well as their language and cultural practices.

These translanguaging strategies are only effective within the context of an instructional design of valorización.

The **translanguaging design** for instruction and assessment is central to the translanguaging classroom; it is what makes it different from a traditional monolingual or bilingual classroom. Designing instruction to set the course of the translanguaging corriente means that you carefully plan its components— the grouping of students, elements of planning (big ideas and questions, content objectives, language objectives, **translanguaging objectives**, texts, culminating project), design cycle (explorar, evaluar, imaginar, presentar, implementar), and pedagogical strategies. It also means including the voices of others, taking into account the difference between content and language and between **general linguistic** and **language-specific performances**, and giving students opportunities to do tasks with assistance from others and other resources when needed. The translanguaging design is the structure that makes the translanguaging classroom purposeful and strategic.

SHIFTS: CHANGING COURSE TO VALORAR

Good teaching is not always planned. In the same way, a good translanguaging classroom does not always follow a strictly planned translanguaging design. Most of the moment-by-moment shifts that teachers make have to do with following the flow of the translanguaging corriente. And most of those on-the-spot moves have to do precisely with ensuring students' socioemotional well-being so that they can learn. For example, recall that when Carla was reading *Lluvia de plata*, Moisés shared the following:

Esta parte que leí me gusta porque los trabajadores que construyeron el ferrocarril le llamaban al tren que venía de Kansas a Chihuahua "si te cansas." Yo creo que no sabían cómo decir Kansas entonces para recordar cómo decirlo solamente mencionaban "si te cansas." [This part that I read I liked because the workers who built the railroad would call the train coming from Kansas to Chihuahua "si te cansas"/"if you get tired." I think they did not know how to say Kansas so to remember how to say it they would mention "si te cansas."]

Carla hadn't planned the larger contexto that emerged in this interaction. However, she could see that the play on words was familiar to the students in the broader contexto of the community. Her students felt valorados when they heard the expression "si te cansas." When one student said, "es como mi familia habla" [like my family speaks], Carla went with the flow. She responded not by immediately going back to her lesson plan, but by encouraging other stories. The dialogue that ensued not only affirmed the students' bilingual socioemotional identities, it also gave Carla further insight into how her bilingual students and their families practiced (bi)literacy.

To separate languages and identities is indeed to segregate and maintain bilingual students as the "other." Carla's shifts were encouraged by her valorización stance, which enabled her to deeply understand her students' socioemotional strengths and work as their ally in the translanguaging classroom.

Translanguaging teachers can use different kinds of unplanned moves to respond to the translanguaging corriente and affirm bilingual students' socioemotional well-being:

- Listen to students and their cuentos, using all their language practices.
- Respond to students' performances in ways that are intimately tied to what students are doing, with whatever language practices.
- Value what students and families have to say (and how they say it) sufficiently to depart from your planned lesson (and your planned language use) as necessary.
- Be willing to change course when students' and families' cuentos bring other perspectives and language choices from the one of your lesson design.

The *shifts* that you make in response to the translanguaging corriente are important. You can use them intentionally and strategically, for example, to valorizar students' experiences, mobilize texts, and seize significant learning moments.

TRANSLANGUAGING AND SOCIAL JUSTICE

Teaching for social justice means working alongside your students to create a better and more equitable world. It means enabling students—especially those who have been historically marginalized—not only to read the word and the world (Freire & Macedo, 1987), but also to write and *rewrite* it using their own voices and unique ways of knowing. These acts of reading and (re)writing are, of course, intimately tied to language. Thus, we see translanguaging as integral to a social justice education. For emergent bilinguals, being able to share their experiences and produce academic work that contributes to a larger sociopolitical conversation can only be achieved when they have access to all of their linguistic resources. For those bilinguals who are proficient in English, translanguaging enables them to put their whole selves into what Stephanie's students call la lucha, the struggle for justice that is carried out through the work of the translanguaging classroom.

We advocate taking up language not simply as an autonomous system of structures, but as "a series of social practices and actions that are embedded in a web of social relations" (García & Leiva, 2014, p. 201). Hence, when we *language*, we are performing a series of social practices that link us to what we want and who we believe we are. Translanguaging goes even further than this idea of *languaging* and acknowledges that within these social practices there are inequalities produced by the social position of speakers. Thus, opening up space for students to language flexibly also means opening up space for a discussion of power relations among social groups at school and in society. To break through the boundaries of language in the ways that society has constructed them, as English and Spanish for example, is also to break ties with the status quo, enabling teachers to embrace new bilingual and other social realities. This, in turn, could lead to the transformation and empowerment of students and teachers, as well as to more authentic learning.

Teaching students to view the world with justice in their hearts requires a new lens that recognizes that there is no "neutral" approach to content, and that traditional textbook explanations are often lacking. Social justice–oriented educators work with students to challenge "common sense" and the status quo. This kind of education opens students' eyes to silent hegemonies, prepares them to resist subordinate positions, and pushes them to work toward educational and societal change. Though *all* students need and deserve this kind of deep and meaningful education, social justice education is especially important for historically marginalized students. Drawing bilingual students' attention to their own languages, and to how those languages are viewed by the school community and society at large, can open their eyes and awaken what Freire (1970) called conscientização, or critical consciousness. As Darder (1991) writes,

> Language represents one of the most significant educational tools in our struggle for cultural democracy in the public schools. It is intimately linked to the struggle for voice, and so is essential to our struggle for liberation. Through language we not only define our position in society, but we also use that language to define ourselves as subjects in our world. (p.107)

To move Latino bilingual students to action, educators must use the approaches—and *languaging*—that encourage and support students on their journeys toward critical consciousness. Taking up a translanguaging stance, design, and shifts in your classroom provides a means of working toward this goal.

Teachers who educate for social justice infuse all parts of their teaching with authenticity, criticality, and the energy that catalyzes action. Rather than set aside specific time for this kind of teaching, teachers can encourage the flow of the translanguaging corriente as they work toward social justice.

Learning and Critical Consciousness

In translanguaging classrooms, teachers facilitate and foster their students' development of conscientização, or critical consciousness (Freire, 1970). They also know that to develop this kind of lens, students must use all of their language practices at all times. Here, teachers' own critical consciousness is a major part of their stance, which in turn helps them go with the flow of the translanguaging corriente and set a course toward social justice. As we did in Chapter 9, we return to Stephanie's classroom to consider how teachers can help each student grow the kind of consciousness necessary to participate in la lucha:

Throughout her unit, *Environmentalism: Then and Now*, Stephanie incorporated readings about Latino historical figures who were given little treatment in the standards-aligned textbook. For example, though the textbook gave a short autobiography of César Chávez and briefly outlined his role in fighting for workers' rights, Stephanie and her students felt it was too cursory for such an important voice in la lucha. Stephanie decided to devote several days to learning about Chávez's life and commitment to both the environmental movement and the fight for human rights.

Stephanie did research of her own and found several websites that had readings about Chávez in English and Spanish. Because she wanted her students to get a full picture of Chávez, rather than the flat rendering she found in the textbook, Stephanie found articles that examined Chávez's legacy from different angles. Some were glowing retellings of his role in the movement. Others highlighted criticism about Chávez and looked at the controversies around his life and work. While some of the readings she found were in Spanish, many were only in English. Thus, Stephanie knew she would have to use different kinds of strategies to help her students— especially emergent bilinguals like Noemí and Luis—access the texts. She knew that her students could handle the content of such nuanced, complex readings; they just needed the language support to do so.

Stephanie's social justice stance is clearly at work as she imagines her approach to a new topic. Stephanie and her students—whose opinions and ideas always inform her choices—identified a gap in their textbook: to them, César Chávez was underrepresented. Rather than simply move on to other content, Stephanie wanted to address the injustice by educating her students about this important figure, who also happened to be Latino. She believed that providing her students with more information on Chávez would not only expand their knowledge of the unit topic, but also help them think critically about why certain people are placed on the margins, rather than at the center, of social studies textbooks.

While the "what" (the varied readings on Chávez's legacy) was very important to Stephanie, the "how" was equally important. This meant providing many of the readings in English and Spanish and encouraging students to use translanguaging to delve deeply into these readings. By approaching this topic with a translanguaging stance, which is *itself* a social justice stance, Stephanie made space for students to access texts, voice their opinions and ideas, and connect with history in a more meaningful way. This kind of access not only made the classroom more engaging, it also opened the doors for Stephanie's students—especially emergent bilinguals—to see themselves as both invited into and important to academic discourse.

Designing Social Justice

Your classroom design—everything from the physical space to instruction and assessment—is where translanguaging for social justice becomes a reality. When your stance informs how you design your classroom, you set up opportunities for students to use all of their language practices at all times and to work together as a community to become agents for change.

Approaching Instruction with a Social Justice Lens

Here we focus on Stephanie's planning process as she begins a new unit of instruction. This insider view of one teacher's design gives us insight into the kind of thinking that leads to the creation of a social justice–oriented, translanguaging unit.

Once Stephanie found. . .Common Core standards that lent themselves to the unit, she moved on to the New York State Social Studies Standards. She thought about the resources she already had—and the understandings she wanted the class to grasp—and, again, found standards that met her students' needs. For example, Stephanie knew she wanted her students to use their understanding of environmentalism and sustainability to locate a problem in the school or community and come up with possible solutions. With this in mind, she found a standard that asked students to prepare a plan of action that defines an issue or problem, suggests alternative solutions or courses of action, evaluates the consequences for each alternative solution or course of action, prioritizes the solutions based on established criteria, and proposes an action plan to address the issue or resolve the problem. This standard, along with ones that asked students to explain how technological advances affect people, places, and regions, understand the nature of scarcity and its link to economics, and explore how citizens influence public policy, helped Stephanie align her vision to those standards that would help structure her students' learning.

Teaching in a translanguaging classroom means that *you* use the standards, not the other way around. This also extends to teaching for social justice. Stephanie knew that she wanted her unit on the environmental movement to culminate in an action-based project that pushed students to imagine a more sustainable and environmentally friendly community. Rather than start from the textbook or from a set of standards, Stephanie started with her own social justice vision and found standards to support that vision. The standards helped Stephanie align and organize her instruction; they did not dictate what she would teach. By encouraging students to meet standards and engage with curriculum using all of their language practices, and providing them with opportunities to language critically, you are also offering them increased access to academic success and the chance to extend their existing understanding to new learning experiences.

Holistic, Authentic, and Enriching Assessment

Assessment should also reflect a social justice orientation. Because so much of our students' educational experience is tied to measuring student performances, it is important that what students know and can do is authentically represented. If students are to remain engaged in the work of the classroom and in their own learning, they must feel that their teachers (and others) see their potential. When we assess our students holistically, in a way that enriches—rather than stifles—their learning, we are engaged in an act of social justice. In Carla's classroom, this belief resulted in incorporating families, the students themselves, and peer groups into the assessment process. The following excerpt looks at the use of the Family Assessment Tool: La conexión (see Appendix A.6.4).

Carla evaluates her students with multiple assessment tools, including her own, students' self-assessments, and their family members' assessments, to get a more just picture of students' full potential. She used the Family Assessment: La conexión to enrich her students' data folders by including the voices of family members and students. In la conexión, families provide Carla with feedback about what they learned from their children about different instructional topics. For example, after an activity in which students learned how to "put a jardín to sleep," families ask their children to show them or tell them what they learned that day. Parents wrote down what their children expressed in either Spanish or English and their children returned the handouts to Carla the next day.

La conexión refers not just to the connection between what students learn at school and what they show their families at home, but also to the connection and integration of home and school learning, practices, and understanding. This type of assessment practice reflects the assumption that knowledge is not simply deposited into students and then measured on a standardized test. Rather, authentic assessment is based on students' performances at school, at home, and in the community.

These types of assessment tools also invite families—arguably the very first "assessors" of their children—into the conversation around their children's progress and growth. Rather than mystify assessment by distancing it from students and their families, la conexión and tools like it send the message that students' growth is *everyone's* responsibility and can be measured in various ways by different people. In addition to spanning the common gap between in-school assessments and the kind of learning that goes on at home, this type of assessment gives students multiple opportunities to demonstrate what they know. Instead of measuring students' knowledge in discrete ways, often using English-only tools, the translanguaging design for assessment provides insight into the whole child, making assessment more just.

Setting the Course with, and for, Social Justice

There are many ways that teachers can set the course of the translanguaging corriente to work with, and for, social justice:

- Involve your students in decision making about curriculum and language use, as well as the day-to-day workings of the classroom.
- Provide students with a variety of choices for demonstrating their learning, and make space for them to justify those choices (e.g., let students make decisions about what language to use in a piece of writing and have them support that choice).
- Make projects and other assessments as authentic and local as possible, and include students' multiple ways of knowing in all classroom work so that they are better able to demonstrate their learning (e.g., flexible language use for meaning-making, culturally relevant assignments, projects that encourage students to go into the community).

Enacting a Democratic Classroom

In the science class where *Justin*, the ESL teacher, co-teaches, students speak a number of different languages, most of which he does not speak. This presents a particular challenge and requires creativity and flexibility on Justin's part, two characteristics that are reflected in his **translanguaging shifts**. As we discussed in Chapter 5, in addition to gauging his students' comprehension and engagement and making on-the-spot shifts in response to their performances, Justin helps students understand new content by making some translanguaging moves that shape the conversation:

Justin was going over students' homework for their science class. As he discussed the topic, heredity, he got the sense that his students, especially *Fatouma* and *Yi-Sheng* who had recently arrived, did not understand what he was explaining. There were blank looks, some off-task behavior, and very little participation. Rather than plow forward, he stopped and asked students to talk to one another in Spanish, Mandarin, French, Vietnamese, Tagalog, or any of their languages about whether they looked like people in their families or not. Though he did not speak most of these languages, Justin could tell from the shift in energy in the room and the excited conversations that students were engaged. After they had spoken to one another, Justin asked them to share some of their ideas in English. *Danilo*, with the help of his Tagalog-speaking classmates, said that he had dark skin but his sister was fair and even had freckles! A student translated for Fatouma that though both her parents had brown eyes, she had green eyes but no one knew why. Some students even shifted the conversation to the many names for different skin colors in Spanish. Jumping off from these comments, Justin connected the idea of looking like (or not looking like) a family member to the work students had done that day with Punnett squares. Suddenly students started to make connections to concepts like dominant and recessive alleles, phenotype, and genotype that they had not tapped into before.

Justin's translanguaging shifts provided students with *access* to the new content. By talking with one another in their home languages, students were able to move from the abstract concept of heredity to the specific, relatable question about whether they looked like people in their families. As has already been discussed, providing emergent bilinguals with access to academic content is part of creating a social justice–oriented classroom. By granting all students, and especially those who are often left out of academic conversations, access to content, you are creating a more just classroom that focuses on students' strengths and potential.

In addition to increasing access through his translanguaging shifts, Justin also made his classroom more democratic by allowing his students' connections and interests to shape the conversation about content. Justin did not know that his students knew so much about a science topic like phenotype (even if they didn't know what it was called). It was only through his flexibility that this kind of knowledge was released in the classroom, making content-area learning more interesting and connected to students' own experiences. Suddenly, Justin was not the sole "keeper of knowledge" in the classroom—his role as expert was shared with his students—who then used their own "local" knowledge and experiences to help the class understand these science topics in a more meaningful way. This kind of moment helped students see that their opinions, ideas, and stories were welcome and important to the academic conversation.

There are many ways that teachers can go with the flow of the translanguaging corriente and stimulate action for social justice:

- Have students turn and talk, brainstorm, free write, or make connections in their home languages so that they can better access content in a new language.
- Remember that your students are your greatest linguistic resource! Ask them for on-the-spot translations or explanations of content-area vocabulary or concepts and then have them (or a peer) translate what they said back into the new language.
- Elicit students' stories, experiences, and connections to new content whenever possible. This helps create a strong classroom community and makes space for students to teach one another through their own experiences.
- Have students share their own linguistic resources with others. This helps students see the languages of others as a resource and promotes linguistic tolerance and commitment to the struggle against linguistic discrimination.

When educators take up translanguaging in their classrooms, we can begin to challenge injustices experienced by bilingual students at school and in society.

CONCLUSION

We have seen how a translanguaging classroom works to **leverage** bilingual students' socioemotional strengths to learn. The valorización stance that we have described is enacted in instruction con respeto, con cariño, como familia, y con acompañamiento. Teachers can support bilingual students' socioemotional well-being and their social standing through their choices of appropriate textos and contextos, as well as the ways they encourage students to interact with those texts and contexts. Teaching with translanguaging to enhance bilingual students' learning is itself an act of social justice—releasing voices, languaging practices, and experiences other than the dominant ones of the classroom.

We also emphasize that translanguaging classrooms do not simply work for individual bilingual student's success. Remember that a translanguaging classroom goes beyond traditional definitions of a monolingual or bilingual classroom. And a teacher in a translanguaging classroom goes beyond the definitions of a monolingual or a bilingual teacher. Translanguaging has the potential to develop bilingual students' sense of critical consciousness. Translanguaging classrooms can prepare teachers and students juntos to identify inequities at school and in society, and then challenge and potentially transform them.

QUESTIONS AND ACTIVITIES

1. How does translanguaging open up space to support and leverage bilingual students' socioemotional development?
2. How does the translanguaging corriente relate to social justice? In what ways is translanguaging itself an act of social justice?
3. How can translanguaging contribute to the valorización of students' socioemotional strength? Describe the elements of valorización and how translanguaging contributes to each element.

TAKING ACTION

1. Look closely at a unit plan or lesson that you have implemented in your class (ideally the unit that you have developed as you work through this book).

   • How does your unit reflect con respeto, con cariño, como familia, y con acompañamiento?

   • How does your unit relate to your students' socioemotional well-being?

   • How does your unit work to advance social justice?

   • What action steps can you take to ensure that your translanguaging unit designs and assessments advance bilingual students' content and language learning, leverage their bilingualism, promote stronger socioemotional identity, and work toward social justice?

Appendix

A.3.1 PROMOTING AN ECOLOGY OF MULTILINGUALISM CHECKLIST

Instructions: Check off the actions you currently take to promote a multilingual ecology in your school. Identify areas that need attention, make plans to address them, and check them off as you do.

For School Administrators

☐ Ensure that your school has Welcome bulletin boards that include all of the languages of the community so that families can see them when they enter the school.

☐ To accompany the Home Language Survey, have a family member from each of the different language groups represented in the school translate a short welcome message into their home language that emphasizes the importance of bilingualism.

☐ Have students who speak languages other than English (LOTE) prepare a multilingual PowerPoint or short video about the school in the different LOTE represented. Provide important information about the school that families and community members need to know, and include a section that emphasizes the value of bilingualism.

☐ Adapt the Home Language Survey for the needs of your school.

☐ Ensure that the information on the Home Language Survey is given to the teachers and entered into a database that all teachers and administrators can access.

☐ Ask family members whether they can volunteer to serve as interpreters or translators.

☐ Hire office staff members who speak the languages of the community.

☐ Purchase translation pens or software programs for the office staff.

☐ Put together a list of school personnel who are bilingual and the languages they can use.

For All Educators

☐ Insist on getting information from the Home Language Survey.

☐ Engage students in an initial discussion of bilingualism in their families and communities.

☐ Have students write their language biography.

☐ Have students write a short journal entry about their use of oral and written English (and varieties thereof) and LOTE (if applicable) at home and in other contexts.

☐ Engage students in a classroom activity in which different varieties of English and home languages would be needed.

☐ Have a pair of students ask each other questions about their language and literacy use at home and in the community.

☐ Have students teach others to say a common phrase such as "good morning," "thank you," or "happy birthday" in their home languages or to sing songs.

A.3.2 BILINGUAL STUDENT IDENTIFICATION AND PROFILE

PART 1: BILINGUAL STUDENT IDENTIFICATION CHECKLIST		
Name of bilingual student _____		
		Score (0–2, according to the numbers in parentheses)
1. Bilingual use at home	Does student/parent say that household members ☐ Speak English exclusively (0) ☐ Speak English and LOTE (2) What languages? _____ ☐ Speak LOTE exclusively (2)	
2. Bilingual friends	Does student say his/her friends speak ☐ Speak English exclusively (0) ☐ Speak LOTE exclusively (2) ☐ Speak both languages (2)	
3. Bilingual exposure in the life of student	Does student say he or she ☐ Never travels to a country where a home LOTE is used (0) ☐ Has traveled, but not every one to three years (1) ☐ Travels to a country where the home language is used every one to three years or has been in the United States less than 3 years (2)	
4. Education in the LOTE	If this student is entering a grade other than kindergarten (if yes, skip no. 4), was this student: ☐ Educated mostly in the LOTE in another country (2) ☐ Educated mostly in any type of U. S. bilingual program where the LOTE was used as medium of instruction (2) ☐ Taught the LOTE as a subject in a U.S. school or program (1) ☐ Never taught the LOTE in school (0)	
5. Literacy in LOTE	Does this student say that he/she knows how to read and write the LOTE: ☐ Yes, well (2) ☐ Yes, but not well (1) ☐ No (0)	
		Total score of bilingualism _____ (Add up totals for nos. 1–5. The higher the score, the more exposure to bilingualism) Maximum score = 10 (8 for kindergarten) Minimum score = 0

PART 2: BILINGUAL STUDENT PROFILE	
Name of bilingual student _____	
1. LOTE spoken or heard consistently at home	
2. Country(ies) where the student has lived since birth	
3. Country(ies) where the student has gone to school since birth	
4. Nativity and residence	Was/did this bilingual student ☐ Born in the United States of U.S. born parents ☐ Born in the United States of immigrant parents ☐ Arrive before 1st grade ☐ Arrive during middle school ☐ Arrive during high school
5. Education in English	Has this bilingual student been taught English ☐ In their country of origin ☐ In their country of origin and in the United States ☐ Only in the United States
6. Education in LOTE	Has this bilingual student been taught the LOTE: ☐ In their country of origin ☐ In their country of origin and in the United States ☐ Only in the United States (indicate where) _____
Teacher observations on student's performances in English and LOTE:	

LOTE, language(s) other than English.

A.3.3 CLASSROOM BILINGUAL PROFILE, GENERIC

Students	Languages Used at Home	English Language Learner Status (yes or no)	Proficiency and Performance in English[*]	Proficiency and Performance in Language Other Than English
1.				
			Student can[†]	
2.				
			Student can	
3.				
			Student can	
4.				
			Student can	

*Teachers should adapt these columns on language performance in ways that accommodate all of the student proficiency and performance data they collect in their program, district, and state in English and the language other than English (LOTE). For example, for state-mandated English language proficiency we find the following categorizations: reading, writing, listening, and speaking in the WIDA system; interactional, interpretive, and productive in the California system; and receptive and productive in the New York system. Some systems number their levels and others name their levels. Some bilingual elementary schools collect DRA2 and EDL2 as evidence of students' reading development in English and Spanish.

†Teachers can make observations about what students can do with language relative to the language demands of academic standards and to the goals of the language education program.

A.3.4 DYNAMIC TRANSLANGUAGING PROGRESSIONS FORM

Directions: Use this form to document your bilingual students' performances on specific tasks. Be sure to record the nature of the task (e.g., writing a persuasive essay, comparing and contrasting the results of two experiments, talking with friends about everyday activities), the observer of the task (i.e., who observed or described the performance), and the date of the performance. You can represent as many languages on this form as are in the students' linguistic repertoire.

Student name _____

Date _____

Task-based performance _____

Observer _____

Entering ←———————————————————→ Commanding

Oracy
Listening
Speaking

Literacy
Reading
Writing

Use the following key to place students:
- Language-specific performance in Language A
- Language-specific performance in Language B
- General linguistic performance

A.3.5 CLASSROOM CHECKLIST OF BILINGUAL STUDENTS' GENERAL LINGUISTIC AND LANGUAGE-SPECIFIC PERFORMANCES

Standard:				
Student's Name	**Task**	**General Linguistic Performance***	**English-Specific Performance**	**Other Language-Specific Performance†**

*To annotate these performances, teachers can place bilingual students along progression categories that make sense to them. For example, in Table 3.2 Carla used *entering*, *emerging*, *developing*, *expanding*, and *commanding*.

†To be filled out by a speaker who is an experienced user of the language other than English (e.g., bilingual teacher, heritage language teacher, world language teacher). An English-medium teacher in a translanguaging classroom may not be able to appropriately assess this one. But he or she will be able to assess the student's performance when he or she uses English only (English-specific performance) from when he or she uses the full features of the linguistic repertoire (general linguistic performance).

A.5.1 TRANSLANGUAGING UNIT PLANNING TEMPLATE

Essential Questions		
Content Standards		
Content and Language Objective(s)	*Content Objectives*	*Language Performance Objectives* *General-Linguistic* *Language-Specific*
Translanguaging Objective(s)		
Culminating Project and Assessments	*Culminating Project*	*Other Assessments*
Texts	*In the Home Language(s)*	*In English*

A.5.2 TRANSLANGUAGING INSTRUCTIONAL DESIGN CYCLE

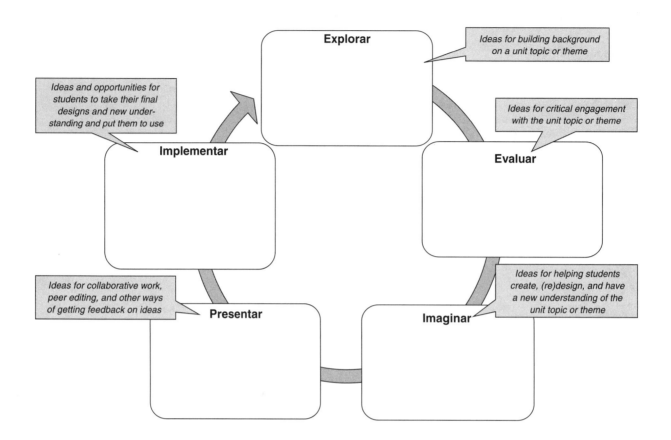

A.6.1 TEACHER'S ASSESSMENT TOOL FOR TRANSLANGUAGING CLASSROOMS

Name of student				

Instructions
- Indicate the type of linguistic performance (general linguistic or language-specific) that student demonstrates in performing each task by indicating whether students can do each task *with assistance* or *independently*.
- Indicate in the appropriate box
   PMA, performance with moderate assistance. Can do task with assistance from other people (peers or teachers) or resources (technology, books, posters, etc.).*
   IP, independent performance. Can do task without assistance from other people or resources.
   NP, novice performance. Only beginning to emerge, even with assistance.

Leave blank if it doesn't apply

	General Linguistic Performance	**Language-Specific** *Performance* **(English)**	**Language-Specific** *Performance* **(LOTE)†**	**Observations/Comments**
Translanguaging Design for Assessment	Using all language resources	Using features from English only	Using features from the LOTE only	
Essential Ideas How is the student demonstrating know-how of the essential ideas of the content?				
Creativity/Curiosity Has the student done something that demonstrates further curiosity about or transformation of the topic?				
Reading Can the student: • Focus on providing text-evidence of key ideas • Make inferences • Identify main ideas and relationships in complex texts • Recognize the text's craft and structure (chronology, comparison, cause/effect) • Associate knowledge and ideas from multiple sources and texts • Conduct research to build knowledge.				
Writing Can the student: • Produce texts of opinion • Produce texts of information • Produce texts of explanation • Produce narrative texts				
Speaking and Listening Can the student: • Comprehend knowledge and ideas • Orally present knowledge and ideas collaboratively.				

LOTE, language(s) other than English.

*For more on IP and PMA, see Bodrova and Leong, 2007.

†To be filled out only by bilingual teachers or world/heritage language teachers.

A.6.2   STUDENT SELF-ASSESSMENT TOOL
WHAT AND HOW I LEARNED/LO QUE APRENDÍ Y COMO

Student name _____
1. ¿Qué ideas esenciales comprendes ahora? ¿Qué preguntas esenciales puedes ahora contestar?   [What essential ideas do you now understand? What essential questions can you now answer?]
2. What vocabulary or language structures did you learn? Did you learn those in one or two languages? If you learned bilingually, what do you notice about how English works that is different from or the same as how Spanish language works?   [¿Qué vocabulario o estructura lingüística aprendiste? ¿Lo aprendiste en una o dos lenguas? Si estudias en dos lenguas, ¿Qué notas de cómo funciona el inglés en comparación con el español?]
3. Reflexiona sobre tu uso lingüístico. Si usaste translanguaging cuándo, por qué, y cómo te hizo sentir? Si no lo usaste, por qué no?   [Reflect on your use of language. Did you use translanguaging at any time? If so, when, why, and how did it make you feel? If not, why not?]
4. Can you identify any reading, writing, listening and speaking, and content standards to which your learning were linked?   [¿Podrías identificar algún estándar de lectura, escritura, comprensión o expresión oral que se enlace con tu aprendizaje?]
5. ¿Cómo te ayudaron tus compañeros para aprender? ¿Cómo colaboraron? ¿Qué podían haber hecho diferente?   [How did your classmates help you learn? How did you all collaborate? What could you have done differently?]
6. What role did your family play in your learning? What could they have done differently?   [¿Qué rol tuvo tu familia en tu aprendizaje? ¿Qué podrían haber hecho diferente?]
7. ¿Qué rol tuvo tu maestra(o) en tu aprendizaje? ¿Qué podría haber hecho diferente?   [What role did your teacher have in your learning? What could he or she have done differently?]
8. What external resources did you use to learn? Texts, the web, videos, newspapers, dictionaries, realia, and so forth?   [¿Qué recursos externos usaste para aprender? Textos, el web, videos, periódicos, diccionarios, realia, etc?]
9. ¿Cuáles de tus actuaciones durante este tiempo demuestra mejor lo que has aprendido?   [Which of your performances during this time better demonstrates what you have learned?]
10. Was the culminating project appropriate to evaluate your learning?   [¿Fue apropriada el proyecto culminante para saber qué aprendiste?]
11. ¿Cómo evaluarías tu actuación en el área de contenido? ¿Pudiste expresarte oralmente o a través de la escritura con éxito? ¿Pudiste expresarte usando solamente las formas de una lengua específica?   [How would you evaluate your performance in the content area? Were you able to carry it out orally and/or in writing successfully? Were you able to carry it out successfully using only the features of a specific language?]
12. What new question do you now have about this topic?   [¿Qué nuevas preguntas tienes ahora de este tema?]

A.6.3 PEER GROUP ASSESSMENT TOOL WHAT AND HOW DID WE LEARN?/ ¿LO QUE APRENDIMOS Y CÓMO?

Names of individuals in group _____

1. ¿Qué se discutió en tu grupo (en términos de contenido y/o lengua)? ¿Qué aspectos fueron más fáciles o difíciles para el grupo?

   [What did you discuss among yourselves in the group (in terms of content and/or language)? What aspects were easier or more difficult for the group?]

2. What essential questions can you now answer (about content and/or language) after having discussed it in the group that you couldn't have answered before?

   [¿Qué preguntas esenciales (sobre contenido y/o lengua) puedes ahora contestar después de hablarlo en el grupo que no hubieras podido contestar antes?]

3. Reflexiona sobre el uso lingüístico de tu grupo. Si usaron translanguaging ¿cuándo, con quién, por qué, y cómo te hizo sentir? Si no lo usaste, por qué no?

   [Reflect on your use of language in the group. Did you use translanguaging at any time? If so, when, with whom, why, and how did it make you feel? If not, why not?]

4. How did your classmates help you learn? How did you all collaborate? What could you have done differently?

   [¿Cómo te ayudaron tus compañeros para aprender? ¿Cómo colaboraron? ¿Qué podían haber hecho diferente?]

5. ¿Qué recursos externos usó tu grupo para aprender? Textos, el web, videos, periódicos, diccionarios, realia, etc? ¿Qué fue más útil para tu grupo y por qué? ¿Qué no fue útil?

   [What external resources did your group use to learn? Did you use texts, the web, videos, newspapers, dictionaries, realia, and so forth? What was most helpful to the group and why? What was unhelpful?]

6. How did your group do with the culminating project? Was it appropriate for evaluating your learning?

   [¿Cómo fue el proyecto final para tu grupo? ¿Fue apropiada el proyecto final para saber qué aprendió tu grupo?]

7. ¿Cómo evaluarías la actuación de tu grupo en el área de contenido? ¿Cómo se expresaron oralmente y en escritura? ¿Cómo se expresaron cuando tuvieron que utilizar una sola lengua?

   [How would you evaluate your group's performance in the content area? How did the group do using oral and written language? How did the group do using only one language or the other?]

8. What new question does your group have about this topic?

   [¿Qué nuevas preguntas tiene tu grupo ahora sobre este tema?]

A.6.4 FAMILY ASSESSMENT TOOL: LA CONEXIÓN

Name/Nombre _____	Date/Fecha _____

1. Hoy su hijo(a) le mostró algo que aprendió en la escuela. **Muéstreme con un dibujo, escriba o dígale a su hijo(a)** lo que aprendió de él/ella. Puede usar la parte de atrás para el dibujo.

   [Today your child showed you something he or she learned in school. *Show me* in a drawing, *tell me,* or *write* what you learned from what your son or daughter shared. You can use the back of the paper for the drawing.]

2. ¿Cree Ud. que su hijo(a) comprendió la lección bien o no? ¿Cómo lo sabe?

   [Do you think your child understood the lesson well or not? How do you know?]

3. ¿En qué lengua le habló su hijo(a)? ¿En español? ¿En inglés? ¿En los dos? ¿Qué opina Ud. del lenguaje que usa su hijo(a)?

   [In which language did your child speak to you? In English? Spanish? Both? What do you think of the language used by your child?]

4. ¿Qué otra cosa le gustaría saber de este tema a su hijo(a)? ¿A Ud.?

   [What else would your child like to know about this topic? How about you?]

5. Tal vez Ud. sepa algo que se relacione a lo que su hijo(a) aprende en la escuela. Por ejemplo, tal vez Ud. sabe cómo hacer algo, conoce una canción, un dicho, un cuento, que nos ayude a entender major la lección. ¿Podría compartirlo con la clase? Díganos.

   [Maybe you know something that is related to what your child is learning in school. For example, maybe you know how to do something, or maybe you know a song, a saying, or a story, that would help us understand the lesson better. Would you be able to share it with the class? Tell us.]

A.6.5   TEACHER'S INTEGRATIVE CLASS ASSESSMENT TOOL

Indicate for each of these five measures whether the student's performance has been evaluated as:

   3 = Advanced
   2 = Satisfactory
   1 = Needs work
Leave blank if you do not have the data to make this determination

1. Add up each column for a *total sum per constituent.*
2. Divide by the number of categories you can assess in the column. This gives you the total *average per constituent.*
3. Add the averages per constituent and divide by 4.
4. Give the *integrative score* in the next line.

Student's name _____

CATEGORIES	Self	Group	Family	Teacher
		Constituents		
Content use *Essential ideas*				
Language use *General linguistic performance*				
Language-specific performance				
Use of resources				
Creativity/Curiosity				
Total sum per constituent				
Total average per constituent				
Integrative score and comments				

A.7.1   REFLECTING AND PLANNING FOR A TRANSLANGUAGING PEDAGOGY

Strand of Translanguaging Pedagogy	Reflected in My Teaching?*	How Can I Adapt My Current Pedagogy to Make Space for Translanguaging?
Stance To what degree do I • Think of students' languages and cultural practices as equally valuable and interrelated? • Value and include students' families and communities in their education? • Challenge traditional hierarchies (e.g., teacher/student, English/additional language, native/non-native speaker) and work toward a more just classroom (and society)?		
Design To what degree do I • Design the physical space of the classroom for collaboration; design a multilingual and multimodal ecology? • Design instruction so that all learning promotes translanguaging (e.g., in unit planning, classroom activities, strategies)? • Design assessments that include different constituents? • Design assessments that differentiate between general linguistic and language-specific performances? • Design assessments so that they can be performed with or without assistance?		
Shifts To what degree do I • Allow for flexibility and changes to my design that are responsive to students' needs, interests, and language practices?		
Comments		

*1, none; 2, some; 3, a lot.

Glossary

additive bilingualism: The traditional view of bilingualism as adding one whole language to an existing whole language.

bilingual education: Using two languages for instructional purposes. *See also* **dual-language bilingual education** and **transitional bilingual education**.

bilingual zone of proximal development: Offering assistance to students bilingually to mediate their learning and stretch their performance (Moll, 2013).

biliteracy acompañamiento: At all times, even when students are reading or producing monolingual texts, they are using all their language resources, including the other language, to make meaning.

code-switching: Switching back and forth between language codes that are regarded as separate and autonomous. It considers language only from an *external perspective* that looks at bilinguals' language behavior as if they were two monolinguals in one.

continua of biliteracy: A theoretical model conceived by Hornberger (2003) that posits an L1/L2 continuum in which bilingual learning is maximized when students can draw from all their existing language skills in two languages.

convergent biliterate model of language and literacy: A model of biliteracy where the interaction with a written text follows the language of the text but where minority literacy practices are calqued (copied) on majority literacy practices.

convergent monoliterate model of language and literacy: A model of biliteracy where the text is only in the dominant language but the interactions around the text can occur using the minority language.

corriente: Spanish word for current, used here to indicate different and fluid language and cultural practices that flow through classrooms, even when invisible.

critical metalinguistic awareness: Refers to the ability to consciously reflect on the nature of language.

dual-language bilingual education (DLBE): A type of bilingual education where the objective is for students to become bilingual and biliterate and achieve academically through two languages.

> **one-way:** Also called developmental maintenance bilingual education, one-way DLBE programs include only students who have a common home/heritage language.

> **two-way:** These DLBE programs, by definition, include equal numbers of students who are learning English and students learning the language other than English.

dynamic bilingualism: In opposition to additive bilingualism, dynamic bilingualism posits that the linguistic features of what are considered two languages are entwined and adapt to the communicative circumstance at hand.

dynamic translanguaging progressions: A flexible construct that teachers can use to look holistically at the bilingual performances of their students. Teachers can also place their bilingual students' performances as more or less experienced along those progressions. Teachers' evaluations of students' bilingual performances are always grounded in the communicative circumstance at hand, and always distinguish between general linguistic and specific linguistic performances.

emergent bilingual(s): Refers to those students whose bilingualism is emerging. In this book it is used to refer mostly to students who are developing English, but can also be used to refer to students developing the language other than English.

English as a second language (ESL): Programs of instruction for emergent bilinguals where only English is used.

> **pull-out:** ESL programs where teachers take out a small group of emergent bilinguals for intensive English work.

> **push-in:** ESL programs where teachers work collaboratively with classroom teachers to support emergent bilinguals in the English-medium mainstream classroom.

> **structured English immersion:** Considered an ESL program in which instruction is in English only. It is only for emergent bilinguals, and teachers modify the language used and the curriculum.

experienced bilinguals: Refers to those students who can use two or more languages with relative ease, although their performances vary according to task, modality, and language.

flexible multiple model of language and literacy: A model of biliteracy that uses two languages together to interact with texts written in both languages and in other media, according to a bilingual flexible norm capable of both integration and separation.

general linguistic performance(s): Refers to the ability to use language without focusing on specific conventions associated with one or another national language. This includes, for example, the ability to use language to express complex thoughts, joke, argue, and explain.

heritage language education: Term often used to refer to teaching of languages other than English as a subject to those who speak or understand the language because of a common ancestry.

juntos: Spanish word for together, used here in relation to the **translanguaging stance** to refer to the teacher's core beliefs that a bilingual student has one language system with features that need to be leveraged together/juntos.

language features: Lexical and structural features of language, such as words, phonemes (sounds), morphemes (word endings), tense systems, pronoun systems, case distinctions, gender distinctions, syntactic structures, discourse markers, and so forth.

language repertoire(s): Refers to the totality of linguistic features that individual speakers have, without identifying them as one language or another.

language-specific performance: Focuses on linguistic performance with language features that have been preapproved for school use: standard grammar, vocabulary, and usage.

leverage: To use something to gain a desired effect and maximum advantage; in this book appears in connection with the use of the home language to amplify learning and gain a higher return.

long-term English language learners (LTELLs): Term used to identify students who were designated as English learners when they entered the school system and have yet to be categorized as fluent, usually after seven years.

monoglossic ideology: A belief that languages are autonomous wholes, and thus bilingualism is just two separate languages. It is the opposite of heteroglossia, the Bakhtinian concept that recognizes different voices regardless of what society deems as appropriate language.

multilingual ecology: Refers to the ways in which the different language practices of a community are reflected in schools and classrooms. It can refer to visual features (e.g., bulletin boards, signage, posters, and student work in multiple languages) and audible features (e.g., talk, announcements, and songs).

separation biliterate model of language and literacy: Uses only the specific language in which the text is written to interact with that text, according to appropriate sociocultural and discourse norms.

students with incomplete/interrupted formal education (SIFE): Refers to immigrant emergent bilingual students who have not received an adequate education in their countries of origin and therefore have low literacy in their home language.

transitional bilingual education: A type of bilingual education where the home language is used progressively less and less, until such time as a student is deemed fluent in English and can transfer to a monolingual classroom. The goal is for these emergent bilinguals to achieve academically in English as they develop English for academic purposes.

> **early-exit:** Refers to transitional bilingual education programs where students are transferred to monolingual instruction as soon as they are deemed fluent in English.

> **late-exit:** Refers to transitional bilingual education programs where, although English is progressively used more frequently, students are not transferred until they finish the program of instruction, usually the end of elementary school.

translanguaging: The theory that posits that bilinguals have one unitary language system that enables them to use all the language features fluidly. It also refers to the pedagogy that leverages that fluid language use.

> **classroom:** Refers to the space built collaboratively by the teacher and bilingual students as they leverage their different language practices to teach and learn in deeply creative and critical ways.

> **corriente:** The flow of students' bilingual language practices, which is always present wherever we find bilingual students, even in so-called English-only classrooms.

> **design:** The planning of the classroom space, the elements of instruction and assessment, and the strategies to be used with bilingual students.

> **design cycle:** Refers to the planning of the sequencing of instruction into five stages: explorar, evaluar, imaginar, presentar, and implementar.

> **objectives:** Planned ways of leveraging bilingualism and ways of knowing so that students can better access both content and language practices valued in school.

> **shifts:** Refers to the many moment-by-moment decisions that teachers have to make all the time.

> **stance:** Refers to the belief that bilingual students' different language practices need to be leveraged together and performed collaboratively with others.

zone of proximal development: In this zone, students can learn and do *more* than they can on their own because of the "boost" they receive from their peers (Vygotsky, 1978).

References

American Educational Research Association, American Psychological Association, and National Council on Measurement in Education (2014). National Council on Measurement. The standards for educational and psychological testing. Washington, DC: American Psychological Association.

Anaya, R. (2004). *The santero's miracle*. Albuquerque: University of New Mexico Press.

Baker, C. (2001). *Foundations of bilingual education and bilingualism*. Clevedon, UK: Multilingual Matters.

Bartlett, L., & García, O. (2011). *Additive schooling in subtractive times: Bilingual education and Dominican immigrant youth in the Heights*. Nashville: Vanderbilt University Press.

Bartolomé, L. (2008). Authentic cariño and respect in minority education: The political and ideological dimensions of love. *International Journal of Critical Pedagogy*, *1*(1), 1–17.

Bodrova, E., & Leong, D. J. (2007). *Tools of the mind: The Vygotskian approach to early childhood education* (2nd Ed.). Columbus, OH: Merrill/Prentice Hall.

Canagarajah, S. (2011). Translanguaging in the classroom: Emerging issues for research and pdagogy. In Li Wei (Ed.), *Applied linguistics review* (Vol. 2, pp. 1– 27). Berlin: De Gruyter Mouton.

Canagarajah, S. (2013). *Translingual practice: Global Englishes and cosmopolitan relations* London: Routledge.

Carini, P. (2000). Prospect's descriptive processes. In M. Himley & P. Carini (Eds.), *From another angle: Children´s strengths and school standards. The Prospect Center´s descriptive review of the child* (pp. 8–20). New York: Teachers College Press.

Celic, C. (2009). *English language learners day by day K–6. A complete guide to literacy, content-area, and language instruction*. Portsmouth, NH: Heinemann.

Celic, C., & Seltzer, K. (2012). *Translanguaging: A CUNY-NYSIEB guide for educators*. Retrieved from http://www.cuny-nysieb.org

Creese, A., & Blackledge, A. (2010). Translanguaging in the bilingual classroom: A pedagogy for learning and teaching? *The Modern Language Journal*, *94*, 103–115.

Cummins, J. (1979). Cognitive/academic language proficiency, linguistic interdependence, the optimum age question, and some other matters. *Working Papers on Bilingualism*, *19*, 121–129.

Cummins, J. (2008). Teaching for transfer: Challenging the two solitudes assumption in bilingual education. *Encyclopedia of language and education, 5*, 65–75.

Cummins, J. (2010). Foreword. In O. García & J. Kleifgen, *Educating emergent bilinguals: Policies, programs and practices for English language learners* (pp. ix–x). New York: Teachers College Press.

Darder, A. (1991). *Culture and power in the classroom*. Westport, CT: Bergin & Garvey.

Escamilla, K., Hopewell, S., Butvilofsky, S., Sparrow, W., Soltero-González, L., Ruiz-Figueroa, O., & Escamilla, M. (2014). *Biliteracy from the start: Literacy Squared in action*. Philadelphia: Caslon.

Fairclough, N. (1995). *Critical discourse analysis*. Boston: Addison-Wesley.

Fitts, S. (2006). Reconstructing the status quo: Linguistic interaction in a dual-language school. *Bilingual Research Journal*, *30*(2), 337–365.

Flores, N. (2014). *Let's not forget that translanguaging is a political act*. Retrieved from https://educationallinguist.wordpress.com/2014/07/19/lets-not-forget-that-translanguaging-is-a-political-act/

Flores, N., & Schissel, J. (2014). Dynamic bilingualism as the norm: Envisioning a heteroglossic approach to standards-based reform. *TESOL Quarterly*, *48*(3), 454–479.

Flores-Dueñas, L. (1999). Plática as critical instruction: Talking with bilingual students about their reading. *Educational Considerations*, *26*(2), 44–49.

Freeman, D., & Freeman, Y. (2007). *English language learners: The essential guide*. New York: Scholastic.

Freire, P. (1970). *Pedagogy of the oppressed*. New York: Herder and Herder.

Freire, P. (2008). Teachers as cultural workers: Letters to those who dare teach. In M. Cochran-Smith, S. Feiman-Nemser, D. J. McIntyre, & K. E. Demers (Eds.), *Handbook of research on teacher education: Enduring questions and answers in changing contexts*. New York: Routledge (original work published in 1990).

Freire, P., & Macedo, D. (1987). *Literacy: Reading the word and the world*. Westport, CT: Praeger.

García, O. (2009). *Bilingual education in the 21st century: A global perspective*. Malden, MA: Wiley/Blackwell.

García, O. (2011a). Educating New York's bilingual children: Constructing a future from the past. *International Journal of Bilingual Education and Bilingualism*, *14*(2), 133–153.

García, O. (2011b). From language garden to sustainable languaging: Bilingual education in a global world. *Perspectives*. Sept/Oct, 5–10.

García, O. (2012). Theorizing translanguaging for educators. In C. Celic & K. Seltzer (Eds.), *Translanguaging: A CUNY-NYSIEB guide for educators*. Retrieved from http://www.nysieb.ws.gc.cuny.edu/ files/ 2013/ 03/ Translanguaging-Guide-March-2013. Pdf

García, O. (2013). From diglossia to transglossia: Bilingual and multilingual classrooms in the 21st century. In C. Abello-Contesse, P. Chandler, M. D. López-Jiménez, M. M. Torreblanc López, & R. Chacón Beltrán (Eds.), *Bilingualism and multilingualism in school settings* (pp. 155–178). Bristol, UK: Multilingual Matters.

García, O. (2014). Countering the dual: Transglossia, dynamic bilingualism and translanguaging in education. In R. Rubdy & L. Alsagoff (Eds.), *The global-local interface, language choice and hybridity* (pp. 100–118). Bristol, UK: Multilingual Matters.

García, O., & Kleyn, T. (Eds.). (2017). *Translanguaging with multilingual students: Learning from classroom moments*. New York: Routledge.

García, O., & Leiva, C. (2014). Theorizing and enacting translanguaging for social justice. In A. Blackledge & A. Creese (Eds.), *Heteroglossia as practice and pedagogy* (pp. 199–216). New York: Springer.

García, O., & Li Wei. (2014). *Translanguaging: Language, bilingualism and education*. London: Palgrave Macmillan Pivot.

García, O., Woodley, H. H., Flores, N., & Chu, H. (2013). Latino emergent bilingual youth in high schools: Transcaring strategies for academic success. *Urban Education, 48*(6), 798–827.

Gibbons, P. (2009). *English learners, academic literacy, and thinking: Learning in the challenge zone*. Portsmouth, NH: Heinemann.

Goizueta, R. S. (2001). *Caminando con Jesus: Toward a Hispanic/Latino theology of accompaniment*. New York: Orbis.

Goldbenberg, C., Tolar, J., Reese, L., Francis, D., Ray Bazán, A., Mejía-Arauz, R. (2014). How important is teaching phonemic awareness to children learning to read in Spanish? *American Educational Research Journal, 51*, 604–633.

Gort, M. (2015). Transforming literacy learning and teaching through translanguaging and other typical practices associated with "doing being bilingual." *International Multilingual Research Journal, 9*(1), 1–6.

Gort, M., & Sembiante, S. F. (2015). Navigating hybridized language learning spaces through translanguaging pedagogy: Dual language preschool teachers' languaging practices in support of emergent bilingual children's performance of academic discourse. *International Multilingual Research Journal, 9*(1), 7–25.

Grosjean, F. (1982). *Life with two languages*. Cambridge, MA: Harvard University Press.

Gutiérrez, K. D. (2008). Developing a sociocritical literacy in the third space. *Reading Research Quarterly, 43*(2), 148–164.

Gutiérrez, K. D., Morales, P. Z., & Martinez, S. C. (2009). Remediating literacy: Culture, difference, and learning for students from nondominant communities. *Review of Research in Education, 33*, 212–245.

Haugen, E. (1953). *The Norwegian language in America: A study of bilingual behavior*. Philadelphia: University of Pennsylvania Press.

Heller, M. (1999). *Linguistic minorities and modernity: A sociolinguistic ethnography*. London: Longman.

Hornberger, N. (1990). Creating successful contexts for bilingual literacy. *Teachers College Record, 92*(2), 212–229.

Hornberger, N. (Ed.). (2003). *Continua of biliteracy. An ecological framework for educational policy, research, and practices in multilingual settings*. Clevedon, UK: Multilingual Matters.

Hornberger, N. (2005). Opening and filling up implementational and ideological spaces in heritage language education. *Modern Language Journal, 89*(4), 605–609.

Johnson, S. I. (2013). *Dual language teachers' changing views of Spanish literacy teaching and learning as influenced by critical dialogue*. (Unpublished doctoral dissertation.) University of New Mexico.

Johnson, S. I., & Meyer, R. J. (2014). Translanguaging: A language space for multilinguals. In R. J. Meyer &

K. F. Whitmore (Eds.), *Reclaiming writing: Composing spaces for identities, relationships, and action* (pp. 164–168). New York: Routledge.

Lee, J. S., Hill-Bonnet, L., & Gillispie, J. (2008). Learning in two languages: Interactional spaces for becoming bilingual speakers. *International Journal of Bilingual Education and Bilingualism, 11*(1), 75–94.

Lewis, G., Jones, B., & Baker, C. (2012a). Translanguaging: Developing its conceptualisation and contextualisation. *Educational Research and Evaluation, 18*(7), 655–670.

Lewis, G., Jones, B., & Baker, C. (2012b). Translanguaging: Origins and development from school to street and beyond. *Educational Research and Evaluation, 18*(7), 641–654.

Li Wei (2010). The nature of linguistic norms and their relevance to multilingual development. In M. Cruz-Ferreira (Ed.), *Multilingual norms* (pp. 397–404). Frankfurt, Germany: Peter Lang.

Li Wei (2011). Moment analysis and translanguaging space: Discursive construction of identities by multilingual Chinese youth in Britain. *Journal of Pragmatics, 43*, 1222–1235.

Li Wei (2013). Conceptual and methodological issues in bilingualism and multilingualism research. In T. K. Bhatia & W. C. Ritchie (Eds.), *The handbook of bilingualism and multilingualism* (2nd Ed., pp. 26–51). Oxford: Wiley Blackwell.

Li Wei (2014). Who's teaching whom? Co-learning in multilingual classrooms. In S. May (Ed.), *The multilingual turn: Implications for SLA, TESOL and bilingual education* (pp. 167–190). New York: Routledge.

Linquanti, R., & Cook, H. G. (2013). Toward a "common definition of English learner": A brief defining policy and technical issues and opportunities for state assessment consortia. Council of Chief State School Officers. Retrieved from http://eric.ed.gov/?id=ED542705

Makoni, S., & Pennycook, A. (2007). *Disinventing and reconstituting languages*. Clevedon, UK: Multilingual Matters.

Martínez, R., Hikida, M., & Durán, L. (2015). Unpacking ideologies of linguistic purism: How dual language teachers make sense of everyday translanguaging. *International Multilingual Research Journal, 9*(1), 26–42.

May, S. (Ed.). (2013). *The multilingual turn: Implications for SLA, TESOL and bilingual education*. New York: Routledge.

McTighe, J., & Wiggins, G. P. (2013). *Essential questions: Opening doors to student understanding*. Alexandria, VA: Association for Supervision and Curriculum Development.

Moll, L. (2013). *L.S. Vygotsky and education*. New York: Routledge.

Moll, L. C., Amanti, C., Neff, D., & González, N. (1992) Funds of knowledge for teaching: Using a qualitative approach to connect homes and classrooms. *Theory into Practice, 31*(2), 132–141.

Otheguy, R., García, O., & Reid, W. (2015). Clarifying translanguaging and deconstructing named languages: A perspective from linguistics. *Applied Linguistics Review, 6*(3), 281–307.

Otheguy, R., & Stern, N. (2011). On so-called Spanglish. *International Journal of Bilingualism, 15*(1), 85–100.

Palmer, D., & Henderson, K. (2016). Dual language bilingual education placement practices: Educator discourses about emergent bilingual students in two program types. *International Multilingual Research Journal, 10*(1), 17–30.

Palmer, D. K., & Martínez, R. A. (2013). Teacher agency in bilingual spaces: A fresh look at preparing teachers to educate Latino/a bilingual children. *Review of Research in Education, 37,* 269–297.

Palmer, D. K., Martínez, R. A., Mateus, S. G., & Henderson, K. (2014). Reframing the debate on language separation: Toward a vision for translanguaging pedagogies in the dual language classroom. *Modern Language Journal, 98*(3), 757–772.

Paris, D. (2012). Culturally sustaining pedagogy: A needed change in stance, terminology, and practice. *Educational Researcher, 41*(3), 93–97.

Popham, J. (2008). *Transformative assessment.* Alexandria, VA: Association for Supervision and Curriculum Development.

Ruiz, R. (1984). Orientations in language planning. *NABE Journal, 8*(2), 15–34.

Sepúlveda, E. (2011). Toward a pedagogy of acompañamiento: Mexican migrant youth writing from the underside of modernity. *Harvard Educational Review, 81*(3), 550–619.

Street, B. (1984). *Literacy in theory and practice* (Vol. 9). Cambridge, UK: Cambridge University Press.

Valdés, G. (1996). *Con respeto: Bridging the distances between culturally diverse families and schools.* New York: Teachers College Press.

Valdés G. (2017). Entry visa denied: The construction of symbolic language borders in educational settings. In O. García, N. Flores, & M. Spotti (Eds.), *Handbook of language and society.* New York: Oxford University Press.

Valenzuela, A. (1999). *Subtractive schooling: U.S.–Mexican youth and the politics of caring.* New York: State University of New York Press.

Velasco, P., & Johnson, H. (2014). New York State Bilingual Common Core Initiative: Creating scaffolds for the successful education of language learners. In L. Minaya-Rowe (Ed.), *A handbook to implement educational programs, practices, and policies for English language learners* (pp. 29–62). Charlotte, NC: Information Age.

Vertovec, S. (2007). Super-diversity and its implications. *Ethnic and Racial Studies, 30*(6), 1024–1054.

Vygotsky, L. S. (1978). *Mind in society: The development of higher psychological processes.* Cambridge, MA: Harvard University Press.

Walqui, A. (2006). Scaffolding instruction for English learners. A conceptual framework. *International Journal of Bilingual Education and Bilingualism, 9*(2), 159–180.

Weinreich, U. (1979). *Languages in contact: Findings and problems.* The Hague: Mouton.

Williams, C. (1994). *Arfarniad o ddulliau dysgu ac addysgu yng nghyd-destun addysg uwchradd ddwyieithog* [An evaluation of teaching and learning methods in the context of bilingual secondary education]. (Unpublished doctoral thesis.) University of Wales, Bangor.

Williams, C. (2002). *A language gained: A study of language immersion at 11–16 years of age.* Bangor: University of Wales, School of Education. Retrieved from http://www.bangor.ac.uk/addysg/publications/Ennill_Iaith.pdf

Index

Note: Page numbers followed by b, f, or t refer to boxes, figures, or tables, respectively.

A

Academic contexts, providing opportunities to develop linguistic practices for, 11–12, 75–76

Academic language, 11

Acompañamiento, 158

Activities, structuring of, 101–104

Additive bilingualism, 19–20, 20f

Argumentative essay, 153

Assessing Comprehension and Communication in English State-to-State (ACCESS) for ELLs test, 3, 33

Assessment, 80–98
  based on authentic, performance-based tasks, 82
  bilingual students' profiles in, 83–84
  dynamic translanguaging progressions in, 80, 84–86, 85t
  family, 88b, 94–95, 180
  general linguistic vs. language-specific performance in, 80, 82, 87b, 91–92
  integrating instruction and, 86, 87b–88b, 89f
  management of, 95
  from many angles, 81–82, 92–96, 92n3, 93f, 114
  peer group, 88b, 93–94, 179
  principles for translanguaging in, 81–82
  social justice orientation of, 164–165
  student self-, 71, 88b, 92–93, 178
  Teacher's Assessment Tool for, 86–92, 90t, 177
  teacher's integrative, 95, 96t, 181
  translanguaging design for, 70–71, 82–92
  translanguaging shifts in, 80, 96–97
  in unit plan, 88b

B

Backward design, 64

Baker, Colin, 2

El barrio y la tierra, 4

Bilingual(s)
  emergent. See Emergent bilinguals
  experienced, 2, 32
  self-identification as, 30–31

Bilingual classrooms, transcending traditional notions of, 23–24

Bilingual Common Core Initiative (BCCI), 5, 34–35

Bilingual education, types of, 3n2, 23
  dual-language. See Dual-language bilingual education (DLBE) classroom
  transitional, 23, 142–143

early-exit programs, 23
late-exit programs, 23

Bilingual identities, support for, 14–16, 76–77

Bilingualism
  additive, 19–20, 20f
  creative ways to gather information about, 38
  as double monolingualism, 23
  dynamic. See Dynamic bilingualism
  making space for, 12–14, 76

Bilingual pedagogy, 2

Bilingual performances, evaluation on different tasks from different perspectives of, 35–39, 36f–38f

Bilingual profiles
  classroom, 32–34, 33t, 172
  development of, 31–35
  student, 31–32

Bilingual repertoire vs. two monolinguals in one, 18–19, 19f

Bilingual storytelling, 4

Bilingual Student Identification and Profile form, 31–32, 170–171

Bilingual Student Identification Checklist, 31–32, 170

Bilingual Student Profile, 31–32, 83–84, 171

Bilingual students, 1–2

Bilingual texts, 144

Bilingual ways of knowing, making space for, 12–14, 76

Bilingual zone of proximal development, 8, 62, 82

Biliteracy, 142–155
  broad notion of texts and literacy for, 143–144
  continua of, 144
  dynamic, 142–145
  flexible model of, 142–143
  multiple pathways to, 144–145
  read-aloud to link language and cultural practices for, 148–151, 149f
  re-mediation of literacy juntos for, 145–146
  strategies for deep engagement with texts for, 153–154
  translanguaging design for, 145, 146–154
  translanguaging shifts and, 154
  translanguaging stance for, 145–146
  using full features of linguistic repertoires in close reading for, 152–153
  writing argumentative essay to assess learning for, 153
  writing research report to assess learning for, 151